Queer in Russia

Queer in Russia

A Story of Sex, Self, and the Other

LAURIE ESSIG

DUKE UNIVERSITY PRESS

Durham and London

1999

© 1999 Duke University Press

All rights reserved

Printed in the United States of American on acid-free paper ♾

Typeset in Quadraat and Quadraat Sans with Industria

display by Tseng Information Systems, Inc.

Library of Congress Cataloging-in-Publication Data

appear on the last printed page of this book.

To Liza for always being there
and to our children, Willa and Georgia,
for knowing when to arrive

contents

preface

I have been traveling to Russia for almost fifteen years now. I have been writing this book, if only in my head, for nearly as long. In the mid 1980s, I would ask everyone I could about "gays and lesbians" (my term, not theirs). Usually I was told that lesbians did not exist in Russia (*ne sushchestvuet*). I was told a "joke" about gay men, over and over again, repeated as a litany, a plea for me to stop asking: "In the U.S. you send all your gays to Camp San Francisco; here we send ours to Camp Siberia." In Soviet Russia, what was spoken and what was lived were not necessarily the same thing. In Soviet Russia, there were no lesbians and gay men went to jail. Of course, as in the United States, there was more to sex in Soviet Russia than was apparent at first glance. Over the years, I met women who desired women; some called themselves lesbians, but most did not. I lived long enough in Soviet Russia to know where men cruised other men.

No one spoke publicly about their own queer desires, although certainly there were private whispers. In the public realm, queers existed only as objects of laws and cures. Legal, psychiatric, and medical "experts" attempted to label, punish, and even change those whose sexual practices were non-normative. Men who engaged in homosexual sex were subject to imprisonment.[1] Women who desired other women were placed in psychiatric hospitals where they were forced to undergo drug therapies. In some cases, women with persistent lesboerotic desire were encouraged to undergo sex reassignment surgery (since desire for a woman was posited as "male" even when experienced by a "female" body).

The "experts" labeled those who desired queerly a minority, a "sexual minority." The term "sexual minorities" (*seksual'nye men'shinstva*) is somewhat analogous to "queer" in the United States. Sexual minorities are all those engaged in sexual practices that are not socially acceptable/dominant.

Sexual minorities can be, among other things, prostitutes, transsexuals, transvestites, lesbians, all (or none) of the above. The term can also signify those who engage in nonnormative sexual practices but do not necessarily identify on the basis of those practices. "Sexual minorities," then, is a more general and a less stable term than "homosexual," since it does not rely on a simple binary opposition—hetero/homo. Instead, nonnormative sexualities are multiple and can easily overlap with heterosexuality (e.g., prostitution).[2]

At the same time, the term "sexual minorities" is rarely used in the first person but is instead associated with Soviet officialdom, a medical term that both separates queers from the society at large (the sexual majority) and does so in a society that does not value difference.[3] Russians who desire queerly, when they do feel the need to self-identify, often use very specific terms to describe themselves (e.g., "transsexual" or "passive homosexual"), while using very inclusive and ill-defined words to describe those who are sexually "other." Women who desire other women (whether they describe themselves as "active lesbians," "transsexuals," or "heterosexuals") are "pink" (*rozovaia*) and men who desire other men are "light blue" (*goluboi*), and together they are "our people," or "on the theme," or "people of the moonlight."

In order to convey the fuzziness and inclusiveness of such terms, I try to use "queer" rather than "sexual minorities." I wish I had a better word. "Queer" is a very troublesome term. It is offensive to many, politicized to most. Using "queer" allies me with certain political impulses and alienates me from others. But I do not wish to alienate those who believe in a "gay and lesbian" culture or politics since I do too, sometimes. I just want a word that will describe nonnormative sexual practices in Russia without making the mistake of assuming those practices are "homosexual." I have yet to find that word in English. The best I can do is "queer." I am asking you to always read the quotation marks (even if they are not there). The quotation marks acknowledge that "queer" is not the exact term I want, but it is the best I can do. "Queer," like "our people," does not rely on a fixed and bifurcated sexuality as straight or gay, but includes a variety of sexual others. "Queer" is also increasingly a site of sexual selves, at least in American English. Many objects of this term, persons who have been labeled "queer," are using it in the first person. There are now activist and academic endeavors to say I am, rather than you are, queer.[4]

After my initial, clumsy searches for Russian gays and lesbians, I returned to live in Moscow. It was 1989 and the USSR was crumbling, but I was too busy searching for (and finding) queers to notice. It still wasn't easy since there were no political or social organizations, no bars or discos, no classified ads. Men still went to jail for having sex with other men; lesbo-erotic desire went unseen. But the Russian "iron closet," which had long confined queer desires, was slowly opening.[5] I experienced increased queer visibility on one of the last nights of that stay in Russia. I was at a restaurant with several Russian friends. Apparently we were visibly "queer," since the thugs who ran the restaurant decided to hold us at gunpoint until we paid them several hundred dollars. They kept shouting at the men in the group, telling them that since they were "faggots" they could not possibly go to the police for help. The shouts were eventually punctuated by beatings, and I began to realize that we might be killed for being publicly queer in a place where queer was invisible.

In 1990, I was safely back in New York City. A phone call in the middle of the night announced the collision of my American and Russian worlds. A queer political organization, the Moscow Association of Sexual Minorities, had been formed. It is difficult to convey to you what this news meant. It meant that for the first time queers had begun to speak aloud about themselves. It meant a new form of identity politics in a country where the only politically viable identities had been as worker or party member. It meant the cracks in the foundations of Soviet power had become large enough to allow some of the most invisible and marginalized members of society to emerge from the shadows of law and psychiatry.

Five years later, that moment when objects of expert knowledge and public hostility became subjects of their own desires seems both more monumental and more complex. There is no Soviet Russia. The Soviet legal and psychiatric system that created "sexual minorities" is no more. The antisodomy statue was removed from the Russian legal code. There is also no sign of a mass movement forming around sexual identity. Queer activism appeared, then faded. Sitting in my Moscow apartment with the same

Russian friend who five years earlier had phoned me with the news of the Moscow Association, I was not surprised to find out that she is no longer interested in the politics of sexuality. She no longer identifies on the basis of her desires. She is not alone. Much of the original excitement of sexual politics has been replaced with disappointment. There are new laws being written that could be used to imprison those who engage in homoerotic acts.[6] I continue to meet women who have been hospitalized against their will for lesboerotic desires. The Russians are not hurrying down the path of U.S. gay/lesbian activism. I do not see Stonewall in Russia's future, nor in its past. The more things change, the more they stay the same.

Or do they? In fact, Russian queerdom is experiencing a shift of seismic proportions, the aftershocks of which are yet to be felt. Russian queers have been coming out in all sorts of public ways. Queerness is taking up more and more space in the public sphere. Queer discos, movie festivals, even restaurants now exist in large urban areas like Moscow and St. Petersburg. Queerness makes public appearances in Novosibirsk and Rostov-on-the-Don. The meaning of queer desires is no longer solely determined by those who speak about "them." Instead, Russian queers have begun to speak for themselves.

The work begins here, at the point in social time and space when objects become subjects. The transformation from object to subject, from "identified" to "identity" is a complicated tale. It is a story of power, the power to create stories (by experts about the meaning of sexual practices). It is also about the power to resist those stories (by the identified producing their own mythologies). The setting is great social and economic dislocation, a setting conducive to but not causing such an object/subject transformation. The plot is a twisted one, since the cast of characters is not our self-identifying subjects (i.e., Russian queers), but the sets of stories, the "discourses," being produced both from without and within. These stories not only interact with the social and economic, but with other sets of stories, such as gender and nationality.

ORGANIZING THE WORK

I am working within certain traditions and against others.[7] I am not trying to "build" a theory of sexuality as much as to describe to you the theories that shaped this work.[8] First, if there is no fixed sexual self, then our sexuality must be enacted over and over again in order to be "real" both for the actor and the audience.[9] Second, acting queer selves out publicly creates queer "culture" and this culture is readable.[10] Third, the culture of queer contains accounts in both the first and the third person. But even spoken in the same person, the accounts do not create a monolithic whole, since the readings of them are so various.[11] To look more closely at queer culture in Russia, I organized the work around two sets of oppositions: public/private and self/other. These oppositions are, of course, simplistic and are not meant to reflect the full complexity of social space.

Public/Private

Thus my first task was to limit the work to queerness in the public sphere.[12] I made up a test of "publicness": If a highly motivated person (e.g., a KGB agent) wished to see this queerness, could s/he? Sometimes the test made the divisions obvious: a disco that promotes itself as "gay" is a public event, while a party at my Moscow apartment with thirty queer activists is not. Sometimes the border was much less distinct: a folk concert by a lesbian singer, where neither the lyrics nor the singer spoke overtly of a queer self but a large portion of the audience is there because they heard her music as lesbian, is surely part of queer culture, but it fails my test of "publicness." My hypothetical, but highly motivated, KGB agent would probably not find out about such an event.

Most of what fell within the rubric "public sphere" was about urban queerness. Queerness outside of large cities was not, at the time of my research, being publicly expressed. There were no queer newspapers or organizations in rural areas. Although I occasionally heard of a few discos or cruising strips in small towns, they usually disappeared as quickly as they appeared. And most of the urban queerness was about men, by men, or for men. Women who desire women were rarely caught in the public eye, whether as objects or subjects.[13] Despite these limitations, I limited my research to the public realm for both organizational and ethical reasons.

Like all researchers, I had to find ways to focus my work. By dividing queerness into public and private, I was spared the daunting task of looking at queer sex in the bedroom. Research into what people actually do with their bodies would require considerable resources in order to get a large enough survey of the population. Rather than try to describe queer sex or even some imaginary community of queers, I limited myself to public queerness.

Then there were the ethical considerations. I did not feel comfortable outing Russians who hide their queerness from the public eye. I have met many people over the years who privately identify as queer, but would never participate in public queerness. Consider my friends Y and V. They are two women who have lived together for over two decades. Y and V must know you well before they tell you they are "lesbians," even if you are one yourself. They have never gone to a gay disco or a meeting of a queer organization. They are not out to their families or most of their friends. Y and V are mystified by those who publicly identify as queer. They laugh at these "professional homosexuals," but their laughter is mixed with fear. I cannot begin to speak of queer identities invisible to the public eye. What would make queer subjects like Y and V speak to me, an unknown researcher, about something they consider none of my or your business? If I convinced them to speak, when speaking is for them a danger, am I telling them their fear is merely the result of false (closet) consciousness? What happens if tomorrow or next month a newly energized Russian state renews its systematic persecution of queers? Suggesting they remake themselves in my own image in order to set them free to imitate me is not a road I want to travel. I do not want to speak of queerness when it is unspoken. More importantly, even if I could convince them to give voice to their private selves, it tells me nothing of how a sense of self becomes a public subject.

Self/Other

I distinguish between self and other because much of the speaking about desire in the public sphere is done in the third person. That is, experts (whether popular or institutional) speak of what "they" do and who "they" are (e.g., "offenders of public morality," "sexually titillating"). Speaking in the third person creates objects of expert knowledge. Sometimes the speaking is done in the first person. In the first person, the stories create a self-speaking subject.[14]

My second task, then, was to divide talk in the public sphere into first- and third-person accounts, queer subjects and queer objects. This division, too, demanded false distinctions. Sometimes openly queer subjects objectify queers, that is, they speak about queer others, not their queer selves. For example, an openly gay publisher wrote an article about "those" homosexuals. Sometimes queer culture is enacted by those who simultaneously speak as straight. A lesboerotic band, The Morality Police, acts out lesbian desire on stage while identifying themselves in interviews as straight.[15] Again, I turned a blind eye to the bodily sexual practices of the producers of queer culture, choosing not to divide these producers, but their products.

Once I had focused the research on public queerness, and divided that queerness into representations of self and other, I had to decide which portions of public queerness were worth further investigation. Work on sexuality in the United States and Europe pointed toward "expert" discourse, particularly the legal and medical/psychiatric professions.[16] My own experiences in the field also indicated the importance of the law. I had spoken with many persons who in some way had been "objects" of this "expert" knowledge (e.g., men who had been sentenced under the antisodomy statute). At the same time, experience in the field as well as the revolutionary changes that were occurring within Russian society forced me to develop a more complex understanding of objectifying practices. In post-Soviet Russia, the "expert gaze" is not as strong as it once was. On the other hand, queer desire is increasingly spoken (in the third person) in the mass media. Also, increased opportunities for Western lesbian/gay/bisexual activists to organize within Russia meant that Russian queers are increasingly subject to a set of practices that are not only objectifying, but colonizing as well. In other words, what is spoken by Western sexual identity activists about Russians attempts not only to determine the meaning of homosexual acts but to replicate a Western sense of self and identity in Russia.

It is not just Western activists who attempt to colonize the meaning of queer desires. My initial approach to subjectivity was limited to subjectivity as identity, particularly identity politics. Thus much of my original research was on "organized" groups of self-identifying queers. I assumed that representations of queer in the first person would mostly center around a "movement." Such an approach not only attempted to force queerness in Russia into my own experiences, but it was also based on a misunderstanding of U.S. queer. I was too willing to overemphasize the importance of highly visible organizations in the United States like ACT-UP. I did not understand the importance of the much more diffuse and more difficult to pin down queer images that permeate our culture. These moments of queerness flicker into our public consciousness, in a music video, or an advertisement, a television show, or movie, and disappear just as quickly.

METHODS

What, then, did I actually do? Most of the research was conducted in 1994, although preliminary fieldwork as early as 1989 shaped subsequent research. Preliminary research and a large part of the 1994 research consisted of "participant observation." [17] My first research strategy was to listen. I listened for those persons speaking in the loudest voices. Once I had a sense of who was being heard, who was leading the way in creating public queerness, I began interviewing. I tried to speak to those leaders of groups, journalists, publishers, artistic and literary figures who had come to my attention in the course of my fieldwork. [18] The interviews were themselves open-ended, but I did try to get these "leading voices" to speak about what was shaping their sense of self. I asked them what movies, or books, or political events, or personal interactions influenced their decisions to be publicly queer. These interviews gave me a sense of which cultural productions were the most important, specifically, which newspapers, journals, books, plays, songs, discos, and so on were both shaping and being shaped by these loudest of queer subjects. From there, I began to collect as many of these cultural productions as possible, including going to political meetings, plays and concerts, discos and cruising strips. In addition to these regularly occurring productions of queer culture, I attended as many singular queer events as I could while in Russia. For example, I attended a "gay and lesbian film festival" in St. Petersburg and an attempt to register a same-sex marriage in Moscow.

The interviews and the subsequent participant observation helped me create a survey that asked those who took part in these public enactments of queerness to tell me which cultural productions they themselves saw as relevant to their sense of self and desire. The survey was distributed within queer organizations in St. Petersburg and Moscow. I also gave it to some of the people I encountered publicly enacting queerness, such as queers at gay discos or cruising strips.[19] The survey was not in any way an attempt to describe all Russian queers, or even all public queers but to lead to other queer productions and to provide multiple readings on the productions I had already collected.

Together, the survey, interviews, and participant observation helped me decide what objectifying practices were important. I tried to obtain as much literature as I could about the antisodomy statute, Article 121.1. In addition, I attempted to speak to psychiatrists and other sexologists, particularly about the meaning of lesbian desires and whether those desires can be "cured" through drug therapy or sex change operations (the two procedures most often mentioned by women with whom I spoke).[20] The mass media proved to be an increasingly important source of expert knowledge of queerness. I was able to collect most mentions of "sexual minorities" in the mainstream press for a period of ten months. Over thirty journals and newspapers spoke at least once, and several more often, of the queer Other. The mass media collected covers a wide spectrum, from advertising circulars to internationally respected publications such as *Nezavisimaia gazeta*.

The sources, then, consist of various textual accounts, first and third person, as well as texts I myself produced (i.e., field notes and surveys). Each of the following chapters relies on some combination of these texts, which are not meant to serve as evidence, transparent to both the reader and the author. Instead, the evidence (rather, the support) for this work resides in my own inquiries into what is being said about being queer. Sometimes the same text can be combed for clues to different queer moments. Sometimes eclectic textual combinations, like bathroom graffiti and James Baldwin, are thrown together. Always the chapters return to the theoretical and imaginative landscape I have just drawn.

The first part, "The Other," explores third-person narratives about queer sexual practices. "The Law" describes how laws prohibiting queer desires were for a long time the only site of public queerness. These laws were more effective as a metaphor for the criminality of male-male desires than as an actual threat. Women were absent from "the Law." Instead, female-female desires were diseased, not criminal, and were thus susceptible to medical and psychiatric intervention. Chapter 2 explores how women were subject to "the Cure." The next part, "Self," looks at how queers represent themselves. In chapter 3, "Identity Politics and the Politics of Identity," I consider reasons for the unexpected igniting and then slow extinguishing of sexual identity politics in Russia. In chapter 4, "Queer Subjects and Subjectivities," I argue that although fixed and stable "identities" are less viable today than five years ago, queerness is both more visible and more vibrant than ever before. The public queerness that is thriving does not require a fixed self-identity but instead provides images of queer desires that remain unattached to individual bodies. These images constitute what I call "queer subjectivities." The third part, "Intersections," considers how sexuality gets entangled in other taxonomies. In "Clothes Make the Man" and "Patriots and Perverts" I untangle some points where queer sexuality seeps into gender and national identities and vice versa. In part 4, "Sex," I conclude by questioning the dichotomies that structure this inquiry: public/private, self/other, Russian/Western, male/female, truth/fiction, and sex the act/talk of sex.

acknowledgments

This book would not have been possible without the support of a number of institutions and individuals. None of them is responsible in any way for the content of this work, but all of them provided me with invaluable support—financial, intellectual, and emotional. The International Research and Exchange Board (IREX) provided funding for nine months of dissertation research in Russia during 1994. A Social Science Research Council (SSRC) dissertation-writing grant allowed me to write full-time in 1995. A postdoctoral grant from Columbia University's Harriman Institute in 1997 allowed me to transform the dissertation into this book. I would also like to thank Ken Wissoker and all the wonderful people at Duke University Press for seeing this manuscript through two years of revisions and reader reports and computer viruses. Ken stuck to it through deaths and births, career changes, and hurricanes.

In Moscow, friends and acquaintances too numerous to mention took time to talk with me, dance with me, and drink with me. Masha Gessen and David Tuller were not only comrades in queerdom, but true friends. Viktor Oboin's archival research with the Moscow Gay and Lesbian Library made my research a much easier task. My Moscow family, the Shakhnaroviches, not only helped me find computer parts and formulate survey questions, but have always opened their home and their hearts to me and all of my queer friends. Between New York and Moscow was Mark von Hagen, an always encouraging and supportive presence in either city. In New York, several individuals have been patient enough to read through several very rough drafts of this work. I would especially like to thank Guenther Roth, Mary Ruggie, Anders Stephanson, Harrison White, and Priscilla Ferguson for their stamina and support. Priscilla not only read the drafts, but provided detailed commentary on them. Fifteen years ago, Anton Ugolnik led me to Russia for the first time. Since then, he and I have been having an ongoing conversation about sex, self, and the other. Finally, I would like to thank my partner, Liza Cowan, for her unflagging enthusiasm for this project, even in the face of my own disdain for it. Liza read drafts, walked dogs, took care of our daughters, and did everything else within her power to bring this book into being.

part I: the other

chapter 1

The Expert Gaze 1: The Law

THE MAKING OF THE HOMOSEXUAL

When I told my mother I was a lesbian, her response was curious. She told me that I did not deserve to be an American. Somehow she saw my sexual practices as a threat to the nation in which we lived. I was completely unprepared for her response. I believe I began to laugh. The connection between having sex with women and the United States of America seemed so absurd to me. None of my friends' mothers had responded this way. Most of my friends who came out to their mothers experienced tears and anger, but the recriminations were more psychological than national. "This is what I get for letting you wear your brother's clothes" or "I knew I shouldn't have let you play sports" or "You're this way because your father left us" were all fairly common responses. These responses said that homosexuality was a personal, not societal, disease. My mother never once blamed herself or our family structure. To her, my lesbianism was clearly an act of treason against the healthy society in which I live. Had I known then what I know now, I might not have found her response so incomprehensible. The problem with my mother's response was not that it was illogical; it was merely out of context. Had we been living in Russia, she would have made perfect sense. In Russia, homosexual acts are read differently than they are here.

In the United States, homosexual acts have, in the last century, congealed into the homosexual person. The birth of the homosexual person was the result of science: biology, demography, medicine, and psychology. The science of sex insinuated itself into the bodies of individuals, who in turn were disciplined to confess their sexual practices. A variety of experts—political, legal, psychiatric—identified the sexual other, who, in turn, learned to self-identify. Sexual identity came from without and then from within. The homosexual was born.[1]

In Russia, despite the development of a similar matrix of disciplinary sciences, the birth of the homosexual species was much more belabored.[2] Homosexual acts did not metamorphose into the homosexual person until much later, and even then, the homosexual was seen as a temporary aberration, always capable of being cured or eradicated with the advance of socialism. Legally, homosexual acts first came under public scrutiny in the Military Articles of 1716. The articles, also known as Peter's Code, marked the first time consensual sex between men was prohibited,[3] but the Code only applied to active-duty soldiers and spoke only of acts, not persons. Later, the act of anal penetration between two men became stabilized in the specificity of the term *muzhelozhstvo*, man lying with man. The prohibition of muzhelozhstvo, Article 995 in Tsar Nicholas I's legal code, forbade anal intercourse between men. Other homosexual practices did not warrant prosecution under Article 995.[4] As Laura Engelstein points out, "The nineteenth-century codes substituted nouns for verbs but were no more precise in their definition."[5]

It was, of course, the very possibility of being subjects before the law that allowed men to be the objects of legal punishment. In 1872, the anti-sodomy code was interpreted as etymologically and traditionally about men. Like American and English legal codes, it left out same-sex contact between women. Instead of being punished by the law, Russian experts were more interested in curing sexually transgressive females. "Admission to the system of criminal justice, the ability to qualify for criminal status, was in fact a mark of acceptance into civil society, a sign of inclusion, not marginalization." Men who desired other men became criminals because they were citizens; women were treated as less than full legal subjects, weaker and therefore more susceptible both to perverse desires and their necessary correctives.[6]

The beginnings of this century saw a Russian juridical complex that still did not have the homosexual object locked firmly in its gaze. Legal prosecution was extremely rare and public tolerance was generally high. In literary and artistic circles, many men and women explored their homoerotic desires in popular venues. Ballet masters Sergei Diaghilev and his protégé,

Vaslav Nijinsky, writer Mikhail Kuzmin, and the poets Marina Tsvetaeva and Sophia Parnok ushered in the twentieth century with a host of textual and mimetic explorations of queerness.[7]

After 1917, the antisodomy law, like the rest of the tsarist legal codes, was discarded. But dark clouds were forming over homosexual expression, whether symbolic or literal. Soviet legal and medical experts tried to find "cures" for this degenerative disease of the terminally bourgeois. For the first time, prominent homosexuals were encouraged to marry women. The Bolshevik State also encouraged highly visible homosexuals to commit themselves to psychiatric institutions in the West.[8] Within the ideological scope of Bolshevism, homosexuality, along with other nonprocreative forms of sex, had no place.

The Bolsheviks rejected earlier Russian constructions of homosexuality as an act, not a species. The Soviet experts were also distancing themselves from their Western counterparts, who saw homosexuality as indicative of a deviant personality. Under the Soviets, the homosexual person was finally born in Russia, but he came out a criminal. Homosexuality was a crime not just against "nature" but against society. Homosexual acts were treasonous in the (dis)utopia of the Workers' State.

THE POLITICIZATION OF DESIRE: THE TREASONOUS HOMOSEXUAL

Eliminate homosexuality, and you will make fascism disappear.

—Maksim Gorky, 1934

By the end of the 1920s, daily life under the Soviets was increasingly politicized.[9] Conversations, letters, diaries, dress, and, of course, desire were becoming matters of state.[10] In the panopticon of Stalinist Russia, sexual practices were no longer affairs of the individual, but indicative of political systems. Sex was political and politicized. The state must intervene in desire, or desire will intervene in the state.[11] As in the West, desires described the person: same-sex desire was more than a momentary lapse, but a perversion of the individual. In Stalinist Russia, the pervert was never a patriot. Queers were fascists, fascists were queers. Good citizens—always straight—must control, punish, and eventually eliminate treasonous desires.

In 1933, a Union-wide law made consensual sex between men punishable by up to five years of hard labor.[12] The law was introduced to the public by Maksim Gorky. In an article, nearly hysterical in tone, that was published in both *Pravda* and *Izvestiia* on 23 May 1934, Gorky warns that the capitalist world is "sick." Capitalism's exploitation of labor incubates social disease. The symptoms of capitalism's disease are visible to everyone, including the capitalist exploiters. As evidence, Gorky cites a German newspaper's account of the murder of a fourteen-year-old boy by his classmate. Next Gorky cites the opening of the first pet food store in England. Continuing in this vein, Gorky offers the most obvious example of the corruption of Western society: "Not tens, but hundreds of facts speak to the destructive, corruptive influence on Europe's youth. To recount the facts is disgusting, but . . . I will point out the following, however, that in the country which is bravely and successfully ruled by the proletariat, homosexuality, the corruption of youth, is socially understood as a crime and punished, but in the 'cultured' country of great philosophers, scientists, musicians, it exists openly and unpunished."[13] Gorky's argumentation leads him to conclude that the time is near for the proletariat to "crush, like an elephant" the immoral minority, which stands in the way of a truly ethical system.[14]

The Soviets continued to regard homosexuality as a vestige of bourgeois mentality analogous to the exploitation of workers. It would be naive to argue that all of Soviet officialdom believed this, especially since some of Soviet officialdom could surely have been charged under Article 121.1, but the official position for the next fifty years was that homosexuality was a crime. A survey of the *Great Soviet Encyclopedia*, a rich source of state-sanctioned opinions, reveals a remarkably consistent attitude toward homosexuality. In 1952, a relatively long entry on homosexuality described it as an "unnatural attraction to persons of the same sex, seen in both women and men." The entry goes on to criticize "bourgeois" scientists in the West for seeing homosexuality as an individual illness caused at either a psychological level or a biological level (i.e., hormones), while ignoring societal influences. Homosexuality is, of course, spreading in capitalist countries while decreasing in socialist countries, where it is limited to those suffering from other "psychiatric anomalies." "In Soviet society, with its healthy morality, homosexuality, as a sexual perversion, is considered both shameful and criminal."[15]

The politicization of same-sex desire did not end with Stalin's death, but homosexuality, like many other treasonous crimes of daily life, was no longer worthy of much notice from the state. The 1972 version of the encyclopedia contains an entry about one-tenth the size of the previous edition's entry, limited to "[S]exual perversion, including an unnatural attraction to persons of the same sex. Seen in both sexes. In the criminal code of the USSR, socialist countries, and also a few bourgeois states, it is punishable under the law." This entry does not discuss homosexuality in overtly political terms. In fact, an entry on *muzhelozhstvo* in the same 1972 edition describes intercourse between two men as a "crime against the person." But the underlying assumption in both texts is that homosexuality is more prevalent in capitalist systems.[16] There is no citation at all on lesbianism in either edition of the encyclopedia, perhaps because lesbianism was assumed to have already withered away.

Despite sporadic mentions of homosexuality in publicly accessible texts such as the encyclopedia, homosexuality was almost completely invisible in Russian society. As Russian sexologist Igor Kon explains, after "[t]he initial anti-homosexual campaign in the Soviet press (in the 1930's) . . . a complete and utter silence had fallen over the entire issue. Homosexuality was simply never mentioned anywhere; it became 'the unmentionable sin' in the literal sense of the words." [17] Homosexuality was now invisible, even if ever present. For five decades, homosexuality existed outside the public's view, glimpsed only fleetingly in a law that forbade it. This chapter explores the objectifying practices of the Soviet and post-Soviet juridical complex,[18] objectifying practices that produced (male) homosexuals as subjects before the law.

THE LAW

I was pulled out of bed in the middle of the night. . . . I was interrogated by the KGB . . .

[T]he man I had slept with worked for the KGB . . . his job was to seduce foreigners who could then be used to inform on other homosexuals.

—*Gay man from the United States in Gorbachev's Russia, 1989*

As long as the Soviet Union existed, the law against male homosexuality, in one form or another, would remain in effect. The 1987 version of the Criminal Code's Article 121.1 read: "Sexual intercourse between men [*muzhel-ozhstvo*] is subject to imprisonment for up to five years. *Muzhelozhstvo*, carried out with the use of physical force, threats, or in relation to an underage person, or by using the dependent position of the victim, is subject to up to eight years' imprisonment."[19] It is the version that sent hundreds of men to labor camps each year before 1993.[20]

The article had an almost mythical ability to silence anyone who wished to speak about or live out homosexual desire. Except for the antisodomy statutes, there was no public presence of queer desires—not in the mass media, nor in the art or literary worlds, not even in the medical or psychiatric professions. And most of all, those who were the objects of the law never ever spoke aloud about their lives. Instead, the entire imaginative realm of unsanctioned desires became concentrated, confined, limited to the law. Queers were completely erased, except as objects of a law that demanded they disappear.

No one knows exactly how many men were jailed for desiring other men. Not all the files are accessible, and even those records that are public are often difficult to read. Part of the problem is that there were no separate records kept for those sentenced for consensual adult relations (under Article 121.1) and those sentenced for sex with a minor (Article 121.2). Also, men were often sentenced for a number of different violations at the same time and the crimes were not necessarily cross-listed. A look at recently declassified files for 1962–1970 indicates that the Russian Republic sentenced an average of 560 men annually under Article 121.1. In the Soviet Union as a whole, an average of 1,414 men went to jail each year for *muzhelozhstvo*.[21]

Men sentenced under Article 121 were part of the lowest caste of the Soviet prison society, the *opushcheny*.[22] *Opushcheny* comes from the verb for descending or sinking. In the argot of Russian prisoners, *opushcheny* are the degraded ones, the lowest stratum in the merciless hierarchy of convicts.[23] Many other prisoners became *opushcheny*, not because they were sentenced under Article 121 but because they violated the unwritten rules of prison life. The warden of the St. Petersburg Colony ITU 20/7 (also known as Yablonevka) explained:

> The meaning of *opushcheny* is highly complex. It means not only those
> sentenced under 121 or homosexuals 'by choice,' but also those who

were forcibly, violently 'degraded,' 'humiliated.' A person can be degraded in many different ways and for many different things. It's not necessary to rape him, it's enough to publicly run the penis along his lips. This person might simply be weak or crippled, or maybe he's degraded because of his not 'prestigious'—by criminal standards—crime, and maybe for informing, or for treachery.[24]

Thus all sorts of persons are "degraded" in the Soviet/Russian penal colonies. According to one study of 1,100 prisoners between the ages of eighteen and eighty and serving sentences of one and a half to ten years, 90 percent of them had homosexual contacts. Of these men, only about 8–10 percent were *opushcheny*. But *all* men sentenced under Article 121, as well as "homosexuals by choice," were automatically placed into the lowest caste of prison society.[25] Perhaps even more revealing is that the method of placing someone into the caste consisted of forcibly putting a man in the position of a "passive" homosexual. Whether through the violence of rape or the violent symbolism of placing a penis on the man's face, even the momentary position of "passive homosexual" was sufficient to permanently "degrade" a fellow prisoner.[26]

Jailers treat the "degraded" more harshly than other prisoners, giving them the dirtiest tasks—like cleaning the outhouses—and the least protection. The jailed force the *opushcheny* to hand over their belongings, their bodies, even their lives. Sometimes the *opushcheny* are separated from the other inmates, sometimes they are not. If they are not separated, they are subject to beatings, rapes, blackmail, and starvation. Former prisoners tell of witnessing gang rapes that led to a "degraded" prisoner's death. "I will always remember how they raped him, all of them, the entire barracks, even after he was dead, even after there was so much blood."[27] A degraded prisoner can never lose his status. Even transfer to another prison cannot help, since if a member of the *opushcheny* caste does not confess his position, the other prisoners will sentence him to death upon discovering it.[28]

Article 121 worked on several different levels, paradoxically annihilating the homosexual in society and creating him as a stable, if criminal, entity. There is no single history of the law, no seamless account of the prohibition of intercourse between two men. Various first-person accounts can, however, reveal something of the way this law disciplined homosexual desire into a self. This is not to say that the oppression written into law also created the law's eventual downfall. To the contrary, political failure was more responsible for Article 121.1's eventual repeal than the protests of those who suffered under it.[29] But the law did create resistance, and resistance created survival and tales of surviving. The power of these tales is in the telling. We hear them and know that even the most repressive legal regimes can be resisted through the formation of self.

Unfortunately, much of this history has vanished from view forever. Too few of the "degraded" survived, and many who did would rather die than discuss their prison experiences. A few brave men, most of them leaders in nascent gay rights organizations, have spoken publicly of the nightmares they lived as *opushcheny* in the Soviet gulag. These are some of the stories of Article 121.1 and those who lived under it, figuratively and literally bearing the weight of the law. Some of the narrators are those who feared being sent to prison under it, some of these accounts are by those whose fears were realized in three to five years of hard labor. The accounts are not meant to reside in the past. Instead, they provide some clues to the meaning(s) of Article 121.1 in the present.

One of the first accounts from someone sentenced under the antisodomy statutes came in 1977 in the form of an open letter from Gennadi Trifonov. Trifonov, a Leningrad writer, was sentenced to six years under Article 121.2 (i.e., homosexual sex with a minor). From a prison camp in the western Ural region, Trifonov wrote a plea to *Literaturnaia gazeta*, beseeching them to print his account. The Brezhnev-era journal did not, of course, publish Trifonov, but his letter was published in the United States. Although not part of the public discourse on the law and homosexuality, Trifonov's letter was widely circulated among homosexuals in Russia and continues to be cited by many homosexuals as an important event and thus merits a closer look:

> I have experienced all nightmares and horrors, but to get used to them is not possible. At the present time, when I have become known in the West, they treat me less barbarically. But in the course of the past year and a half I have daily witnessed what it is to be a convicted homosexual in the Soviet correctional system. In comparison, this system makes the position of its counterparts in the death camps of the Third Reich look like child's play. They had a clear perspective—the gas chamber;

we have—our half-animal existence, doomed to a death from starvation with each one of us secretly hoping for any sort of fatal disease so that we could have a few days of peace in a hospital bed of the camp's infirmary. . . .

The administration of the places of interment, working within the overall parameters of the state's conception of a "relationship" to homosexuals, dismisses without the least bit of attention any of our protests or complaints, allowing the other prisoners to torture us unpunished. . . . The majority of homosexuals . . . are forced to feed off of food thrown into the garbage piles, we are not allowed to sit at the general tables in the camp mess hall, in the jails we must go completely without food. I myself . . . during three months of awaiting an investigation—while they threw me from cell to cell, where each time I was cruelly beaten and forced to sleep on a cement floor for only thirty minutes a day—did not have anything hot to eat for a month and a half. . . . Many of the homosexual prisoners are without any sort of place to sleep and at any time of the year forced to sleep outside the walls of the barracks and then are cruelly punished for this by the administration.[30]

Pavel Masal'skii was also among the first to speak out as a man sentenced under the antisodomy statutes. For Masal'skii, being gay was never something he tried to hide. "I was very open. When I was fifteen years old . . . I went and announced to my group home [Internat] that I was gay. I thought that they couldn't do anything to me as long as it was just words. At eighteen I told the militsia I couldn't fulfill my military service requirement because of my homosexuality. I asked: 'What do you want to do? Has the army become a house of ill repute?'" Despite his youthful optimism, Masal'skii was imprisoned under Article 121.1 from 1984 until 1987. His time in prison, from the ages of nineteen to twenty-one, was spent as a "degraded" inmate. Masal'skii survived the ordeal by finding protectors among the inmate population. By "prostituting" himself for protection, food, cigarettes, and his life, Masal'skii was able to survive his prison sentence and then serve four more years of forced exile from his family home in Moscow.[31]

For Iuri Ereev, the leader of a St. Petersburg–based sexual minorities' rights group, imprisonment under Article 121 seemed doubly unfair, since it resulted when the boys who had burglarized his home were allowed to go free in exchange for testifying against him. Although the boys lacked any evidence, they accused Ereev of plying them with liquor and (unsuccessfully) attempting to seduce them. Because his guilt was not proven, the court sentenced him to four rather than eight years. Like Masal'skii, Ereev was sent to a camp where *opushcheny* were not separated from the other prisoners. Ereev was subject to beatings, but not rape, since his open homosexuality was perceived by the other prisoners as a source of contagion. A prisoner who risked sexual contact with him was himself subject to being "degraded." "I learned to be brave in jail. There I was before thousands of people who hated me . . . who wanted to kill me for who I was because although there are many homosexual relationships in the camps, very few men are actually imprisoned under 121. . . . I never thought that my life would hold such difficult lessons. It's been a school of hard knocks." [32]

For other men, prison sentences were not realized except as an ever present threat. Aleksandr Kukharskii, a founder and leader of another St. Petersburg gay group, had what he describes as a good relationship with the Soviet authorities. In fact, Kukharskii is convinced that no men were sentenced under Article 121.1 after 1985 (despite evidence to the contrary). Nonetheless, in 1987 he himself was the "victim" of a "ferocious attack . . . by the assistant prosecutor." According to Kukharskii, the prosecutor couldn't find any evidence against him of violating the law against homosexual sex with a minor (Article 121.2). Instead, the prosecutor focused on a semipublic distribution of pornographic images. "On New Year's Eve of 1986/87 I had distributed some gay pornography among my guests at a party and I was thus charged with 121.2. The case eventually collapsed . . . but I lost my professorship at the university [Leningrad State University]." [33]

Many of the men over thirty with whom I spoke related similar stories of intimidation. Consider V, a middle-aged man who for nearly two decades had carefully recorded and reported all homosexual contacts he had with foreigners because the KGB threatened him with imprisonment. Then there is S, who always kept the keyhole in his door taped so that none of his neighbors in his communal apartment could actually witness a criminalized sex act being committed. Once, a neighbor broke into his room and caught him and his boyfriend anyway, and she blackmailed him into signing over his extra room to her.

The law against sodomy embedded itself in the bodies of queer men and insinuated itself into their lives. The terrifying nature of imprisonment as a "degraded one" ensured that the effect of Article 121 was always out of proportion to the actual number of men prosecuted under it. Its power was always more symbolic than actual. It created fear and mistrust. It created a series of lacunae in Russian society. Homosexuality was denied, unseen, forced to remain hidden, but it was always in danger of getting caught in the world.

THE "NEW" RULE OF LAW

On 29 April 1993, President Yeltsin signed a bill that eliminated the law against consensual sex between adult men. Additionally, the maximum sentence for homosexual sex with a minor was reduced from eight to seven years. The reversal of the antisodomy law lightened the psychological burden of both men and women who desired queerly. Although it is unclear how many men were actually released from prison,[34] there is no evidence that men continue to be sentenced for consensual homosexual sex. Many saw the fact that Article 121.1 was retroactively repealed rather than as part of an amnesty as an admission that there should have never been a law against consensual homosexual sex.[35] Many men and women describe feeling vindicated, feeling as though they could now be openly queer without fear of (state) reprisal.

Just as the fear of Article 121.1 was always far greater than the law's actual reach, rejoicing at its repeal was far greater than was warranted. The "new" legal system is hardly a safe haven for queer desires. Even after the article's repeal, the remaining law still stated that "[s]exual relations between men committed with the use of physical force, threats, or with a legal minor, or by exploiting a dependent position or helpless state of the victim shall be punishable by up to seven years in prison."[36] Clearly, the law remained ambiguous enough to allow prosecution in the case of "exploiting a dependent relationship," since such a relationship could include any employee/employer or teacher/student relationship, as well as numerous others. Also, the law continued to treat heterosexual and homosexual relations as completely separate, creating all sorts of meaningful, if not purposeful, inconsistencies. For instance, heterosexual rape was paradoxically subject to a higher penalty than homosexual rape. Heterosexual contact with a seventeen-year-old, however, was fully legal, while homosexual contact with a seventeen-year-old was subject to seven years of imprisonment.[37] The current Criminal Code of the Russian Federation (effective 1 January 1997) is far more "fair." The new laws put both men and women at risk of criminal prosecution for same-sex relations and do not create separate punishments for heterosexual acts. Article 132, "Violence Acts of a Sexual Nature," allows prosecution for "[s]odomy, lesbianism, or any other acts of a sexual nature which use force or the threat of force to the victim or any other persons or take advantage of the helpless position of the victim." The vague term "helpless position" of the victim is repeated in Article 133 as "taking advantage of material or any other dependence of the victim." Article 132, subsection 3b, also allows prosecution for "recklessly endangering the health of the victim . . . with HIV-infection." [38] Despite the more equitable wording of the law, its ambiguities allow the government a lot of leeway in deciding what sorts of sexual acts are punishable.

Many other laws exist that allow for harassment of gays and lesbians, including articles that make not seeking treatment for a sexually transmitted disease a crime.[39] Indeed, public misconceptions about AIDS and its transmission provide the most obvious point for state intervention in queer desires. A recent proposal by the Committee for Health Protection would allow for mandatory testing of any persons suspected of having the AIDS virus, as well as the possible imprisonment of such persons.[40] In addition to laws regarding sexual disease, the articles against "hooliganism" as well as "pornography" seem ready made for the harassment of sexual dissidents.[41] During the course of my research in Russia, two separate prosecutions occurred that illustrate the "new rule of law" in Russia. In one, a publisher of an erotic newspaper was charged with distributing pornography; in the other, a gay journalist was charged with hooliganism.

Case Studies of State Intervention into Desire

Eshche: Pornography and Politics   During the Emergency Rule that descended on Moscow after the 1993 attempted coup, the Yeltsin government temporarily shut down those newspapers it deemed "oppositional." Unexpectedly, the erotic newspaper *Eshche* (*More*) was shut down along with *Pravda* and *Sovetskaia Rossiia.*[42] Forty thousand copies of the erotic paper were confiscated from the apartment of Zufar Gareev. The paper's publisher, Aleksei Kostin, was also arrested. According to press accounts, no official warrants were presented to justify either the arrest or the search. Two of the persons involved in the arrest did offer their own justifications. One, an arresting officer who did not give his name, said: " 'We should have destroyed the sexually anxious a long time ago.' " A certain Detective Matveev was even more to the point: "I . . . am categorically against the sex act."[43] After three days, Kostin was released, although the confiscated papers were never returned. After his release, Kostin managed to produce several more issues of the paper. Then, on 3 February 1994, Kostin was arrested again. This time he was charged with violating Article 228 of the Criminal Code, which prohibits "the manufacture and sale of pornographic materials" and carries a prison term of three years. During the course of the arrest, a fax machine, private correspondence, and letters to the paper were taken.[44] Even before any trial Kostin was placed in a general holding cell in Moscow's Butyrskii Prison. Kostin continued to be held in this cell, one described as so overcrowded that the prisoners are forced to sleep in three shifts.[45] Even more shocking, Kostin remained in prison for over a year awaiting a trial, despite the fact that the Russian Processing Code only allows for a maximum pretrial imprisonment of nine months. Criminal proceedings were launched against the editor and a distributor of the paper.[46]

The charge of pornography seemed ludicrous on several levels. First, *Eshche* can hardly be described as a marginal publication, especially given the number of other erotic/pornographic publications that can be bought at any metro station in Moscow. By comparison, *Eshche* seems much more like *Playboy* than *Screw.*[47] Second, Kostin is the publisher (i.e., neither the creator nor distributor) of *Eshche*. Neither the paper's editor nor the persons selling it were immediately charged. Third, Kostin never received any warnings that his paper was in violation of the Criminal Code. In fact,

Eshche had been legally registered with the Ministry of Publications for several years.[48] Finally, Kostin's arrest seemed like a clear violation of the new laws protecting freedom of speech and the press.

The reasons for Kostin's arrest remain unclear. The weekly *Ekspress khronika* claimed that Kostin was the victim of a legal contradiction that put him between the Ministry of Internal Affairs (MVD) and the Ministry of Publications, between a law against pornography and a law guaranteeing freedom of the press.[49] Others suggested that Kostin's real crime was participating in a roundtable discussion the day before his arrest. The roundtable, organized by the journal *Ogonek*, was to explore erotica in the mass media. It was also meant as a press gathering to discuss the case against Kostin.[50] At the roundtable, Kostin apparently offended the MVD representative by insisting that "pornography contains everything that the government would like to forbid." [51] Yet another possible reasons for Kostin's arrest was his connection to former Vice President Aleksander Rutskoi and the former head of the Supreme Soviet, Ruslan Khasbulatov. These connections are what *Komsomol'skaia pravda* referred to as the "political subtext" to Kostin's arrest.[52]

Uncovering the actual directives/intentions behind the state persecution of an erotic newspaper is undoubtedly the task of future historians. Regardless of what the future reveals, the historical moment of Kostin's arrest says volumes about sexual otherness in Russia. I first heard about Kostin's case a few days after his arrest. It was a typical evening in Moscow: huddled around a table drinking tea, or perhaps it was vodka, four of the country's top queer activists and myself discussed the case. Two of them insisted that *Eshche* was being targeted not because of Kostin's political affiliations, nor because of the paper's possible pornographic nature, but because *Eshche* had always published a lot of articles by and for queers.[53] I was unsure whether my friends' fears were justified or paranoid (or both). I did, however, hear the same sentiment echoed again and again, whenever Kostin's name was mentioned among queers.[54]

The suspicion that Kostin's "real" crime was publishing articles about homosexual desire became even stronger once his trial actually began in February of 1995. At the trial, Kostin was led into the courtroom hand cuffed and forced to sit in a steel cage, one usually reserved for violent criminals. According to a report by Masha Gessen for the Committee to Protect Journalists (CPJ):

> The judge droned on to a fidgeting, giggling courtroom, reading the reports of some ten different expert committees called together to determine whether the newspaper was pornographic: There is no definition of pornography in Russian law. (Judge): "The newspaper places a conspicuous focus on the satisfaction of sexual desire in *perverted* ways. . . . It should be noted that the editors pay particular attention to male and female homosexuality. . . . The editors are interested only in the unusual sides of sexual life. . . . The images of heterosexual group sex and *female homosexuality should be considered pornographic.*" [55]

Regardless of the government's intention, the prosecution of Kostin was read by many as an attack on public queerness. The *Eshche* prosecution appears to be an attack not just on freedom of the press, but on the freedom of desire.

Mogutin the Hooligan   In November of 1993 charges were brought against openly gay journalist Yaroslav Mogutin. Mogutin was charged under Article 206.2 of the Russian Legal Code: "criminal hooliganism with exceptional cynicism and particular impertinence." Anyone convicted of "hooliganism with exceptional cynicism" is subject to imprisonment for up to five years.[56] This highly publicized case began with an ironic twist: Mogutin came to the attention of the prosecutor's office when he tried to obtain legal redress after one of his articles was plagiarized by another paper.

The article, "Dirty Peckers," was first published in Kostin's *Eshche*.[57] "Dirty Peckers" openly discussed the homosexuality of Boris Moiseev, a popular performer. Moiseev not only spoke as a gay man, but spoke about the sexual attraction men in the audience feel for him. Perhaps even more disturbing to the prosecutor's office was Moiseev's "confession" of performing oral sex on "aging Komsomol members' dirty peckers."[58] A highly edited version of the interview was later used by *Moskovskii komsomolets* (MK),[59] Russia's largest circulation daily,[60] without the permission of its author.[61] At this point, Mogutin tried to press charges and published segments of the interview under the same title in the independent newspaper

Novyi vzgliad (*A New View*) in November of 1993.[62] Instead of charging MK for the unauthorized use of another publication's material, the prosecutor's office used the *Novyi vzgliad* article to charge Mogutin with "criminal hooliganism" (i.e., Article 206.2). According to an article in *Kuranty*, both Mogutin and the editor of *Novyi vzgliad*, Evgenii Dodolev, were charged for hooliganism because the "judicial organ was not at all pleased with the article's glaringly foul language illustrated by naked 'gay' he-men [*muzhiki*]."[63]

Several persons and groups protested that the prosecution of a journalist for published material, no matter how offensive, constituted an extreme violation of the principles of freedom of speech and freedom of the press. The Russian chapter of PEN, in a letter of protest to the prosecutor's office, pointed out that the leaders of Russia have publicly declared their support for a freedom of the press that is only limited in the case of "the incitement of racial and national enmities, propagandizing violence and hatred between people. Any other prosecution of an author, particularly criminal prosecution, is impermissible."[64] When Mogutin mentioned the danger to freedom of the press that his prosecution would bring, a person from the Moscow Prosecutor's Office replied that the sort of language used in "Dirty Peckers"[65] and the homoerotic pictures that accompanied the article were comparable to "summoning the public into the editor's office, climbing onto the desk, pulling down his pants, and telling the onlookers to suck his dick."[66]

Mogutin was actually brought to trial for "criminal hooliganism" several times, each time facing a possible conviction and prison sentence. I attended one such trial on 14 April 1994. The following is a highly edited version of my notes from the trial:

> The trial is held in a courtroom intended for criminal cases. A large cage takes the place of a defense table, although Mogutin and his co-defendant Dodalev are mercifully allowed to sit in the spectator seats. Mogutin is represented by Genrikh Padva, a lawyer whose fame in Russia is comparable to William Kunstler in the U.S. Under the Soviets, Padva represented dissidents, today he represents the likes of Alexander Rutskoi [leader of the failed 1993 coup]. Both lawyer and his client are dressed extremely well, in expensively tailored suits. In contrast, the judge, a middle-aged woman, wears a Russian-made suit. The

cheaply outfitted judge and shabbiness of the courtroom, in dire need of new paint to cover the peeling lime green walls, make the trial look more like a clash between the newly successful and the formerly elite. Slava [Mogutin] asks to acquaint himself with the charges because he received no official notification. Padva argues that the case should be dismissed because of a variety of technical errors on the part of the prosecutor's office. . . . He points out that this is not just "a minor point, but . . . a violation of his human rights."

During a break Padva spoke to the reporters, mostly Russian, in the room. He pointed out that the gay theme of the article was certainly one of the reasons for the prosecution. Asked by a reporter why the state withdrew Article 121.1 from the legal code, Padva replied that "the prosecutor would happily put them [queers] all in jail . . . but world opinion and some understanding that this is not a criminal matter [prevent him from doing so]. Although there are certainly people still in jail for this . . . we have to ask in what way is this a crime." After about forty minutes the judge returned with her ruling that although the defendants were obviously guilty, the case would not be pursued (although it could be reopened later).

Ironically, the trial was held in the Krasnopresnskii Regional Court, the same legal district in which the October Events, the failed overthrow of the Yeltsin government, took place in 1993. Mogutin himself pointed out to me the absurdity of the legal office responsible for prosecuting the putsch organizers relentlessly pursuing a case of "hooliganism." Why the prosecutor's office decided to prosecute this case in the first place is unclear, but why they decided to close the case and eventually drop it[67] is even less clear. Perhaps the answer lies in a part of the story which I left out of my edited version: the night before the trial Mogutin and his partner were visited by a very large man accompanied by a police officer (from the militsia). The man insisted they pay him money and in exchange he would make sure the case against Mogutin was dropped. The man also insisted that he was a member of Zhirinovskii's quasi-fascist Liberal Democratic Party, hated "pederasts," and would be just as happy to kill them if they did not pay the bribe.[68]

Public homosexuality continues to be subjected to Russian law,[69] but Russian law is intersected and dissected by paralegal entities, political powers, and personalities, all of whom bend it and shape it to their own will. The juridical complex is, as it turns out, not as stable as it seems. The homosexual subject is certainly produced by the Law. But the Law itself is never completely whole. There are constantly breaches in the Law's security, wars over borders and margins that may end up being the site of more central battles. Perhaps this is even more true in a legal landscape as highly contested as post-Soviet Russia.[70]

According to Michel de Certeau, there are always a variety of "tactics" available to those who are not in a position of power.[71] In terms of the Law, the most visibly queer "tactic" is the (mis)use of the very legal system that subjects them in the first place. It was just such a tactical skirmish that took place in the spring of 1994, when two men tried to officially register their marriage. The men, Mogutin[72] and his American partner, Robert Filippini, first told me of their plans to "marry" in March of that year. Filippini wanted to get married because the "bottom line is that two men love each other and that's it. . . . [L]ove is love and I have as much a right to my love as my mother has to hers. . . . It's not our sexuality that's different, it's the presumption that there is a difference . . . that the grace of our love should not be allowed." For Mogutin the reasons were more overtly tactical: this was to be an "iconographic act against the homophobia and sexism of the regime." Mogutin was not convinced of a "right" to marriage as much as he was the opportunity to get a lot of press coverage. Both agreed that any coverage of queers in the press is a good thing because the media is a public space, accessible even in the deepest of closets.[73]

The would-be honeymooners set the date for 12 April, a holiday that commemorates the USSR's cosmonauts. Both believed this to be a very "manly" day. It also happened to be Mogutin's twentieth birthday.[74] The day before the wedding, the two went to the U.S. Embassy to register their intended marriage as per U.S. law (again, Filippini is an American citizen). Surprisingly enough, they were not refused. Instead, after completing the required forms, a stunned Filippini asked the embassy worker if he understood that this was a same-sex marriage. The man answered that the "same-sex" nature of the relationship did not concern him.[75] Buoyed by the nonchalance of the U.S. government, the two lovers drove the next day to the Palace of Weddings Number 4.[76]

I arrive around 3 p.m. There is a huge contingent of press, including CNN and AP and a lot of the Russian papers and television. The doors are not yet open [*i.e., the Palace is on a lunch break*]. . . . Evgeniia Debrianskaia [*probably the most famous of the gay and lesbian leaders in Russia*] and her girlfriend arrive looking very visibly queer. The three of us stand out in the crowd of reporters with our black leather motorcycle jackets, combat boots, short hair. The Russian press immediately notes Debrianskaia's arrival and several reporters surround her. They ask what she thinks of the wedding. She answers that she does not understand the point of imitating heterosexuality, but as an "act which reveals the innate homophobia and sexism of the state" she supports it. . . . The grooms arrive. Mogutin is dressed in a tee shirt and motorcycle jacket. . . .[77] After about thirty minutes the crowd (about 60 people, most of them apparently reporters) moves into the Wedding Palace, which is lit in fluorescent light with pictures of happy, if tacky, heterosexual couples on the wall. The people who work there seem a bit overwhelmed by all the press attention. The director of the Palace, Karmin Boreva, seems well prepared for their visit. She gives a statement that seems to be sympathetic: she understands love, she herself thinks that love should be recognized by the state, but according to the Family Code adopted in 1969 marriage is between a man and a woman and this code remains in effect. Boreva suggests that the grooms address themselves to their representatives in the Duma. They kiss anyway and Filippini tells the press that they exchanged vows and rings this morning. . . . Afterwards the director answers a few questions. She says that this is *not* the first time two men have tried to get married, although no women have ever tried. When asked why, she says because men are "more romantic somehow." She also mentions how she has read a lot of ancient Greek poetry and therefore she personally saw nothing wrong with their marriage[!], but she cannot break the law.[78]

As Mogutin predicted, press accounts of the affair were indeed numerous. *Ekspress gazeta, Kuranty, Segodnia, Komsomol'skaia pravda, Inostranets,* and the English-language *Moscow Tribune* all wrote of the event within a few days. Not only was this decidedly queer action spoken about publicly, but all of the newspapers contained supportive, if sarcastically so, accounts of the young couple's attempt to be wed. The article in the moderate *Segodnia* was entitled "The Setting Right of Russian-American Relations Is Delayed." The article goes on to say that "unlike its legislative counterparts in European countries, Russia does not anticipate the possibility of registering same-sex marriages." The director of the Palace is described in decidedly derogatory terms as advising the young pair to address themselves to the legislature without removing her "happy *dezhurnaia's* [gatekeeper] smile." When asked to whom in the Duma they should address themselves, the director apparently answered, " 'To anyone of the exotic politicians, there are plenty of them there.' "[79] *Komsomol'skaia pravda* was even more gay-positive, describing the refusal to register the marriage as "callous" and reminding the lovers that "happy marriages are made in heaven" (i.e., not in the Palace of Weddings Number 4).[80]

As spectacular as the wedding was, there are other, less "newsworthy" tactical maneuvers to use laws to subvert the Law. Many of the gay/lesbian rights organizations have worked very hard to become legally registered. Although no organization has yet registered as an organization *of* queers, many have registered as an organization *for* the rights of sexual minorities. Moscow's Triangle saw registration as an organization *of* "gays, lesbians, and bisexuals" as a primary goal. According to Triangle's Debrianskaia, it is unacceptable to register in any other way since it does not force the state to recognize the legitimacy of sexual minorities coalescing into groups.[81]

ENDGAMES

The workings of the Law on the homosexual body and the body politic are similar under the "new" rule of law and the Soviet regime. In the past, Article 121 transformed same-sex desire into a sort of person: the homosexual. The homosexual was then separated from the majority by a law, which sometimes actually removed his body from the social realm, but, more often than not, Article 121.1 worked in the body politic. The homosexual was a subject before the Law. As a subject, the homosexual could now speak/act in his own behalf.[82]

The "new" rule of law must contend with that self-speaking homosexual, but it does so in ways that reproduce him. Homosexual desire is still separate, ready to be criminalized if it transgresses its allowed public space. This separation is codified in laws that create a higher age of consent for homosexual acts, which target those who speak too gay-ly, which create legislative bills that would make "homosexuals" and "lesbians" a separate population in need of state intervention.[83]

The Law also continues to reproduce its misshapen offspring, the demi-legal entities that are enough a part of the Law to blackmail, extort, and commit other acts of violence against those they identify as sexual minorities. This quasi-legal subjugation often reeks of the Law when it takes the form of powerful nationalists who are closely allied with the militsia, or judges, or prosecutors (as it did in the Mogutin case). At other times, the connections are much more tenuous, as in the case of militsioneers who look the other way during a gay bashing.[84]

The Law is not just repressive, it is productive as well. It remains a powerful source of public queerness. The power of the Law to subject simultaneously produces self-speaking subjects. It is the double sense of subject, subjected to and a subject before, which creates the paradoxical situation of the legal system as a producer of homosexual identity.[85] The Law, old and new, cultivates queer identities as well as queer fears.

ENGENDERING SUBJECTS

When discussing the creation of the homosexual subject, the personal pronouns are decidedly gendered—as male. Russian/Soviet laws against homosexual desire were always gendered. The very term for illegal homosexual acts, muzhelozhstvo, literally means "men lying together" and has always been interpreted to mean a penis entering the anus of another man.[86] Legal experts created the homosexual criminal and they created him male. Transgressive female desires were not the object of legal knowledge, women were not subjects before the Law.

Although women were never sentenced under the law, prison camps played a large role within lesbian and popular conceptions of female-female relationships.[87] Some Russian specialists on female homosexuality in prison estimate that nearly one-half of all female prisoners are sexually engaged with other women.[88] In interviews, many women suggested that their own lesbianism was the result of either reform school or camp experiences. Often, they themselves were not interned but learned about lesbianism from women who were.[89] Olga Zhuk has argued that *all* lesbians in Russia were highly influenced by the sexual roles developed in the camp system. These roles consisted of an active partner, who attempted to "imitate a man" in bed. "All that was female is repressed and hidden; they do not completely undress nor do they allow their genitals to be touched." "Active" lesbians paired only with "passive" ones, who were considered by themselves and others to be "naturals" (i.e., heterosexual).[90]

But if many women who desire other women feel tied to criminal systems, it is not the same tie that binds men. Women may experience lesbian relationships in female prisons, just as they may experience these relationships in single-sex worker dormitories. Women, however, do not become criminals for the expression of their desires. Lesbianism is not against the Law. Instead, according to this (il)logic, lesbianism is against Nature: unhealthy, diseased, needing a cure. The next chapter explores diseased desires and those who would cure them. Although medicopsychiatric experts certainly attempted to cure men, it was women who were their most likely patients. For a man to speak of his desire for other men was a dangerously illegal act. For a woman, it was often a mandatory part of the "Cure."

chapter 2

The Expert Gaze 2: The Cure

All her actions, it is clear, were entirely expedient and rather well thought out. She showed absolutely no signs of psychopathology or neuropathology in anything she did but only a persistent attraction to the female sex.

—*A doctor writing the only known clinical history of lesbianism in tsarist Russia, 1895*

In tsarist Russia, the Law created not a homosexual person but a prohibition of certain sexual practices. Pre-Soviet medical and psychiatric professions showed a similar refusal to make homosexuals a separate species. Certainly the Russian medical/psychiatric understandings of sexual "deviance" were shaped by European literature, but Russian experts did not exhibit the same obsessive interest in nonnormative sexual practices as did many of their colleagues in the West. Most psychiatric journals in fin-de-siècle Russia rarely spoke of homosexuality. Even on those rare occasions when queer desires were taken up by these journals, homosexuality was not necessarily seen as pathological.[1]

The Russian medicopsychiatric complex may have been more reluctant to evaluate desires than their Western counterparts because of their very different positions in society. According to Laura Engelstein's analysis, the intelligentsia in Russia was radicalized by the fact that it did not have access to state power. The intellectual elite, which included medical and psychiatric experts, was thus "more likely to use socially marginal groups to exemplify their own disempowered condition than to affirm a monopoly of power they did not possess."[2]

The relative indifference to homosexuality changed after the 1905 Revolution, when class, ethnicity, and gender were both more fluid and more embattled. Set adrift in postrevolutionary uncertainty, experts latched onto various evaluations of homosexuality. Homosexuality was now often "en-classed" as elite depravity or equated with certain groups, particularly Jews. At the same time, many foreign writings on sexuality were being imported into Russia.[3] One European text that was widely read in turn-of-the-century Russia and continues to be cited in post-Soviet Russia is Sex and Character by Otto Weininger.[4]

By 1914, thousands of copies and numerous editions of Sex and Character had been issued in Russia.[5] Sex and Character is a complicated book. In it, Weininger equates Jewishness with femaleness, and both with uncon-trolled desires. Both Jews and women undermine the rational self-control of the (non-Jewish) male, and thus both must be controlled, even elimi-nated, by (non-Jewish) men. Yet Weininger's work is much more than the ramblings of an anti-Semitic misogynist. It is also a defense of homo-sexuality. Weininger begins by separating gender from sex. In other words, gender and sex divide "naturally" into masculine and feminine, but gen-der attributes are randomly distributed onto individual bodies, regardless of sex. Weininger uses his radical theory of gender to support his poten-tially radical view of homosexuality: homosexuality is neither a perversion nor an illness, but instead the result of the "naturally" random distribu-tion of gender. In other words, homosexuality occurs when "biological" sex as male or female is not in agreement with gender attributes as mascu-line or feminine. That is, some women are "naturally" masculine and some men are "naturally" feminine. Homosexuality cannot be "cured" since the "natural" sexual object choice of a mannish woman or a womanly man is someone of her/his own sex.[6]

Not only were Western thinkers like Weininger widely read, but so were native philosophers of sex, gender, and desire. Vasilii Rozanov wrote a satirical account of all the "shocking clinical histories from the then popu-lar books of German psychiatrists who specialized in sexual pathologies."[7] In People of the Moonlight: The Metaphysics of Christianity[8] Rozanov also offered his own theory of desire and gender, and his account is surprisingly similar to Weininger's. Masculinity and femininity are not exclusive of each other. Instead, "they can occur in a person in any proportion."[9] Like Weininger, Rozanov saw homosexuality as the "natural" result of "naturally" randomly distributed gender attributes. But Rozanov goes further than Weininger by searching for latent or subconscious homosexuality (which he calls "spiritual homosexuality"), locating it in the words of famous men as diverse as Jesus and Lev Tolstoy.[10]

Although hardly the beginning of a "gay liberation" movement, medical and psychiatric experts did read texts like Weininger's and Rozanov's. These experts "read" that homosexuality should not be punished—since it is not a perversion of the soul, but a contradiction between the psychic and physical selves. The Expert Gaze, then, had more than one look. As I argued in chapter 1, the Law set out to punish transgressive sexual acts and ended up creating a species of transgressor: the homosexual. But the medical and psychiatric experts gazed upon homosexuality from a different point of view; they did not want to punish homosexual acts but to cure them. Homosexuality—both female and male—was to be located, analyzed, and corrected.

Not only did medical/psychiatric experts intervene in desire differently from legal experts, but the Cure produced a different sort of object from the Law. Instead of the Legal Subject, the Cure erased any individual subjects and produced in their stead diseases of desire. The results were not the same. Disease is different from crime. The individual "I" is not responsible for illness, but its victim. The victim must be cured, and if not cured, comforted. "They cannot help it if they are sick, perverted, queer. They have been infected: by a sick society or a perverted family" (e.g., a society/family "unnaturally" dominated by a mother/women). The victims did not create the disease themselves. They are not its authors, so they have no authority with which to speak. They cannot act as subjects before the Cure, since not they, but diseased desires, are what the Cure imagines. Thus began a long and arduous search for "cures."[11]

DIAGNOSING DISEASED DESIRES

One early cure for homosexuality was to transplant the testicle of a "healthy" heterosexual onto the "diseased" homosexual.

—As quoted in the Bol'shaia meditsinskaia entsiklopedia, 1929

I didn't even know there was such a thing as lesbianism in our country and when I found out I was so shocked. After all, there has been a cure for that for some time. There's no need to suffer when we can cure such things with an operation.

—A Moscow AIDS specialist to a shocked New York audience at the Soviet/U.S. Women's Summit, 1990

The first part of any cure is the correct diagnosis.[12] Diagnosing desire is not a simple task, since the same behaviors can signal both healthy and diseased bodies. A married man, a father of children, can fondle another man in the bathhouse. A man who lives with his mother or his male friend should not spend too much time in a public toilet. The gaze of medico-psychiatric experts was not, however, generally focused on men. Most of those who became objects of psychiatric and medical intervention during the Soviet regime were women.[13]

It is difficult to know just how many women were "cured" because Soviet psychiatrists did not wish to name that particular disease. Instead, lesbian behavior was treated as "sluggishly manifesting schizophrenia"(*vialo-tekushaia shizofreniia*). "Sluggishly manifesting schizophrenia" is a uniquely Soviet term. As Masha Gessen points out, this diagnosis is often compared with the Western "borderline personality" disorder when, in fact, it has no equivalent outside the former Soviet Union. Instead, "sluggishly manifesting schizophrenia," which was invented by Andrei Snezhnevskii at the height of Stalinism, is an umbrella term, a disease that does not reside in any fixed behaviors. Anything from sleep disturbances to making copies of censored literature can fall under "sluggishly manifesting schizophrenia."[14] Significantly, lesbians were treated not for homosexuality, but for this most fluid and flexible of diseases. "Sluggishly manifesting schizophrenia" made sure that love between women dare not speak its name because lesboerotic attraction literally had no name of its own.

The possibility of being diagnosed as sexually/mentally ill and the resulting forcible interment in a Soviet psychiatric institution worked primarily at a symbolic level. The Cure, like the Law, circulated as a threat. The diagnosis/cure symbolized removal from normal society into illness, perversion, and disease. It kept women on the *straight* and narrow. Even women who enacted same-sex desire generally also enacted—or at least *play-acted* —heterosexual desire. Many lesboerotic women married men and/or had children, sure signs of "health." [15] If a woman stepped too far out of line, the threat of the Cure could force her to return to the family of man. Many women told me of threats from the internal security apparatus as well as the KGB: if the women did not "cooperate" they would be outed to their families, at their place of employment, to their neighbors. Places of employment would fire them, neighbors would blackmail them, families would shun them, or worse, commit them to a psychiatric institution.[16]

Some women gave themselves over to the Experts, secure in the knowledge that only with medical intervention could they go on living. More often, women were committed by their "loved" ones. Psychiatric experts evaluated the behaviors and chose the appropriate cure. A girl who had an "unnatural" attachment to her girlfriend might "grow out of it." If not, forced hospitalization might "help" her do so. Usually the cure involved drug therapies and even aversion therapies, including shock therapy. After the treatment, the patient was forced to register with a walk-in psychiatric clinic where she was supervised. The supervision, which was imposed for the lifetime of the patient, often included continued medication and a curtailment of legal rights.[17] Sometimes a patient could not be completely cured of same-sex desire. The disease had to be contained so it would not infect the whole body social. One method of containment was confinement to a psychiatric institution for the chronically ill. Another cure for such "persistent schizophrenia" was a sex change operation. If the Experts could not change the Object of Desire, they could change the Sex of the Desirer.

But that was then, and this is now. Now, it is illegal to hospitalize someone against her will. Of course, the new rule of law in Russia is anything but complete. Now, too, the psychiatric diagnostic manual still lists same-sex attraction as a personality disorder and most psychiatric textbooks and courses either ignore homosexuality or treat it as a pathology in need of intervention.[18] If most psychiatrists continue to consider homosexuality a disease, then they will continue to find willing and unwilling patients. Underage women are still vulnerable to psychiatric hospitalizations and treatments against their will, but not against the law.[19] Even if adult women (and men) who experience same-sex attractions are not forced into treatment, they are certainly drawn into it.[20] Today many homosexual men and women place themselves into the medicopsychiatric complex, desperately seeking a cure. The Cure, then, works not just as a threat, but as a metaphor. The Cure works to teach those who are caught in it that they are diseased, that they are not responsible for the disease, or the cure, but that they must put themselves in the hands of experts who will help them to become "healthy." The medicopsychiatric experts welcome the sexually diseased with open arms, poking and prodding and probing them, looking for causes and cures for their desires.

Causes of Homosexuality

The experts posit a variety of physiological and psychological causes of homosexuality. Although not a comprehensive survey of all of the literature,[21] this chapter explores interviews with and articles by those sexologists who are well known among queers in Moscow and St. Petersburg.[22] Because of their close contact with communities of sexual minorities, these experts tend to be more sympathetic than those who do not specialize in sexual "deviance." On the other hand, even these sympathetic experts are always careful to maintain their own objectifying gaze—insisting that they themselves are speaking in the third person, not the first.[23] When I asked the sexologists why they got involved in such research, the answer was never connected to their own homoerotic desires. One said that his initial interest in sexual pathology led him to understand that homosexuals are not sick.[24] Another answered that he began to be interested in homosexuality after studying men who seduce boys. It soon became obvious to him that homosexuality was not related to pedophilia. Although at first his colleagues reacted with disbelief, wondering if he was not gay himself, they eventually understood that there were a large number of sexual "deviants" in need of psychiatric help and began to send patients to him.[25]

One queerly popular expert, Dmitri Isaev, believes issues of sexuality are fundamental to the psychiatric profession: "I always said that such persons make up a large percentage of the population. . . . [S]chizophrenia [affects] only 1 percent of the population and takes up tens of thousands of psychiatrists, but homosexuality is 4 percent of the adult population and

I don't know a single person who specializes in this. There should be four times as many psychiatrists who study this than study schizophrenia."[26] Like all of the experts I interviewed, Isaev portrays himself as a defender of homosexuals from the cruelty of less enlightened experts. Describing the work of some of his colleagues, Isaev says, "Most of the . . . persons whom they cured were not in fact homosexuals. . . . [T]hey cured [them] with extremely powerful medicines, drugs, some of which are forbidden now—at least they are rarely used, because their effects are very bad. Furthermore, they tell us that while they take these drugs they won't have any homosexual contact, but as soon as they stop taking them, they begin to act as they're used to acting. Such cures are senseless. . . . [T]his is a true police approach."[27]

Like the younger Isaev, Igor Kon is also critical of his Russian colleagues for continuing to define homosexuality as an illness to be treated.[28] But sympathy does not prevent any of these experts from making heterosexuality the standardized norm in no need of explanation while casting homosexuality as that which needs to be located, dissected, and, at least sometimes, eradicated. All of the sexologists known to queers[29] are searching for the causes of homosexual attraction and behavior. Causes, of course, indicate cures. None of these experts spoke of the causes of heterosexuality, nor of its possible cures.

Isaev According to an article by Isaev, "Psychosomatic Relations in the Etiology of Homosexuality," about 4 percent of all men and 2 to 3 percent of all women are of a homosexual orientation and this has been true since ancient times.[30] Isaev defines homosexuality as existing not just when there is sexual contact between persons of the same sex, but when this contact is accompanied by "emotional, erotic attraction which is only directed at persons of the same sex."[31] Thus same-sex contact without emotional attachment, or in same-sex environments, such as prison, does not constitute homosexuality.[32]

Once "real" homosexuals are separated from "situational" ones, Isaev further categorizes homosexuals as either "primary" or "secondary." "Primary" homosexuality has its roots in biology. It is often the result of neurological malfunctioning, a genetic predisposition, or a hormonal imbalance. For male "primary" homosexuals, their sexual orientation is often directly related to "testicular feminization" due to an "androgen deficit in the male fetus." This deficit causes a decrease in sensitivity to testosterone, resulting in "feminine appearance and mimicking, sometimes infantile frail constitution, high-pitched voice, and little hair on body and face." [33] For female "primary" homosexuals, "inborn adrenal hyperplasia" causing prenatal hormonal imbalances is a major source of their desires. Such girls "manifest . . . male behavior . . . accompanied by marked sexual role deviations and high levels of intelligence and ambivalent attitudes toward the same sex." [34]

"Secondary" homosexuality can be caused by dysfunctional familial relations, an incorrect upbringing, or the bad influence of a peer group during puberty. Often "secondary" homosexuality occurs in persons with "anxiety personality traits; . . . a stormy, disharmonious puberty with manifestations of hypersexuality and a diffuse eroticism; [and/or] . . . personal immaturity, lack of critical self-assessment, and a tendency toward situational involvement in deviant activities." For women, secondary homosexuality "is often [the result of] a negative experience in contacts with men, marked by brutality." [35] Evidence from as far back as 1952 is amassed to argue that homosexuality is the result of a variety of factors, both biological and psychological. Single-factor explanations cannot sufficiently explain something as complex as homosexuality. [36] Indeed, Isaev does not find most other work on homosexuality helpful, including the work of Western scholars, since much of the Western literature tends to describe same-sex attraction as either biological or psychological. Instead, Isaev sees a homosexual potential, analogous to mathematical ability, which is either developed or not. The realization of such potential relies on a combination of psychological, biological, and societal factors. [37]

Instead of a monocausal model, Isaev offers a matrix of homosexuality and homosexuals. Armed with a battery of tests, Isaev charts and plots his objects. One set of tests involves a person's self-image, what Isaev calls her/his "I." The questions ask the patients to describe their ideal self, friend, "special person," [38] and sexual partner. The responses are then divided into three groups: men, women, and homosexuals. For this particular study, homosexuals were considered to be men. It is unclear how women became a single group while men were split into "men" and "homosexuals." It is also not obvious why groups were divided by gender as opposed to some other taxonomy, like economic class or education level.

In a later study, the responses, like the respondents, are also divided by gender. Isaev constructed a series of attributes marked as either masculine or feminine. The responses consist of "evaluation," "strength," and "activeness." The higher the level, the more "masculine" the response.[39] Isaev then correlated his homosexual patients' descriptions of "I at the present time," "I as I would like to be," "a close friend," "favorite person," "sexual partner," "homosexuals," "most men," and "most women" with "evaluation," "strength," and "activeness."[40] Isaev found that "primary" homosexuals (i.e., those born that way) differed from "secondary" homosexuals (i.e., those who became that way) in several ways.[41] First, primary homosexuals were much more likely to see themselves as "like women" than were secondary ones.[43] Primary homosexuals were also much more likely to devalue women than were secondary ones, although the first valued homosexuals more highly than the latter. Perhaps most interesting of all, "secondary" homosexuals were looking for "feminine" characteristics in their sexual partners, while primary homosexuals wanted "masculine" lovers. Isaev concludes from his study that primary homosexuals desire men because they actually identify as women, while secondary homosexuals are more like heterosexual men in their desires and probably best described as "bisexual." This is especially true since secondary homosexuals did not seem to have close emotional ties to men. Isaev sees both groups as at risk for maladjustment since the primary homosexuals privilege masculine over feminine—but are themselves feminine; while the second group desires feminine partners—but limits itself to other men.[43]

Isaev's careful studies say more about experts than they do about homosexuals. Isaev is clearly relying on a very rigid model of gender as well as an assumption that sexual attraction is always about gender and not sex. Isaev's gender model, which is never the object of his study, presumes that traits such as strength and activeness (which he also calls "dominance") are masculine and that masculinity belongs to men. Since a person is either masculine or feminine, man or woman, a feminine man is not really a man, but a woman. In other words, his primary homosexuals actually identify as "women" and desire "men" while his secondary homosexuals identify as "men" and desire "women." A truly feminine woman could not desire another truly feminine woman. A truly masculine man could not desire another truly masculine man. Apparently Isaev has never been to a leather bar. Nor has Isaev ever considered the possibility that strength and dominance are the social laws of gender, not the metaphysical ones. "Strength" and "intelligence" are not measures of masculinity, but of Isaev's masculinist worldview. Perhaps even more perverse is Isaev's conflation of gender with sexual desire. Within his theoretical paradigm, a person does not desire a body, sexed but ungendered. Desire is never phallo- or gynocentric. Instead, sexual desire is always desire for the "opposite" gender. Which makes homosexuality heterosexuality, since desire is always desire for the Other (i.e., manly men want womanly women — or womanly men; but manly men never want manly men or manly women).

MIR: A Scientific Community   During 1991 in Moscow a lot of queers were speaking about a place called MIR, an acronym for a private company called Medicine and Reproduction. The word mir resonates at many levels in Russian. Mir can mean the world, peace, or the village community. For many of the city's queers, MIR had become just that: a world that offered them both peace and a sense of community. At a time when the only place to meet other queers was at a cruising strip or public toilet, MIR conducted weekly meetings that not only functioned as support groups but also as social groupings, places to meet others "like you." The meetings were co-sponsored by a group of sexual identity activists associated with a newly formed publishing concern, ARGO. The activists provided the queers; the sexologists provided the answers.[44]

The queers who came were desperately seeking each other,[45] while the sexologists who ran the institute were desperately seeking to make "homosexuals" an easily defined and recognizable group. By 1991, the doctors at MIR had developed a computer program to determine the "percentage of homosexuality" in a person. The method involved monitoring the body (e.g., skin temperature, heartbeat) while simultaneously recording reactions to particular stimuli. The reactions measured were bodily and facial expressions as well as gestures. The assumption was that there are certain bodily movements commonly understood as masculine and others that are feminine. For instance, a man who consciously and frequently poses his body, gestures expansively with his arms, and often changes facial expressions is exhibiting an "instability of his gender role."[46]

Another section of the test attempted to determine whether a person is at "risk" for homosexuality. It contained eleven questions that have a "direct relationship" to homosexuality, such as, "What sort of relationships did your parents have toward sex?" "When was your first sexual awakening?" "What sort of relationship do you have with your father?" "Are any of your relatives homosexuals?" Further risk was determined by asking the patient to look at pictures and describe whether a person is hetero- or homosexual, sexually satisfied or dissatisfied.[47]

CURES
Redirecting Desires

The sexologists at MiR developed such elaborate tests in order to cure the sexually unsuccessful. When persons came to them unable to "start a normal sex life," often deeply depressed, even suicidal, the experts wanted to determine whether the reason was homosexuality. "After all, often it happens that a person doesn't even admit to himself that he has such an orientation." Once the computer determines that a person is "significantly" homosexual, the doctors try to "gradually prepare his consciousness to accept the idea that homosexual[ity] is not a psychiatric illness nor a horrific moral crime. And often it happens that you have to do this [preparation] slowly and not immediately say 'Listen, you're gay, now get out of here and find your own kind.' "[48]

The community of MiR, however, was not a homosexual recruitment center. Instead of "preparing" a patient to accept his/her own homosexuality in order to be a homosexual, MiR sexologists worked to "reorient" (pereorientirovat') the now "admitted" homosexual back to a "normal sexual life." This is because homosexuality does not bespeak "psychiatric health." Although many of the MiR experts believed that the "mental instability" of homosexuals is a result of social prejudices, society does discriminate against homosexuals and the "task of any doctor" is to help a person feel "normal."[49] Since normalcy requires heterosexuality, that is the preferred course of action.[50] Of course, if the computer determines that the person is "highly homosexual" (e.g., over 50 percent) the sexologists have to "consider whether it's worth it to work for 'reorientation'."[51] Thus MiR's testing for homosexuality as well as preparing the patient for the results was analogous to doing a biopsy on a tumor to see if it is cancerous or not and then preparing the patient to both accept the cancer and, if possible, rid him-/ or herself of it.

Transsexualism as Cure   If a person cannot be "reeducated" to normalcy, not all hope is lost. There is another cure, but this cure, like chemotherapy, is extremely invasive and does not ever offer complete recovery of the self. The cure begins with a label: transsexualism. Once the label is acquired, the cure (i.e., a sex change) is guaranteed. In order to obtain the label, a person must submit her/himself to a battery of tests. Over the course of a few months to a year, the experts determine whether or not the patient is a transsexual. Once the diagnosis is given, the patient receives an official declaration (a *spravka*), which is then taken to the local passport office. The passport office changes the sex written in the passport from male to female or female to male. Now the "transsexual" is officially of the opposite sex (regardless of his/her bodily sex).[52] At this point, many transsexuals feel the "cure" is complete. Others go to one of the several hospitals that perform the operation and demand the medical procedure that will force their bodies to match their documents.[53]

Receiving the label is not simple. Transsexualism, like homosexuality, is difficult to pin down. It is often "misdiagnosed" as homosexuality. The border between homosexuality and transsexualism is ill defined. Sometimes those who consider themselves homosexuals are in fact "low-level transsexuals."[54] At other times, those who are "really" homosexuals want to change their sex in order to conform to societal restrictions. It was not unheard of for homoerotic men to have sex change operations to avoid prosecution for sodomy.[55] In the past and the present many young females have sex change operations, not because the doctors diagnosed them as "transsexuals" but because they labeled them "lesbians." Isaev has given twenty women over the past couple of years the necessary permission to change their sex. In none of these cases did Isaev actually believe that the women, usually under twenty-four years of age, were in fact transsexuals.

According to Isaev, transsexuals are those who are under the impression that their bodies are not their own and "cannot actually engage in sexual relations because such intimacy would occur in an alien body. This is the difference between a transsexual and a homosexual."[56] Isaev actually labels these women lesbians. But like many of his colleagues, Isaev believed that because women are "much more conservative" than men and have a much more difficult time living outside of social norms, they cannot (ever) adjust to being labeled homosexual, a perversion, but must become transsexuals, a disease with a cure.[57]

"Transsexuals," then, are those who cannot live as homosexuals. The sexologist from MiR explained that a *homosexual* does not want to change in order to fit into societal norms. A *transsexual*, however, feels that "if he is attracted to other men and is himself a biological male then something must be changed." Even if consciously a "transsexual" accepts that s/he is in fact a "homosexual," a "true transsexual" "cannot subconsciously accept" such a thing.[58] Transsexuals feel as though their personality "does not correspond to the physical, that is, biological [sex]."[59]

What the sexologists mean by "biological sex," however, is much more like the social construction of gender. By the experts' own admission, those they label "transsexuals" rely on a very rigid system of gender differences. The transsexual is a "worshipper of sharply defined sex roles, and he cannot escape them. . . . [H]e believes a man ought to be a man with capital letters. . . . For them polarity is absolutely necessary: м/г."[60] Although generally there are no physical differences between "transsexuals" and "homosexuals," even when there are, as in the case of "transsexual syndrome," the transsexuals are sometimes content to live as homosexuals. It is only during periods of extreme crisis in their lives, that "the thought occurs to them, perhaps I should change my sex."[61]

If the experts' understanding of transsexualism is true, then it offers a partial explanation of why there are ten times as many female-to-male transsexuals as male-to-female in Russia.[62] In a society as gendered and masculinist as Russia, women are surely more likely to face crises *as* women. But the experts' explanation for the ten-to-one ratio is different: women are either too conservative to live as lesbians or, as lesbians, they have the necessary "maleness" (i.e., "balls") to pursue the operation. That is, in order to get through all the required bureaucratic and societal barriers, a person "must be more masculine than feminine. Femininity for this? Well, he would cry, and worry. . . . Or most tragic of all, go and hang himself." This is because a person, regardless of sex, who is psychologically male is better adapted to society and less likely to get depressed than a person who is psychologically female.[63]

Transsexualism and Sexual Hierarchies   "Transsexual" is much more powerful in Russian than in English. As in the United States, it is born of expert knowledge that sees same-sex desire through a prism/prison of gender. The expert tendency to pathologize gender transgression and then correlate such transgression with homosexual practices is hardly absent among U.S. experts. For example, according to the American Psychiatric Association's (APA) diagnostic manual, unwillingness to conform to gender roles may indicate gender identity disorder. The symptoms of this disorder in children include insistence on wearing clothing stereotypical of the opposite sex, "strong and persistent preferences for cross-sex roles in make-believe play . . . intense desire to participate in the stereotypical games . . . of the other sex; [and a] strong preference for playmates of the other sex." Although no studies have been done among women, for men the correlation of gender identity disorders with homosexuality is quite high (three-fourths of boys with this disorder grow up to be homosexual or bisexual men).[64] But the Russian experts are more likely to categorize individual bodies as incorrectly sexed, rather than forcing every body into the hetero/homosexual divide of our own society.

It would be too easy to slip into a self-righteous tirade against the "tyranny of transsexualism." Even the Russian experts argue that transsexuals are those so trapped by gender that they are forced to cut themselves out/up.[65] Too many homosexuals argue that transsexuals should confess that they're "really" gay/lesbian. Both experts and queers offer the Cure to transsexuals: surgery or homosexual identity. I have no Cure. It is not obvious that a system that offers only two sociosexual choices (straight or gay—and sometimes bi) is more liberating than one that offers other possibilities. We all wear our own straitjackets.[66]

Thus, while transsexualism is certainly a label that originates in the imagination of experts, like other labels of deviance it is most powerful for those who wear it. The fact that transsexuals realize their "true" selves within webs of expert interventions and objectifying practices does not seem substantially different than how one comes out as a lesbian or gay man (or a straight person, for that matter). It might be argued that even if a homosexual is just as much a product of expert discipline as a transsexual, the former does not have to undergo radical surgical procedures and a lifetime of hormone treatments. Yet this ignores the decisions we all make in order to become *ourselves*. Some women have breast implants or take diet pills or have all their body hair removed in order to be heterosexually embodied. These are practices that do not necessarily reside in more "sane" individuals, but they are practices that receive less judgment from experts and queers alike. Sexual hierarchies that make certain choices normal and others bizarre are not nearly as compelling as the stories of some of those identified and identifying as transsexuals.[67]

Transsexual Subjects

It was the summer of 1991 when I first met women who identified as transsexuals in Russia. My partner and I were interviewing women whom we might have called lesbians, had they ever used the term themselves. We had heard about a group of women-oriented women in St. Petersburg who had formed a social club, which met once a week in an ice-cream parlor (*moloknyi kafe*). We found our way to the café one hot and dusty July evening. To our surprise, the women were young, very young. Of the twenty or so women there that evening, well over half were younger than sixteen years of age. Most of the women were divided into pairs and in almost every pair one partner identified as transsexual. The transsexuals did not appear any different than their partners: none of them was particularly tomboyish, none was wearing obviously masculine clothing, and few even had short hair.

As we spoke to the club members that evening and on other evenings, it soon became clear that their definition of transsexual was quite different from our own. We had expected women who wanted male bodies. Instead, we found girls who seemed like any other girls, except that they had female lovers. All of these girls risked scorn from their families, psychiatric hospitalization, arrest, and violence for their love. All of them wanted to live lives free from state/societal/familial interventions. Transsexualism seemed to afford them that. It meant that they were not really breaking any rules. Instead, one of them was "ill" and needed to be "cured."

I remember hoping that these girls would not go through with the operation, that they would not make such an irrevocable stand at such a malleable age. I wanted them to be "lesbians," to free themselves of the shame and humiliation I read on their faces each time I suggested it to them. I have grown a lot since that summer, and so have those girls. Some of them have grown into women, others into men. Some identify as lesbian, others as straight, still others survive in a liminal space they call transsexualism.

Zhenia Zhenia[68] is a tall, thin woman with translucent white skin and piercing black eyes. As a boy or a girl, she is beautiful. When I first met her, she was seventeen years old. She had just come to St. Petersburg from a provincial town in the South. She was enrolled at one of the local institutes, but had not gone to class for months. Zhenia was studying the repair of musical instruments. She loved this work and had since she was a child who liked to fix broken violins for her own pleasure. But only boys got work as craftsmen. Zhenia felt frustrated, but she was comforted by the other love in her life. Zhenia loved women. She had since she was a child, and now, living alone in a city, Zhenia set out to explore women and herself. But Zhenia was no more allowed to love women than she was allowed to fix violins. "Only boys can do that, but I'm not a boy"—or so she thought. Then she read about a wedding in India where a man, who used to be a woman, married a woman. The man who had been a woman was called a transsexual, and that is what Zhenia began to call herself.[69]

Zhenia went to see a therapist, who began a lengthy diagnosis to determine whether she was a he. Zhenia began to dress more and more like a man, he cut his hair short, he started using masculine endings when he referred to himself. He played only the role of a "man" with other women.[70] Before Zhenia could officially become a transsexual, he changed his mind and became a she. She decided she was, after all, just a woman who loved women. She didn't want a man's body; she preferred her own boyish one.

I last saw Zhenia in August 1994. I took her and her girlfriend out to dinner to talk about a lesbian organization in which the girlfriend was active.[71] In the course of the evening I realized I had met Zhenia before, in her 1991 incarnation as a transsexual. Rather than discussing the organization, she told me of the path that had led her to her current self, one she feels is both more and less true. She still was not able to find work as a craftsman, but she was enjoying being a woman in love with a woman who was just as butch and just as femme as she. The woman she loves called herself a lesbian, but Zhenia did not feel like one of those either. To her, the word sounded alien and "harsh." Her girlfriend suggested that Zhenia has internalized society's homophobia and that she should see the label "lesbian" as an honor, not an insult. "It's not that," Zhenia said, "it's just that I don't feel like a lesbian. I don't want to be what I do in bed."

Misha   He had always dreamed of having children.[72] "Papa," his daughter called, and he answered with a smile. He always did, because he was her mother. When he was very young he was a girl named Masha. But at an early age, the child felt like a boy, and so Masha became Misha. Growing up in a children's home, Misha waged a "battle for his masculine existence." By the age of fourteen, Misha had come to the attention of a gynecologist. The gynecologist told him that he was "sick" and that he must be "cured" because he would never be "accepted in our society and they'll put you in a psychiatric hospital." The symptoms were visible in the symbolic, not the physical. Misha refused to look or speak like a woman. Even worse, Misha had a girlfriend.[73] The doctor began to give Misha female hormones. "This wasn't in a hospital—he did it privately, more like an experiment." For five years he gave Misha hormones, from thirteen to eighteen. The doctor wanted Misha to "feel like a woman," but Misha never did.

Misha lived as a man, in the body of a woman. Misha found work as a conductor on the railroad. Although he loved his job, he almost lost it for refusing to dress like a woman. "According to the law, conductors who are women have to wear skirts with their uniform. I went to my boss and said I couldn't wear a skirt. . . . He asked why. I answered, 'Imagine if you had to go into the street in high heels, panties—how would you feel? That's how I feel in a skirt.' " By the time he was eighteen, Misha had met the love of his life. They set up house together and lived as a family, even raising Misha's younger sister as if she were their (biological) child. Although not officially sanctioned by the state, the young couple did manage to have a church ceremony, as man and wife.

When asked by an interviewer whether or not his relationship with a woman (while still inhabiting a female body) meant that Misha was perhaps a lesbian, instead of a man, he answered as though he'd thought about it before:

> The word "lesbian" at that time was something horrible, we tried not to even say it aloud. Most of us didn't even know what it meant. My wife did not consider herself a lesbian, she considered herself a normal woman, and she considered me to be a man. . . . I have always considered myself to be a man. If it hadn't been for the hormonal treatments . . . I would still consider myself a man and not a woman. . . . But because of the hormones' interference, every once in a while . . . I think like a woman. I want to be a man. But here that's not acceptable; here they make it illegal. If I have a woman's name on my passport, then I have to be a woman. So I have to be clever, to resort to trickery.

For three years Misha refused to see the doctor who had tried to turn him into a woman. When he saw him again, the doctor apologized for not understanding. He said "Misha, forgive me, I was mistaken, I did you a lot of harm, but forgive me because I finally understand. Of course, you needed an operation to make you a man because by your nature you should be a man." Misha answered: "You know, everything I have suits me just fine — I have a marvelous . . . wife. . . . Why would I want to change all that?"

A couple of years later Misha's life was no longer all that he wanted. Misha was alone in the world. His wife had died of a massive coronary, and Misha began to wonder if he should have a sex change.[74] Only by becoming a man could Misha find "a second woman like that [since] . . . in a lesbian pair . . . one of them all the same has to be a transsexual, has to take on the role of the leader. Since when there are two women who merely want to live with women, it's difficult for them to have sex. When there is no leader, it's difficult to start — there's some sort of shyness in front of one another. But I don't understand this very well — perhaps I'm mistaken." [75]

Hope of a sex change operation, however, was not enough to lift Misha out of his depression.[76] He decided to kill himself, but just when he had slit his wrists, a friend walked in. As a result, Misha was taken to a psychiatric hospital. Misha thought all was lost until it occurred to him to have a child. "[L]ife was over, and I had to have a child, a person for whom I could continue to live." Misha did have a child, and then had a sex change operation. Now Misha is the father to the child he bore, married to a woman, this time, legally, as a man.

Roma   Roma[77] is a businessman. Each morning he wakes up, gives orders to the twenty or so men who work for him, and then descends to his car. The car, a BMW, is a symbol of his success and his manhood. He drives it aggressively, "like a man," onto sidewalks if traffic is moving too slowly, into oncoming traffic if caught behind a bus. Roma was not always a successful businessman. Roma was not always even a man. When I first met Roma, she was a rough-and-tumble young blackmarketeer, and she lived and referred to herself as a woman. At that time, in the 1980s, Roma made her living by selling stolen flowers. Ironically enough, Roma would steal the flowers from the statue where newly married couples laid bouquets symbolizing their state-sanctioned love.

After a few years, as the economy loosened, Roma was able to sell her flowers more openly and even hired a young woman to help. The woman, Ira, told Roma, who by then was a he, that she was twenty-three years old, though she was really only fifteen. The two of them fell in love, and Ira eventually moved to Roma's apartment. As a juvenile, Ira was still subject to parental intervention—and intervene her parents did. Ira's mother told her she was "going against nature" by being with Roma. Her mother did not consider Ira a lesbian, but someone who had been "perverted" by a "transsexual." The mother felt that "transsexuals should have to live separately from everyone else and not hit on girls." Eventually Ira's parents called the police and had their daughter committed to a psychiatric hospital.

Ira found nothing perverse (read "homosexual") in her relationship with Roma since "[w]e relate to each other like a woman with a man, and not like a woman with a woman." Although she was sleeping with someone who was officially a woman, Ira did not consider herself a lesbian.[78] The authorities did not agree. For two weeks Ira was kept in a semiconscious state by a psychiatric hospital staff. It was even suggested that she might be put into a diabetic coma as a way of "curing" her "persistent schizophrenia."[79] A psychiatrist tried to explain to Ira why she must end her relationship with Roma: "Your [Roma] . . . is not a transsexual, but a transvestite . . . wearing men's clothing and considering herself a boy. They aren't normal people, gays, lesbians, transsexuals. We have to cure them and generally we ought to just put them in jail. They are perverted. And you, [Ira], are a woman and you should not live with someone of the female sex. . . . You shouldn't live with her because you're going against nature, and nature demands that you should have children—that you must live with a man."

During Ira's hospitalization/incarceration, Roma thought he would lose his mind. He was afraid Ira would come back a "zombie." Roma had himself been put in a psychiatric hospital in 1973, when he was fifteen years old. He was told that if he didn't stop calling himself a boy he would be put in the hospital for those with chronic mental illnesses. Roma had seen with his own eyes what the result of psychiatric intervention could be.

Roma and a few friends went to the hospital and convinced the nurses to let Ira go. He convinced the nurses with a knife and threats to kill them, but all the same, Ira was freed. By now, Ira was sixteen, old enough to marry, but Roma could not marry her. Roma decided to change his official sex from female to male. I asked Roma whether or not he wanted to have a penis. He was incredulous: "I don't know. I've never even seen one [a penis]. I don't think so. But I want women, so I can't be a woman." Besides, Roma points out with pride, that as a transsexual without a penis, he is a much better lover than a man with a penis: "I have a dildo (*iskustvennyi chlen*). . . . "I'll never infect a woman . . . nor will there be any unwanted pregnancy. . . . I feel my own body better, and I feel her body better than any man. I know what a woman needs, and what she doesn't need. Not a single man has been in a woman's body, and he does everything only for his own satisfaction." For Roma, then, the goal was not so much a change of sex as much as a legal right to cross gender boundaries. "When I get a legal passport in this stinking, shitty country, then I'll have legal rights. I can marry my girl. No longer will I be kept down in society, people saying that I'm a freak. Everything will change immediately. I'll say: I'm a man, here's my passport. . . . When we're being married, no one is going to ask me: take down your pants, what sort of dick do you have. They'll say: here comes a young man, married to a woman."

Roma managed to eventually get his passport changed. Roma never did get a penis, although now he has several dildos, some of them imported from the West. He calls himself a transsexual, but he hates all the other transsexuals he knows. "What do I need those people for?" he asks when I wonder whether or not his identity provides him with a community. "I have my girl, I have my work." Roma never did marry the girl, but he is rarely lonely. Roma always has several lovers. Once one of his lovers, a woman from Western Europe, told Roma that he was really a lesbian. Roma said: "I'm a man and that's it. What do lesbians do [in bed], I have no idea. I would never allow a woman to touch me. . . . A woman is a passive creature in sex, and a man—an active one. . . . My consciousness and soul are masculine, I'm all man."

NONSUBJECTS OF SEX AND GENDER

[He] ordered them to cut [her tongue] so short that she could not speak . . . whereupon they ripped out her tongue and cut it off at the root.

—The legend of St. Christine as told by Christine de Pizan, The Book of the City of Ladies, 1521

The Cure, then, catches up those who desire queerly and weaves them into the fabric of a binary gender and heterosexuality. Those who are diseased with (homosexual) desires have little choice but to turn to medical and psychiatric experts. The experts work to categorize, stabilize, and cauterize the diseased. The diseased work to survive in a system that, like the Law, both creates and eradicates queer identities and desires. Until now, the Cure has been where women reside. Neither subjected to antisodomy laws, nor subjects before the law, women who do not reside easily within their assigned gender and sexual roles have not been allowed stable identities. Women have not been made into homosexuals by the Law but have "sluggishly manifesting schizophrenia," according to the Cure. Disease is not a stable place for the self to reside because disease is always potentially curable. Women, then, are produced not as sexual subjects but as bodies on which diseased desires can be written and then literally erased.

So it happens that women-oriented women in Russia are confined to a place where it is difficult for self-speaking subjectivity to form, because it is not allowed a language with which to speak. Women-oriented women are subjected to the Cure, not the Law, and the Cure names only the disease, schizophrenia, stubbornly refusing to name the women. When it does name women-oriented women, the Cure names them transsexuals. In Russia, transsexualism is a space between one sex and another, a permanently transitional space on the way from one self to another. If the goal of trans-sexualism in Russia were not gender conformity but combat, if transsexuals were identifying as transsexuals, rather than as one gender or the other, transsexualism might transform into subjectivity. But in Russia, transsexualism provides no permanent housing for transgressive identities. A transsexual is becoming a man or a woman, not a queer.[81] Gender seeps into the gaze of experts and their objects alike, colors their vision, and the result is a shifting landscape of subjectivity and nonsubjectivity. Women's bodies are caught in this twisting landscape, pushing at its borders and boundaries, but never breaking free.

The Marriage of the Cure and the Law: Sex Criminals and AIDS

Somewhere between the Law and the Cure lies another gendered space, one reserved exclusively for men. The Law labels the men in this space criminals; the Cure labels them diseased. Some of the men are HIV-positive or have AIDS. The physical virus is transformed into a social one—those who have it are called homosexuals—regardless of what they call themselves, and having it is a crime. Other men are here for committing violent acts for sexual pleasure. These men are also labeled homosexual—regardless of whether their crimes or their selves are easily categorized as such. In this space of gendered, sexualized, and criminalized selves, homosexuality is read as diseased desire, disease is read as homosexuality, and crime is read as both.

Disease as Crime   The AIDS community in Moscow works hard to not be "too gay." In 1994, the largest AIDS information and support organization in Moscow was Aesop. Its director, Kevin Gardner, was a rarity in Moscow. He managed to receive government cooperation as a foreigner and as an openly gay man. Gardner believes that there is an indigenous Russian impulse to identify on the basis of sexuality. "The concept of identity is here. Look at the names of the gay publications, think about it: *My i Vy, Ia + Ia* [*We and You, I + I*]. All these pronouns are not a coincidence. The new sexuality is within this context of reclaiming sexuality as an individual identity." Although Gardner admits a lot of influence from the West and is extremely careful about his own position as an American gay activist working in the

Russian world of AIDS, he points out that identity "can't be [just] an import because it's not like a kiosk is selling it."[82]

At the same time, Gardner believes that the last thing Russian queers want or need to do is separate themselves from the rest of society. The desire to not become a separate "sexual minority," and the fact that much of Aesop's funding is contingent upon remaining heterosexually inclusive, means that Aesop is decidedly not Moscow's answer to New York's Gay Men's Health Crisis (GMHC). Reading Aesop's safe-sex pamphlets is about as homoerotic as a Harlequin romance novel. One pamphlet, "Aesop about AIDS," begins promisingly enough, with the picture of three young men, wearing the skimpiest of bathing suits, playing on the beach. In the background, a young woman in a bikini reclines, watching and waiting. The next picture shows one of the men leering at the woman. The rest of the illustrations show the man and the woman in the throes of passion. Although the text lists anal sex and homosexual contact as one of several possible modes of transmission, it is not aimed primarily at gays, but at heterosexuals who might think that they are not at "risk."[83] The purpose here is clear: Aesop and other AIDS groups want to stop the spread of AIDS, which means they want to educate everyone about safer sex practices. These groups are also trying to speak about queer sexual practices without losing support, financial and social. AIDS is not presented as a gay problem, even if it is.

As much as the independent AIDS groups try to graphically separate AIDS from "diseased desires," the juridical and the medicopsychiatric experts, the Law and the Cure, consistently conflate the two. An internal memorandum of the Ministry of Health states that "an infected person, who appears to be healthy, cannot only get sick himself, but presents a serious threat to society as well. In this connection, the fundamental task of health organs and institutions is the discovery of those persons infected with HIV, the surveillance of infected persons." The persons most likely to be infected are, of course, "homosexuals, persons who lead promiscuous sex lives, those sick with venereal diseases, and drug addicts."[84]

The current draft legislation on AIDS is just as willing to confuse homosexuality with illness. The draft law, which originally passed the Duma in November 1994, was vetoed by President Boris Yeltsin because of its provisions for the mandatory testing of all foreigners. Testing of foreigners was then limited to those who are in Russia for three months or more and the law passed the Duma's lower house by 276 to none. Neither Yeltsin nor any legislators seemed concerned about what the law would impose on HIV-positive Russians.[85]

In June of 1994 I attended a press conference on the proposed AIDS legislation. The conference was organized by the Aesop center, but included many medical and legal experts. The conference illustrated how queer AIDS activists construct their own closets in order to be heard by various experts as well as the general public. The conference might also be a tale with a moral, like the fables of the other Aesop. The moral is that closets alone will not protect queers with AIDS from becoming the target of the Cure and the Law.

> A female reporter speaking to a couple of cameramen: "There must be some sort of law since we have to do something about AIDS. These people have no control," and the cameramen nod agreement. Next several well-known queer activists arrive and sit down in the audience. [Evgeniia] Debrianskaia [founder of the first sexual minorities organization] arrives in a black leather jacket, motorcycle boots, her hair boyishly short. Next [Masha] Gessen [a well-known journalist as well as lesbian activist] sits down. Gessen is wearing a man's suit, the pants held up by suspenders. [Yaroslav] Mogutin [the gay journalist prosecuted for hooliganism], arrives in black leather and sunglasses. The sartorially "queer" audience is an odd contrast to the "straight" panel, where everyone wears suits and ties or other "unidentifiable" clothes. The panel, all men, introduce themselves. Despite the fact that two of them are well known to many in the audience as "gay," none of them mentions it. Instead, they introduce themselves as employees of anti-AIDS organizations. Gardner mentions journalists, specialists, and all those who are interested in AIDS prevention—but does not mention gays. In fact, no one mentions homosexuals at all until an hour and forty minutes into the conference when an audience member brings it up.
>
> Much of the conference seems to be about establishing true "Russianness." One expert critiques the law for not being written by real Russians because of its obtuse language. G. Rashchupkin mentions that he is proud to be a Russian as well as HIV-positive. The empha-

sis on national identity seems to coincide with a mad belief that AIDS is a disease of foreigners. The scientific director of a medical institute suggests that Russians need to be educated to avoid contacts with foreigners since AIDS is a foreign import.[86]

The proposed legislation relies on juridical institutions to locate those with the AIDS virus. Those who "look suspicious" of having AIDS are to be forcibly tested. Some of the panel members admit privately that no one looks more suspicious of having AIDS than queers. The law also requires mandatory testing of all persons seeking medical treatment. The government has already conducted 120 million tests, but has only found 717 persons with HIV. Obviously there are more than 717 cases of HIV infection in all of Russia. But those most likely to be positive avoid testing, in part because they fear juridical and medical intervention. Those who test positive are forced to reveal all their sexual contacts—including homosexual ones. Homosexual contacts can result in a myriad of interventions, and being positive can result in imprisonment for transmitting a sexual disease.[87]

Even more Orwellian are provisions of the law that make it illegal for HIV-positive persons to have any sexual contact at all.[88] For, once located and tested, those with HIV can be forcibly separated from society by a law that does not allow them to have sex and a medical establishment that believes in isolation rather than prevention.[89] The isolation in a sanitarium of HIV-infected persons, the isolation of Russians from foreigners, the isolation of those who "look suspicious" of having AIDS from those who do not, the isolation of AIDS from homosexual, homosexual from AIDS, all come together to erase queer subjects from the Law. At the same time, the Law continues to subject those who are queer to both the Law and the Cure. The Aesopian fable comes to an end. In the fantasyland of AIDS policy, isolation will work. In the real world, isolation will not prevent AIDS from spreading. In the real world, trying to separate AIDS from homosexuality will not preserve queer men. Instead, AIDS as diseased desire will be written by the Law onto the bodies of queer men, even as these men continue to act as though they cannot read.

Crime as Diseased Desire   The Law and the Cure hide behind the smokescreen of AIDS prevention in order to subject queer men to state and medical interventions. In this way, disease is read as desire, but surreptitiously so. In the case of sex criminals, medical and legal experts go out of their way to highlight the connection between the crime and homosexuality, even if they have to invent that connection themselves.[90] Homosexuals, in the expert imagination, are ill, and their illness makes them more likely to act in desperation, to commit crimes of desire. The connection between criminality and homosexuality was nowhere more evident than in the case of Andrei Chikatilo.

During the 1980s, Chikatilo committed a series of gruesome and sexually motivated murders in the Rostov region. Although most of the victims were women, the Rostov authorities fervently believed that a killer so perverse must be a homosexual. The assumption was that the killer suffered from a sexual disorder, and since homosexuality was a sexual disorder, the killer was homosexual. By 1984, with twenty-four victims recovered, five of them male, investigators began to act on this illogical syllogism. The result for queer men in Rostov, and possibly other areas of Russia, was what one American observer called a "gay pogrom."[91] A dragnet of all of the region's homoerotic men began with one man, who in order to continue taking care of his sick mother was forced to reveal the names of all men whom he knew to be homosexual. The dragnet resulted in 440 men being identified and investigated. Of those men, 105 were sent to jail for sodomy. Several other men chose suicide over imprisonment as sex criminals.[92]

Initially, Chikatilo and other sex criminals were a secret best left to the experts. As the Russian press freed itself of state control, however, it began to print more and more information about sexually motivated murders. The information in the press relied on the expert construction of sex criminal as homosexual (and homosexual as sex criminal). In an article entitled "Chikatilo and Company," a journalist relies on cases from a sexologist to warn parents that if they are too "carefree" about their children's developing sexuality, they may end up with a murderer on their hands. Such murderous tendencies appear "most often in the area of attraction to sexual perversion." Any "innocent exceptions from the norms of sexual behavior," including "narcissism" (i.e., an attraction to one's own body and a euphemism for homosexuality), "may transform into a criminal form" the journalist cautions. Quoting from a conference on "Serial Killings and

Social Aggression" held in Rostov-on-Don in September 1994, the journalist goes on to pronounce the conclusions of the expert studies with all the authority of science. Sex criminals have "long hands, weak sperm, little body hair, femininity in the way they conduct themselves, and often in the way they look." [93] If the description is a familiar one, it is because this is how various medical experts characterized "primary" or "passive" homosexuals. With or without the antisodomy laws, being a visibly gay man or young boy is still criminal, only now it is pathologically so.

Several other articles picked up on the expert description of sex criminals as "feminine." One article began with the title "Sexual Maniacs for Some Reason Always Have Long Hands" and went on to discuss the case of Slivko, a serial killer who made a film of his crimes. Slivko's victims were "without exception pubescent boys," and he feared women as though they were fire.[94] Other experts have spoken to the press about the link between homosexuality and criminality. A doctoral candidate, Elena Topil'skaia, used her dissertation on "Typical Versions of Personalities of a Rapist of Juveniles," to help find the rapist of an eight-year-old boy in St. Petersburg. The rapist was assumed to be homosexual because of his choice of victim and thus known homosexuals were the choice suspects.[95] The press also picked over the case of Akhmat Azimov in gory detail. Azimov, known as the "vampire from Andizhan," killed four young boys. The boys were held captive for several days or weeks during which time Azimov would cut into their veins and drink their blood. The press was only too happy to point out that Azimov's peculiar tastes were developed during a homosexual liaison when he bit his lover's hand during sex and drank blood. "From that moment on Akhmat understood that blood—this was for him. It's tasty. Very tasty." [96]

Homosexual sex can clearly lead to murderous impulses. In another article in the press, accusations of homosexuality can do the same thing. "Sexual Maniac? No, Just a Drinking Buddy" recounts the vicious murder of a man who was found with a sharp stick shoved into his anus. Although the police originally suspected a sex maniac, they quickly realized that the killer was just a "regular guy" who had been accused of being a "certain unprintable word that is usually reserved for men who belong to the sexual minority" (i.e., "faggot"). That the drinking buddy killed his companion and then raped him anally was not a sign of mania at all, merely the under-standable, if unfortunate, result of an unspeakable insult.[97]

From *Identified Identity*   The postperestroika press began to publish more and more articles about "perversions"—homosexual and pathological alike. In the past five years, homosexuality has captured the public's attention, and the media has complied to demand by writing often about this once darkest and deepest of secrets. The result is a public discourse in which homosexuals, no longer illegal, are sources of prurient interest in the pathological. Entering into the public clamor over the meaning of sexual otherness are queer subjects. Queers are beginning to talk back. No longer confined to the Law and the Cure, queer subjects are now represent-ing themselves in a variety of ways. Chapters 3 and 4 will explore queer indentities and queer subjectivities as both a product and a producer of the Expert Gaze.

Russian and American activists protest in front of the Soviet consulate in New York City, 1990. Evgeniia Debrianskaia and author are third and fourth from left. Photo by Michael Wakefield.

Group of young female-to-male transsexuals and their heterosexual partners outside an ice cream café. Leningrad, 1991. Photo by Laurie Essig.

Poster from Roman Viktiuk's production of Jean Genet's *The Maids*, 1994. Photo by Laurie Essig.

ЖАН ЖЕНЕ

СЛУЖАНКИ

САТ ИРИ КОН

Queer activists Masha Gessen and Tanya Miller discuss how best to sartorially signify lesbian desire. Moscow, 1994. Photo by Liza Cowan.

Robert Fillipini (left) and Yaroslav Mogutin speak to a crowd of reporters at Wedding Palace No. 4 about their attempt to legally register their marriage. Moscow, 1994. Photo by Laurie Essig.

Queer activist Evgeniia Debrianskaia explains her philosophical opposition to state recognition of any marriage to reporters at the Mogutin/Fillipini wedding. Moscow, 1994. Photo by Laurie Essig.

Queer activist Olga Krauze meeting with young female-to-male transsexuals in Leningrad, 1991. Photo by Laurie Essig.

Author (left) cruises the streets of Moscow with friends, "Vanya," and queer activist Pavel Masel'skii (right). "Even in a dress, I am often taken for a man, although always a queer one." 1994. Photo by Liza Cowan.

Author at the Bolshoi cruising strip. Moscow, 1994. Photo by Liza Cowan.

part II: self

chapter 3
Identity Politics and the Politics of Identity

After loss of Identity, the most potent modern terror is loss of sexuality, or, as
Descartes didn't say, "I fuck therefore I am."
— Jeanette Winterson, Art and Lies, 1995

In the United States, much of political life is born of the politics of identity. We demand representation *as* women, *as* African Americans, *as* gays
and lesbians. These "particular" identities are counterpoised against the
more "general" identity of not a woman, not black, not queer. Regardless
of whether we are the standard or the deviation, we speak about identities
as though they reside outside of time and culture, floating in some metaphysical truth that merely awaits our discovery (and the discovery of our
"true" selves).

The American faith in identity has created the possibility of mass social
and political mobilization. Identities as blacks, women, and queers have
catalyzed civil rights, feminist, and gay/lesbian movements around the
country. Although the movements themselves have lost much of their mo-
mentum in the 1990s, the belief that we *are* a race, a gender, a sexuality
is stronger today than ever. We now exist in an age of the multicultural
imperative: everyone must have a fixed and stable identity or, better yet,
identities. There is no possibility of maintaining "mobile subjectivities," of
paying attention to the way in which we inhabit identities with our practices, make them ours by acting as though they already were. We are far
more like squatters—in constant danger of losing our seemingly stable
homes—than like landowners.[1]

But if identity has become the unavoidable trope of those who reside in
late twentieth-century America, it is a barely recognized narrative in Rus-

sia. Under the Soviet regime, identity was not a major organizer of social and political actions. Although taxonomies of class, gender, and ethnicity infiltrated every corner of daily life, few persons felt the need to engage in the endless process of publicly self-identifying, in part because few identities were publicly "allowed" in Soviet Russia.[2] As the Soviet Union entered its final decade, a variety of public identities did appear. Peace groups, environmental groups, even self-identified hippies and punks became more and more visible.[3] Then, as the Soviet empire lay dying, this handful of diffuse identities exploded into a multitude of highly politicized identities.[4] Suddenly there were groups of persons organizing around gender, national identity, even around sexuality. It seemed as though Russia was following the United States into an era of identity politics and the politics of identity.[5]

The initial explosion did in part transform into a Western-style identity polity. Certainly, there are many more organizing identities in Russia than ever before. In 1990, sexuality as an organizing identity in Russia seemed to be experiencing a moment similar to Stonewall in the United States[6] Many observers expected the first public acts for the rights of sexual minorities to spark a movement in the same way that the Stonewall Riots inspired U.S. gay and lesbian activism.[7] Yet post-Soviet Russia has not seen a mass movement of sexual identity develop. Instead, a small and disparate group of organizations appear less vital with each passing year.

The rise and fall of sexuality as a politically organizing identity is the story of Western imports clashing with the economic, cultural, and discursive realms of post-Soviet Russia. The clash has produced some truly brilliant moments, when activists acted courageously and humanely. It also produced some truly cynical moments, moments when Westerners and Russians exploited national stereotypes and prejudices for computers, dollars, and fame.[8] In the end, many persons felt burnt from the effort to create a stable movement in a highly volatile context.[9]

It is not just the current economic and societal crises that have stilted the growth of queer identity politics. There are no "gay" geographic spaces in a country where housing is still in terribly short supply and moving often requires registration (propiska). There is no "gay" economic base; there is barely any economic base at all. There are few phones that work well, fewer fax machines and computers. Perhaps most important of all, there is no clearly defined identity around which to organize. As I argued in chapters 1 and 2, expert definitions of the sexual other did not solidify into the homo-sexual species as they did in the United States. Instead, sexual otherness was a temporary fall from heterosexual grace, not a permanent marker of a stable and abiding self. The fluidity of Russian sexual identity is seen in the day-to-day lives of Russians who juggle marriages to someone of the oppo-site sex with lovers of the same sex.[10] It is seen in narrative realms, in the unwillingness of many women and men to "be" a sexuality.[11] Ultimately the experience of sexual identity in Russia speaks not about the "peculiari-ties" of Russian society, but the weakness of "identity" and the politics it spawns more generally. This chapter explores identity politics as one of the most powerful and problematic forms of self-representation by looking at the failure of sexual identity politics in Russia.

WHISPERS OF A MOVEMENT

In 1979 a group of women in Leningrad began to produce a samizdat femi-nist journal. The journal, *Woman and Russia*, was meant to be a "platform for all women" who were linked by their "natural" ability to "give life, to be opposed to war and violence"[12] The essentializing feminism of the journal's editors led them to believe all women were alike,[13] but they did not force all women to desire in the same way. Instead, *Woman and Rus-sia* bravely published fictional and autobiographical tales of female-female sexual relationships such as "The Right to Be Myself," a powerful polemic for the rights of lesboerotic women.[14] By the time of the second and third issues of *Woman and Russia*, both the KGB and Western feminists began to show intense interest in the publication. The KGB warned that further pub-lication would result in arrests, while Western feminists had the journal published in Paris.[15] The last issue of *Woman and Russia* appeared in 1980, along with the harassment, arrests, and eventually expulsion of the four editors/leaders.[16] Despite the brevity of its existence, the journal managed to create a space for some of the earliest first-person expressions of sexual otherness in Soviet Russia.

A few years later, another group of Leningraders began gathering, this time for the explicit purpose of forming a "gay and lesbian" group. A young student by the name of Aleksandr Zaremba had read about the International Gay and Lesbian Association (ILGA) and had decided it was time to form a similar organization in Russia. In 1984, Zaremba gathered about thirty persons together, four of whom were women, and founded the *Gai Laboratoriia* (Gay Laboratory). The main goal of the Gay Laboratory was to change the antisodomy laws,[17] but they also attempted to distribute information on the dangers of AIDS.[18] By July 1984, the group had established contact with Finnish gay/lesbian activists and had been made a member of ILGA. The KGB was dismayed not just by the formation of a Russian gay/lesbian group, but by the constant contact that the group had with foreigners. KGB agents continued to harass the members, eventually revoked the visa entry privileges of the Finnish liaison to the group, and planted informers. By August of 1986 the once optimistic activists decided to disband.[19]

THE MOVEMENT FINDS ITS VOICE

In the winter of 1989–90 queer activism in Russia found its voice. A group of persons working for the Libertarian Party decided to form the Moscow Association of Sexual Minorities. The Libertarian Party, led by Evgeniia Debrianskaia, was itself committed to the rights of sexual minorities.[20] Many of its members were influenced by the ideological platforms of the German Green Party and the Italian Radical Party—both of which advocated an end to state interference in the organization of desires.[21] Before leading the Radical and Libertarian Parties, Debrianskaia had enjoyed a long career as a professional dissident.[22] In the mid-1980s, she was a member of the Moscow-based peace group *Doveriia* (Trust). The Trust group protested the Soviet government's war in Afghanistan as well as the militarization of Soviet society.[23] In 1988, Debrianskaia was one of three cofounders of the Democratic Union, or DS. The DS, an eclectic group of activists, managed to unite feminists, queers, and even Russian nationalists in the first proto-party organization by dedicating itself to the single goal of ending the political monopoly of the Communist Party.[24]

Debrianskaia's work in the dissident movement provided her with a large network of friends and colleagues[25] as well as some idea of how far she could push the Soviet system without ending up in jail.[26] Thus, when a group of queer activists began meeting in the winter of 1989–90, Debrianskaia easily established herself in a leadership position.[27] By the beginning of 1990, the activists staged their first public event—an international press conference. At the press conference, ten men and five women announced the formation of the Moscow Association of Sexual Minorities as well as the publication of its newspaper, *Tema*.[28] Debrianskaia and Roman Kalinin, a young student,[29] were the only members of the association to state their full names, thereby becoming the first "out" queers in Russia.[30] The act of publicly coming out was, of course, extremely significant for many self-identified queers who had never before witnessed someone speaking in the first person about being queer. It was also an extremely important event for the Russian public more generally. Debrianskaia was a dissident, an activist against the tyrannies of the already discredited system. When Debrianskaia spoke for the rights of sexual minorities, the public was forced to listen.[31]

The association's paper, *Tema*, also marked a significant turning point in Russian culture. Although its first edition's circulation was only 527,[32] by the summer of 1990 *Tema* was being printed in runs of 15,000,[33] and was eventually sold openly throughout Moscow.[34] In its first issue, *Tema* combined articles about safe sex with news about the legal status of homosexuals and gossip about famous queers in history.[35] Thirteen issues appeared between 1990 and 1993, when Kalinin announced the end of *Tema*. Those involved in the paper's production felt that it had already "completed its historic mission."[36] The mere fact that *Tema*'s end came about not as the result of government harassment but because its producers moved onto other projects reveals just how important that mission was.

Half a year after their first press conference, Debrianskaia and Kalinin were pushing Russian society in previously unimaginable directions. The association activists succeeded in registering *Tema* with the Moscow City Council despite the obvious opposition of the Communist Party (as stated in the party's mouthpiece, *Pravda*).[37] In the same month Debrianskaia entered the Russian press with a vengeance when she organized a series of demonstrations for the rights of Soviet prostitutes (the association's mandate was promoting the rights of "sexual minorities," a term which includes sex workers). Debrianskaia demonstrated outside the Intourist Hotel in Moscow (a popular place for the purchase of Russian prostitutes by foreign businessmen) and then a few days later handed out the group's literature and condoms near Red Square.[38] TASS, the Soviet news agency, failed to acknowledge the Association of Sexual Minorities, but did describe Debrianskaia as "the leader of the fair half of the controversial Soviet Libertarian Party" and of gays and prostitutes.[39]

Shortly thereafter, Debrianskaia and Kalinin traveled to the United States at the invitation of the Gay and Lesbian Alliance against Defamation (GLAAD) and the Stonewall Foundation. While in the United States, the activists managed to organize a demonstration in front of the Soviet Mission to the United Nations to protest the official indifference to the burgeoning AIDS crisis as well as the continued criminalization of male homosexuality.[40] In addition to the demonstration, Kalinin and Debrianskaia gained a certain amount of fame in the U.S. gay press and among gay/lesbian activists through a variety of interviews and speaking engagements.[41] Kalinin was even named "Man of the Year" by the national circulation gay journal the *Advocate*.[42] These contacts would eventually result in tens of thousands of dollars of support for the group's endeavors (both in the form of cash and technical equipment) being funneled from U.S. gays and lesbians to association activists. It would also result in the group's transformation from the Association of Sexual Minorities to the Association of Gays and Lesbians. The nominal shift meant a much narrower focus for the group, since an entire world of sexual otherness, including Debrianskaia's prostitutes, was now excluded from the group's mandate.[43]

The association continued in its pared-down form for the next year or so. In the summer of 1991, Kalinin was the Moscow organizer for the International Gay and Lesbian Human Right's Commission's (IGLHRC) "Soviet Stonewall" festival. Debrianskaia and Kalinin differed sharply over the usefulness of an American-organized and sponsored Soviet Stonewall. Although they continued to work together, at least occasionally, the Moscow Association was barely functioning by 1993. Debrianskaia helped to create a separate organization, the Soiuz Osvobozhdeniia (Union of Liberation), but it never really got off the ground.[44]

Several activists decided that what was needed was a conference that would be run by and for Russians (in contrast to the American-organized 1991 Soviet Stonewall).[45] By the summer of 1993 they had organized such a conference. According to its organizers, the all-Russian conference managed to achieve several goals. First, activists from all over Russia participated. Second, information was successfully exchanged at a series of roundtable discussions on AIDS, the political and legal situation of "sexual minorities," the role of the mass media in the queer movement, as well as a roundtable dedicated exclusively to lesbian organizations. The result of the conference was not the continuation of the Moscow Association of Gays and Lesbians, but its replacement by Treugol'nik (Triangle). Triangle was to be an umbrella organization for "gay, lesbian, and bisexual" groups and persons throughout Russia. There would no longer be a Moscow-oriented group of activists.[46]

At the same time that activists began organizing in Moscow, several St. Petersburg activists were creating their own, more culturally oriented version of sexual politics. In December 1989, feminist leader Olga Lipovskaia was busy planning the sixth issue of her samizdat feminist journal Zhenskoe chtenie (Women's Reader). The sixth issue was to be a "lesbian issue." Although Lipovskaia was not herself a lesbian, she felt it important for feminism to address all relationships between women.[47] The "Lesbian edition" of Women's Reader contained translations of Adrienne Rich's "Compulsory Heterosexuality and Lesbian Existence,"[48] an article from Lesbian Connections, as well as original fiction and essays by several Russian women.[49]

One of the lesbian contributors to Zhenskoe chtenie, Olga Zhuk, was simultaneously founding her own organization, Fond Chaikovskogo (the Tchaikovsky Fund).[50] Together with about forty other activists, Zhuk managed to stage several well-publicized events, including an art exhibition entitled "Woman as Object and Subject of Art." As a result of the publicity, the Leningrad city council initiated proceedings against Zhuk for violating the antisodomy statute. As I explained in chapter 1, the Russian word for sodomy, muzhelozhestvo, literally means males lying together. Thus the prosecution of Zhuk was eventually dropped as an impossibility.[51] Despite the initial harassment, the Tchaikovsky Fund was eventually legally registered.[52]

In 1991, the fund leaders, Zhuk and Iuri Ereev, like Kalinin in Moscow, helped bring the American-organized Soviet Stonewall to St. Petersburg. Then in 1992 and 1993 the fund managed to stage queer cultural festivals.[53] The festivals, known as "Christopher Street Days,"[54] attracted thousands of the city's queers to a carnivalesque revelry in the form of large queer discos, as well as smaller numbers to seminars on AIDS and the "development of gay and lesbian community." [55] In May 1994, the fund also served as the local liaison for a German gay/lesbian film festival.[56]

The Rise of Queer Politics: Foundations and Fissures

Russian queer activism burst into the public sphere like a bull in a china shop. Many of the new groups were radically queer and did not attempt to make their positions more palatable to a public ignorant of and often hostile to sexual otherness. Not surprisingly, other groups of activists began to form in opposition—not to society at large—but to counter the first groups of sexual minorities. Vladislav Ortanov split from the Moscow Association and started his own organization and journal, RISK (the Russian acronym for Equality, Sincerity, Cooperation, and Compromise). Unlike the Moscow Association's thirst for controversy, Ortanov felt that queer activists should try not to offend either public opinion or government officials. Ortanov argued that most Russians are strongly opposed to homosexuality and the last thing activists should be doing is further alienating them. Ortanov also believed it was much simpler to work within the system, to show the authorities the advantages of decriminalizing homosexuality, rather than remaining permanent outcasts from officialdom.[57]

In August 1991, a group of Moscow lesbians also decided that the association could not adequately represent their interests. To these women, the association's prioritization of ending the antisodomy statute as well as working against AIDS had little to do with the day-to-day realities of being a lesbian in Russia, since neither Article 121.1 nor AIDS had a major impact on them. The women were also frustrated with what they saw as too much emphasis on the political and too little on the cultural. Together they formed the Moskovskaia organizatsia lesbiianek v literature i iskustve (the Moscow Organization of Lesbians in Literature and Art), known simply by its acronym, MOLLI. Although MOLLI began with a primary focus on social support,[58] the group quickly transformed itself into an association dedicated to facilitating woman-centered culture. In this capacity, MOLLI sponsored several concerts of "women's music," and one of its leaders, Liudmila Ugolkova, produced a short documentary program on love between women, which aired on Russian television in October 1991.[59]

At the same time that the Moscow queers were breaking ranks, a group of less confrontational activists in St. Petersburg was forming *Nevskie Berega* (the Banks of the Neva). Led by Aleksandr Kukharskii, a former professor of mathematics at Leningrad State University, the group began with ten women and two men dedicated to *gradually* changing the minds of those who make laws and influence public opinion.[60] Although initially denied registration, Kukharskii's group did manage to gain official recognition in 1991 when they changed their name from the Banks of the Neva to Kryl'ia (Wings).[61]

The appearance of fissures in the earliest building blocks of queer activism in Russia was the result of serious structural flaws in a politics based on identity. Common sexual practices do not create common politics/ideologies. Consider the following example. One compromise-oriented activist, Kukharskii, described his relationship with the government as "extremely positive." In 1994 he insisted that there had been no legal discrimination against homosexuals for at least seven years and little social discrimination either. When in New York for the twenty-fifth anniversary celebrations of Stonewall in June 1994, Kukharskii was angry that few U.S. reporters wanted to hear such glowing descriptions of the position of queers in Russia. Kukharskii felt ignored when a more radical activist, Masha Gessen, was quoted because she told "alarmist" tales of lesbians being put in psychiatric institutions against their will. "This is nonsense, no such thing has occurred in the last few years, but journalists don't want to hear this," said Kukharskii.[62] Gessen, who had just spent a year documenting cases of legal and psychiatric abuses of queers, clearly disagreed.[63]

Radical activists like those who participated in the Tchaikovsky Fund and Triangle would probably not describe their relationship with the government as "extremely positive," nor are they overly concerned with not alienating the "general" public. Faced with state and societal discrimination against sexual minorities, they do not see pleasing an oppressive heterosexual majority as a task of queer activists. For them, the fight for queer rights is a war, not a seminar. Compared to compromise-oriented activists like Kukharskii and Ortanov, radical queers want to move quickly and decisively. Compromise-oriented activists, however, do not want to make public opinion on homosexuality any worse than it is. Instead they prefer moving more slowly, but more safely.

The differences are not only political; they are also personal and material. Many compromise-oriented activists have more to lose in the Soviet and post-Soviet systems than their radical counterparts. Often, compromise-oriented leaders have careers and apartments and families to protect. Many of them perceive radical queers as "criminals." The radicals, on the other hand, see compromise-oriented leaders as being morally compromised by their positions of relative privilege. The differences between the two groups are illustrated again and again in the circulation of rumors.

Rumors about radicals are occupied with criminality. I have heard leaders like Debrianskaia, Zhuk, and Kalinin referred to as drug addicts, alcoholics, and thieves. One compromise-oriented activist told me that when a German delegation came to the Tchaikovsky Fund they were encouraged to drink too much and then robbed not only of their money, but also of their shoes (and this during a Petersburg winter!). This rumor pairs radical criminality with the victimization of Westerners. This theme occurs again and again in the circulation of rumors about radical Russian queers. A particularly popular story involved a well-known activist developing an "obsession" for a German woman. One day the Russian showed up at her door, trying to kick it down, and eventually physically attacked the German woman's lover, inflicting a serious bite wound. The bite was all the more frightening because the Russian was "known" to be an IV-drug user, and thus "probably has AIDS." Here we see violence, drug abuse, and disease as the markers of radical activists. A similar rumor circulated about a Russian activist who demanded money from her English lover. When the Englishwoman refused, the Russian woman beat her lover's head on a cement floor to the point of unconsciousness. A third story also contained violence. In it, an American lesbian and a Russian lesbian went traveling together. When the American woman refused the Russian woman's advances, the Russian woman tried to rape her. Whether or not any of these or the hundreds of other stories told in queer circles are true is unclear. What seems obvious, however, is that many of the compromise-oriented activists do not trust in the integrity of their more radical counterparts. They are afraid that their less "civilized" colleagues will behave in uncontrolled and inappropriate ways. This fear seems particularly great when the radical queers come in contact with Westerners. Most of the stories I heard involve at least one Westerner, usually a gay/lesbian activist. No doubt this is partly a response to my own position as a foreigner in Russia, as well as a fear of losing Western support because of the behavior of others.[64]

It is not only compromise-oriented activists who circulate rumors. Many radical queers tell equally disturbing tales about their more middle-of-the-road comrades. One leader is a well-known "pederast" with a large collection of photographs of young boys and is even rumored to have sex with animals. Several are "clearly" KGB informers, since they managed to maintain careers and gay lifestyles during the Soviet regime. The rumors about them are slightly different than those about the radical queers. In rumors about middle-of-the-road activists, too much willingness to work within the system as well as (moral) hypocrisy sustains the plot. Yet the point to the stories about both groups is similar. They warn the speaker and the listener not to trust "those" people—the ones who are too queer or not queer enough.

The ideological divisions among queer activists generally run along material fault lines. Position in society—particularly class and gender—rattles the foundations of "common identity." Radical activists are generally already marginalized members of society. They do not have prestigious jobs or reputations that they are trying to protect. Indeed, many of them have made careers in opposition to the system[65] or are too young to have careers to risk.[66] In contrast, many of the more compromise-oriented activists are struggling to reconcile mainstream careers with queer sexualities. Ortanov and Kukharskii, the first to break ranks with the more radical queers, are both established professionals.[67] Long after he started RISK, Ortanov continued to live with his wife, further reinforcing his social legitimacy, and has done all his queer activism under a pseudonym (Ortanov).[68] Kukharskii, too, has a career both distinguished and distinct from his queer activism. Kukharskii was a professor at one of the most prestigious universities in the country until he was forced to resign in 1987 over charges of violating Article 121.2 (having homosexual relations with a minor). Despite Kukharskii's expulsion from academia, he has managed to establish himself in the new Russian business world. Even if he had not, Kukharskii has enough class capital to last a lifetime. On the wall of his living room hangs his grandmother's diploma from the St. Petersburg school for young girls of nobility (Catherine's Girls School) as well as a sword his great-grandfather brought back from a war in which he fought at the tsar's personal request.[69] Class distinctions, always highly relevant in the Soviet years, have become even more so as Russian society flirts with a return to monarchy as well as a Western-style system of class reproduction through fiscally restricted access to education and careers.

It is not only class, however, that cracked the veneer of queer solidarity. Gender, too, divided what quickly became a male-dominated movement. Despite the fact that many of the earliest leaders were women, most of the first queer organizations ignored issues like punitive psychiatry and the legal position of lesbian mothers and focused on AIDS and changing the antisodomy laws. Perhaps the focus of the early groups was the result of masculinist leaders, but it also undoubtedly stemmed from imitating Western models of gay activism. Problems like AIDS and laws against sodomy translated much more easily than the uniquely Soviet psychiatric system. Regardless of the reasons for the masculinist focus, many women did not see the queer identity groups as valid representations of their lives and interests.

The divisions among taxonomies other than sexuality that appeared among queer activists are not, of course, unique to Russia. The radical queer/mainstream lobbyist split certainly exists in the United States, where groups like the Republican Log Cabin Association compete in the public imaginings of sexual otherness with ACT-UP and the Lesbian Avengers (whose slogan, "We Recruit," is surely meant to alienate). Any large event that tries to unite queers of every type always creates as much friction among the participants as between the participants and police.[70] But while the divisions themselves are not unique to Russia, the fact is that less than five years after it began, identity politics was floundering rather than flourishing. That the early activists' extremely courageous appearance in the public sphere as self-speaking queers did not develop into a "movement" means that Soviet Stonewall never really occurred. Russian queers are not "just like American queers, just twenty years behind"; there is no universally true path of sexual otherness that follows through the rather unimaginative steps of "the closet, the movement, pride and community."[71] This "standard" Western fairytale is far too simplistic to have ever occurred, even in the United States.[72] To ask why a movement did not develop in Russia is to impose the Western model in the posing of the question. Rather than examine the reasons a movement failed to develop, it seems more important to consider what is, and is not, happening among those queers who believe that common sexual practices and identities produce common social and political agendas.

THE FALL OF QUEER POLITICS/THE RISE OF QUEER SUBJECTIVITIES

"I feel like I'm witnessing the birth of the Russian gay and lesbian movement."

"More like the miscarriage . . ."

—Conversation between two American activists at a meeting of Moscow's Triangle, April 1994

Despite a still tenuous legal position (consensual male-male sex was illegal until 1993), divisiveness among activists in Moscow and St. Petersburg, and an extremely hostile climate, queer activism did flourish in the first years of the decade. (Homo)sexual identity politics surfaced in towns far from Russia's center. Queer activists in Krasnoiarsk and Novosibirsk, inspired by their participation in the Leningrad Stonewall events in the summer of 1991, returned home to begin their own group, Siberian Initiatives. One of the activists, Natalia Ivanova, even began a lesbian-themed radio program.[73] In 1993, in Tomsk the local queer group, Astarta, was officially registered and also held the first gay discos.[74] The city of Omsk managed to hold Siberian Gay Festivals in 1992 and 1993.[75]

These were heady years for those who believed Russia was to follow the road to identity politics that the West had so carefully laid.[76] Many activists, both indigenous and imported, believed Russia would soon be just like the U.S./us.[77] By 1994, however, few activists dreamt so large. There were still many organizations and groups based primarily on sexual identity, but few of these were as successful or hopeful as they had been in the past. In part this was the inevitable result of the massive economic and societal changes which Russian society was undergoing. Many people were too tired and too poor to feel much enthusiasm for any sort of activism, all the more so an activism that cost so much personally. Although homosexuality is no longer illegal, the social costs of being openly queer are still tremendous. A recent poll found that almost half the population of Russia still believes that homosexuals should be either killed or at least isolated from the rest of society.[78] Losing a job, family, even an apartment, as well as opening oneself up to harassment by criminals and police are just part of the costs of being openly queer.[79]

The decline of queer activism, as well as queer optimism, comes from within as well as without. The fissures that appeared early among queer activists have only deepened. Personal, political, class, gender, and other points of difference have increasingly become points of contention. Disillusionment with Western models of organizing and identity, a sharp decrease in interest and funding from Western sources, and a general feeling that the politics of sexual identity was not meant to flourish on Russian soil have all dampened the early glow of queer activists. All of this has meant that the four largest and most successful organizations in St. Petersburg and Moscow, the Moscow Association, MOLLI, the Tchaikovsky Fund, and Wings, were by 1994 barely functioning or not functioning at all. The failure of each of these groups to spark anything like a movement is emblematic of the failure of identity to unite. The mid-century identity movements in the West turn out to be the exception, not the rule.

Treugol'nik/Triangle

Many of the original activists from the Moscow Association later joined together to create Treugol'nik/Triangle in August 1993. Triangle was envisioned as a nationwide umbrella organization that would serve as the informational (and perhaps leadership) center for various activist groups. A national founding conference was held and representatives from various cities attended. Triangle was to issue a bulletin of news relevant to the "movement" as well as organize an annual conference.[80] In the first year of its founding Triangle was largely unsuccessful at being either a national or informational organization. Its informational bulletin was already under its second editor and was being produced sporadically at best. Triangle was de facto not a national organization, but a Moscow one, since its weekly meetings were held in Moscow and were attended almost exclusively by Muscovites. On the anniversary of its founding, Triangle members were discussing whether or not the organization should be disbanded. Although its members ultimately decided to continue, Triangle was clearly occupied with its own survival, not the creation of a national movement.

In the course of six months in 1994, I attended nine meetings of Triangle. There were generally almost as many Americans as there were Russians. These meetings were full of the details of any organization—arguments among members, discussions about what should be done and how. The meetings also exhibited a variety of Russian problems. People were working too many hours just to have enough money to buy food. They did not have much time to spend on activism.[81] In addition, an inordinate amount of hope was placed on the generosity of Western activists in terms of time and money. When Western activists did not supply the necessary initiative or financing, the result was disappointment in Western notions of identity and politics.

The meetings I attended generally occurred at the home of a gay American businessman. His apartment, located in the center of the city, was easily accessible as well as large enough to accommodate the ten or so members who usually attended the meetings (a luxury that none of the Russian activists could afford). These meetings were not exactly "public" since a person had to be informed about when and where they would take place.[82] One of the first Triangle meetings I attended, at the beginning of April 1994, was rife with differences and disagreements. These arguments echoed larger problems with the organization. Triangle members disagreed with each other over how the organization should function, the organization's goals, and most important, whether or not there should be leaders.

Some members had expectations that Triangle would behave as a rationalized organization—with clearly defined goals and tasks—while others advocated a much more ad hoc policy of dealing with things as they came up. This was not an argument between Americans and Russians per se, since some Russians advocated the more rationalized approach, and some Americans advocated the more flexible one. At another level, several misunderstandings seemed to occur between "classes"—between those with exposure to various cultures and technologies and those who came from extremely poor backgrounds with few opportunities for formal or informal education. For instance, for some members, six dollars was a lot of money to spend on mailing out the informational bulletin, for others it was too small a sum to even merit discussion.[83] Although class was not merely a Russian/American divide, all the Americans present were in fact highly educated (and undoubtedly not extremely poor, since Moscow is an expensive city for foreign residents).[84]

The lack of commitment to common goals was evident in the way the group planned and executed a "fundraiser." Actually finding people who had the time (or inclination) to volunteer for various tasks was extremely difficult. Two Russians did offer to find a venue, but contacting potential sponsors, making up flyers, informing the press, and printing up tickets fell to the Americans. There seemed to be no overarching goal besides "fundraising."[85] Fundraising (the word and concept were taught to the Russians by the Americans)[86] was an end in and of itself. The fundraiser also revealed just how divided the organization members were over its purpose or even whether there should be a purpose. Some members felt the fundraiser should support further publication and distribution of the informational bulletin, others thought it should be used to support a newly forming gay/lesbian library and archives, and still others thought it should be used to create a salaried position for members.[87]

The lack of common goals or even an ideology to unite the members was evident when the second annual conference did not take place. A week before the conference was to take place I attended a last, desperate "organizing session."[88] A conversation ensued that laid bare many of the fundamental ideological and tactical differences between queers and the leaders who claim to represent them. The individual speakers are less important than what was said:

> "After 121.1 [the anti-sodomy law] was changed there was no ideology to unite us. . . . I joined [the queer movement] to contest the establishment—there were lots of different movements forming—from Mothers of Soldiers to Farmers and there was some room, a possibility, to take part in the new establishment, but that opportunity is probably gone and we've missed it. It won't exist again." "We lost it because shock tactics [*epatazh*] are all we've really seen from most activists. Who besides those of you who are bicultural wanted this? . . . Debrianskaia and Kalinin are merely shock tacticians." "But shock tactics allowed homosexuality to be visible for the first time, to become part of the public discourse." "But in this way, gays enter the public scandalously. . . ."

"Yet things have changed here. . . ." "Of course they have. When I first started writing here it was not considered okay to write about this, but now homosexuality is part of serious journalism." "But the movement is disappearing. . . ." "Right, because there is no goal to get the work done. Getting a salary and fundraising are not enough." "I left Triangle because it seems there is interest in social organizations but not political ones."

The discussion said a lot: there was little to unite the few persons present, let alone "sexual minorities." Some people wanted to create publicity; others wanted to create a publicly acceptable image. Some wanted political influence; others wanted social networks.[89]

"Ideological" differences between the members seemed less of a problem than personal ones since, as the months wore on, there seemed to be more and more bitterness over certain leaders, including Debrianskaia, Gessen, and the American Kevin Gardener. At the same time, very little seemed to get done without at least one of those leaders present. The refusal of and need for leadership was illustrated by a series of meetings that occurred in June. The meetings were to be more "public" than the others in the sense that everyone was to inform as many persons as possible about the meetings and they were held in a public space (a gay bar).[90] At the first public meeting, twenty-two persons sat in a room waiting to be addressed. Unfortunately, the only two Triangle members there were not the informally established leaders and did not feel competent representing Triangle's interests.[91] None of the leaders showed up and a meeting never took place.[92] The other public meeting also failed since no one outside of the organization showed up.

Without a highly articulate person to lead the meeting and explain the organization's goals and methods, there was little chance of gaining new members at the first public meeting. Leadership was doubly important in this case because of the great divide separating Triangle members from the women who came. Most of these women belonged to an organization that is very different from Triangle. Triangle includes many Americans and the major leaders of the Russian queer movement. It maintains a large number of contacts throughout the world with activists, academics, journalists, and even politicians. The other group, however, is made up entirely of

Moscow-area women, most of whom have had very little formal education or contact with foreigners. They are, as one Triangle member described them, "simple" women (*prostye*)—a word that has many nuances in Russian—working-class, uneducated, earthy, pure, and not terribly bright. For these differences to have been bridged, a full-scale propaganda campaign was necessary. Instead the "simple" women and the few others who came that day found that Triangle said it wanted input from a wider group of people, but in fact was only talking to itself.

By the time Triangle's disastrous "public" meetings were taking place in June, there was already a lot of personal dissension among its members. Although a fundraiser for the organization, a tea dance,[93] raised nearly two thousand dollars, many members were angry that the sum seemed to be getting smaller and smaller with a variety of "incidental" costs. Various leaders were accused of using the money for their own personal expenses. There was also a lot of personal disagreement over who should represent the organization in New York at the twenty-fifth Stonewall celebrations.[94] During these months I was often the object of confidences by members about their colleagues. One person was addicted to drugs, another closely allied to fascism, and most were "only interested in making a career for themselves" as professional activists and therefore not acting in the best interests of the group. Again, the point is not whether any or all of these charges were true, but that the amount of hostility toward individual leaders further incapacitated Triangle at an organizational level.[95]

By August, when Triangle was supposed to be hosting its second annual national conference, it was clear that the group was in danger of disintegrating. The organizational failure was in large part due to leadership failure. The conference never took place, despite the fact that fundraising letters had been sent to groups in the West and announcements to Russian activists. No rooms were rented, no roundtables or seminars organized, no tickets sold. There was, however, enough interest in discussing the future of Triangle that twenty-four persons (including six Westerners) showed up on the Friday night the conference would have begun. The post mortem began with a series of questions about what Triangle had achieved in the last year. The answer appeared impressive—nine issues of the informational bulletin, the opening national conference, and a fundraiser, but Triangle was no longer really functioning. "[P]eople didn't work. No one from the governing board came to a single meeting to plan the conference." Debrianskaia argued that the "time has passed . . . when people will work for free. People who received a salary worked. I've been a volunteer for six years. I can't do it anymore. I'm done." Yet several other people were enthusiastic enough to continue the meeting the next day.

The next day the problem of leadership was on everyone's minds. Debrianskaia, true to her word, did not come to the meeting. Gessen arrived forty-five minutes late, only to discover what anyone who had attended the June public meetings already knew: the meeting could not begin until one of the accepted leaders was present. As soon as a leader showed up, a discussion began over whether or not a leader was necessary. Several people seemed to want a leader, someone to "rally others around him, to inspire others," but Gessen argued that a leader was absolutely unnecessary. Instead, she led the discussion and the discussants to accepting the idea of an "initiative group" of persons willing to take responsibility for various projects. Anyone interested in working on a project would turn to the person in charge, but there would be no leaders per se.[96]

The meeting sparked hopes that Triangle had indeed been resuscitated, but it was merely the illusion of rebirth. Despite initial efforts by Masel'skii to get the organization registered, it never was. The informational bulletin never appeared again, and the early leaders really did seem to be tired of activism. Kalinin continued to run Moscow's only gay bar, the Underground, Debrianskaia her newsstand, but neither one seemed interested in leading sexual minorities to better places.[97]

MOLLI, the Tchaikovsky Fund, and Wings

The case of Triangle was hardly unusual. MOLLI, too, was barely functioning by 1994. Its founder, L. Zinoveva, had left the organization after arguing with Ugolkova, as had several other people. In fact, Ugolkova seemed to be the only consistent (and often just the only) member of the group. Ugolkova felt the main thrust of her organization should be "beauty" and "love," not sexual politics. According to her philosophy, theater and art do more to create space for same-sex love than any amount of protesting or lobbying. Thus MOLLI concentrated on creating a journal and producing concerts. In the first months of 1994 there was a lot discussion between Ugolkova and graphic artist Tania Miller over creating a journal of women's culture. The journal was not meant to be specifically lesbian, although there were to be certain "lesbian-themed" articles and illustrations. Although MOLLI did manage to produce a sample journal, they did not work on finding renewable sources of support, like advertising or subscriptions. Instead, the journal itself was to be financed by a German feminist group. The financing never materialized and therefore the journal never appeared.[98]

In the meantime, Miller decided to quit working with MOLLI, which found itself again down to its only steady member, Ugolkova. As the only active member of the group, Ugolkova did surprisingly well. She managed to produce two concerts of women's music. Again, although the concerts were not lesbian per se, the performers were themselves all lesbians. In addition to various stage presentations, ranging from traditional Russian folk songs to lip-synching, there was a sale of lesbian-produced art at each concert. Although the concerts did not pay for themselves and relied to some extent on outside sponsors,[99] they did manage to attract about forty persons each time as well as present the idea of women's music and art (even if they were never specifically lesbian music or art).[100]

The concerts and journal, however, pointed to deeper problems within MOLLI and its efforts. MOLLI wanted to represent "women's experience" through art, but it simultaneously did not openly admit lesbianism as part of that experience. Since it is in fact lesbians who participate in MOLLI, the effort to represent all women universalizes from the particular. Although this could work to the group's benefit, allowing it to make contact with feminist and women-oriented groups,[101] it presents a problem to queer activism because when MOLLI formed, it was to create a gendered space and gendered critique within the queer movement. For MOLLI to divide queer politics with a critique of its masculinist nature and then to refuse to work toward a less masculinist queer politics is to leave a silence where those who are speaking as queers and as women should be. Finally, MOLLI is not only divided from within, but maintains particularly hostile relationships with other groups and leaders. Ugolkova refused to participate in any Triangle activities, was nearly heckled off the stage by a rival leader at the March concert of MOLLI, and has more former participants than current ones. As an organization MOLLI died a long time ago; as a personality Ugolkova may continue for some time.

The problem of a "cult of personality" is played out again in the two St. Petersburg organizations, the Tchaikovsky Fund and Wings. Although both groups claim hundreds of members, they are in fact centered on particular personalities. The Tchaikovsky Fund's founder, Olga Zhuk, was extremely charismatic. Zhuk was also, apparently, an extremely difficult person to work with.[102] Although Zhuk managed to start the organization and attract members, she moved to Germany soon after the organization was founded. The vice president, Iuri Ereev, took over the presidency of the fund.[103] Under Ereev's leadership, the Tchaikovsky Fund did not so much organize anyone or anything as act as a liaison—providing translation, accommodations, and contacts—to foreign, mostly German, organizations. In this way, the fund was involved with two festivals, several discos, and the American and German film festivals (in 1991 and 1994 respectively).[104] Yet the fund was basically Ereev. Occasionally active members would appear for a short time, but they would not stay long. The Tchaikovsky Fund was functioning as an informal meeting place, a sort of queer salon where foreigners and Russians alike could meet and drink and engage in any mutual affairs they might have. Ereev used money from sponsors of the fund to keep his easily accessible apartment[105] open to just about anyone who cared to drop by, an undoubtedly useful service, but it was not an organization.[106] The fund is often described as a *tusovka*, a Russian slang term for an informal group of persons who get together for primarily social reasons, like card playing or drinking—a nonintellectual salon. Indeed, the fund is basically a *tusovka*, a primarily social group—one that can rally its resources to be useful to those who would be more active, but not an entity with an abiding membership, a leadership structure, or a system of renewing itself. In fact, when funding and initiative from the outside are unavailable, the Tchaikovsky Fund consists entirely of Ereev's apartment and the people who gather there.[107]

The situation with the Tchaikovsky Fund is basically repeated in Wings. Although Wings does not rely on funding from outside sources,[108] it consists primarily of an apartment and a leader. Its leader, Kukharskii, claims that Wings has over three hundred registered members, one half of whom are in St. Petersburg, the rest located throughout Russia. When asked in 1994 what Wings as an organization actually does, Kukharskii referred to the need to answer the thousands of letters the group received when they put a notice in a national newspaper when they were first registered three years previously. Kukharskii ignored the dated nature of answering letters three years old and instead described the project as "supporting gays and lesbians at crisis periods in their lives." In fairness to Wings, most of the actual letter writing seems to have been done by Kukharskii and one or two others, a daunting task given the fifteen thousand letters the group had received by 1994. In addition to the letters, Kukharskii organized two AIDS memorials in May 1993 and 1994. At each service, a small group of persons gathered to mark International AIDS Awareness Day.[109] Often, although not always, Wings hosted a roundtable discussion on the third Thursday of every month. At each roundtable a certain topic was discussed, such as AIDS prevention or crimes against homosexuals. There was also a literary section of this roundtable.[110]

Wings has managed to organize without Western leadership or funding, but it still has many of the same problems as Triangle or the Tchaikovsky Fund. Kukharskii, like so many of the leaders, has been unwilling to work with other groups and leaders. In an interview, Kukharskii insisted that he attempted to work on several joint projects with the Tchaikovsky Fund, but was turned down by Ereev. In the same breath, Kukharskii dismissed Ereev and other queer leaders as criminals who misuse funds from the West for their own personal gain. Kukharskii also criticized Triangle's inability to legally register as "their own fault" for not working within the system. Kukharskii may dislike his counterparts in other organizations, but he shares their fate. Wings' events were less and less popular by 1994, with fewer and fewer men (and almost no women) participating. Kukharskii argued that it was the increased opportunity to meet in purely social venues, such as discos, that discouraged people from coming, but the reality is that the organization had dwindled to Kukharskii, who organized a few events a year, the events themselves of decreasing popularity.[111]

Like Ugolkova and MOLLI, Wings and Kukharskii managed to keep the façade of an organization without any of its substance: no renewable membership, no clear tasks performed by the organization (as opposed to relying solely on an individual who is literally indispensable), and little hope of joining with other persons or groups in order to create more viable and permanent structures. Although Triangle, MOLLI, Wings, and the Tchaikovsky Fund are not the only organizations in Russia, they are by far the largest and most resource-rich (in terms of leadership, financing, and technological support). At the same time, many of the smaller and more indigenous organizations do not seem to be suffering the same sort of decline that their more Westernized counterparts have. The smaller organizations have become more popular, not less, despite the fact that they suffer from many of the same problems as the larger ones (i.e., little organization, too much reliance on a single person, inability to work with other groups or persons). These groups are not the Soviet Stonewall that was heralded in 1991. Instead, they represent a different species of queer activism and queer activists: one based on common interests, rather than identities.

Indigenous Initiatives and Local Queers

In St. Petersburg a group of young women have been working to create a social network since 1991. That group, known as Sappho Peter, organizes women-only dances at bars and discotheques around the city. The "organization" is in fact an informal network of friends and acquaintances. The women in Sappho Peter have not been able to effectively advertise their events, which occur irregularly, nor do they even have an internal system of communication. When I attempted to attend dances in March and April 1994 I was forced to phone several persons to find out where the dance would be. The location, the Café Caprice, was hardly "accessible," since it involved an hour on the metro from the center of town and then a bus ride through a postindustrial wasteland of large apartment blocks and mountains of burning trash. The first time I went to the Café Caprice, I encountered a completely isolated building in a sea of mud and garbage. Despite the fact that there were several expensive foreign cars parked in the mud (a BMW and two Mercedes), the inside of the building was as shabby as the outside. After stumbling through a poorly lit hall that reeked of urine, I knocked timidly on a metal door. It was opened to reveal a bar with several men and women drinking and playing pool. I was immediately told to leave since the disco "for my kind" [112] had been rescheduled for the next night. The semiautomatic strapped to his side persuaded me not to bother the barman for the use of his phone. No one from the organization had notified me of the disco's cancellation, despite the fact that someone had told me at 5 P.M. that the 8 P.M. disco would take place.[113]

In May and August of 1994, I did manage to attend three of Sappho Peter's discos. The discos I attended (at the Café Caprice) usually included about twenty women from St. Petersburg. Most of the women with whom I spoke (about five each evening) tended to be working-class (i.e., had the equivalent of a high school diploma, perhaps a few years at an institute, and occupations ranging from factory worker to kiosk attendant to cashier in a store). They ranged in age from late teens to early thirties. Nearly half of the women identified their sexual orientation as *naturalka* (i.e., hetero-sexual)—which does not preclude their having relationships with other women but rather circumscribes their gender roles to "appropriately" (i.e., conventionally) feminine.[114] No one, including the organizers of Sappho Peter, described the events as helping to form an identity or a politics based on that identity. Most women described the discos as a place to meet other women, but no one described them as a place to organize effectively by sexuality (especially since the women did not necessarily see themselves as sharing a common sexuality).

The lack of even a rudimentary form of communication, like a phone tree, indicates just how much Sappho Peter, like some of its larger counter-parts, was primarily a *tusovka*, a girl gang that sometimes managed to rent a space for an evening of dancing.[115] Yet unlike its larger counterparts, Sappho Peter was an organization by and for local women. It had become more rather than less popular, moving from completely informal gather-ings to much better organized ones, without the initiative or input of out-siders.

Another indigenous initiative in St. Petersburg, which was no less vital in 1994 than in 1992, was the *Klub Nezavisimykh Zhenshchin* (Club of Indepen-dent Women). The Club of Independent Women is not a club as much as it is the obsession of one woman, Olga Krauze. Krauze began to work with Wings for a short time in 1991 as well as some of the women in Sappho Peter, but soon left to form her own organization. Like so many of the queer "leaders," Krauze seemed more able to work alone than in a group. The club never became an organization as much as a one-woman crusade to make her voice heard. Krauze began self-publishing books of her poetry as well as graphics by her then girlfriend, Margarita Bogdanova. Krauze eventually began a small, independently distributed journal, Probuzhdenie (Awakening).[116] Awakening contains political and cultural news relevant to queers, original photos as well as those "borrowed" from Western publications, poetry and prose by Krauze and others, as well as announcements about upcoming events and information on safe sex between women.

It is not Krauze and her journal that represent an important local initiative but the "acquaintance service" (sluzhba znakomstva) provided inside it. Through the classifieds, which usually take up about one-fourth of the journal, readers can contact women from throughout Russia as well as several other countries worldwide. Better still, Krause charged a nominal fee for the service (in 1994, less than one dollar for four lines). Krauze felt it was important to let women from provincial cities or from poor backgrounds to participate in the service, to know that there are others "like them" in this world.[117]

In Moscow, the Klub Svecha (Club Candlelight) is, like the Club of Independent Women, pretty much centered on one person, Valeriia Kurskaia. Like Sappho Peter, Club Candlelight is more a tusovka than an organization. Candlelight grew out of an informal group of lesbians, which began meeting in Kurskaia's apartment in the late 1970's. This tusovka of forty or fifty persons would meet privately but never entered the public world until the 1991 Soviet Stonewall events. Kurskaia quickly became convinced that "meeting in a private apartment is never going to help us [i.e., lesbians] since it always end up in a drinking binge [piianka]."[118] Thus Kurskaia began to organize public monthly events—concerts or "cafés" once a month where women can socialize, hear a lesbian folk singer, or just have a drink. The group advertised events in a local classifieds publication, Krasnaia shliapechka (Red Hat).[119]

Club Candlelight, like its St. Petersburg counterparts, represents a group of women who act in their own interests at their own initiatives. Yet Candlelight marks a different sort of native species, one which is both highly organized and willing to work with other groups and organizations. Kurskaia's system of phoning persons interested in upcoming events seems completely reliable. In the course of several months I was given detailed directions and dates for upcoming "club nights."[120] Kurskaia spends up to six hours a day phoning her "girls," making sure that organization events run smoothly. The result is that Kurskaia can summon large numbers of women to almost any sort of event, even if the women themselves do not particularly want to be there.[121] Kurskaia not only worked hard to create a well-organized if informal group of women, she also worked to create ties with other groups and organizations. She was an active member of Triangle and even served on its governing board. In addition, Kurskaia has participated in various Western-sponsored events, such as the consciousness-raising sessions put on by American activists through the *Golubki* (Doves) center.[122]

These informal networks of women all share certain common characteristics. They are based on local needs, not an attempt to import Western-style groups to Russia,[123] and they work to fill a pressing need for more opportunities for social interaction that is both pleasurable to its participants and does not require a lot of sacrifice or risk. Indeed, a woman can attend Sappho Peter dances or meet someone through an acquaintance service without ever feeling a need to publicly define her sexuality, let alone define it as marginalized (e.g., "lesbian," "sexual minority"). That these three groups have become more rather than less popular is not a surprise. The local groups exhibit many of the same weaknesses as their larger colleagues in queer activism, but the weaknesses are more than counterbalanced by their strengths. Thus it is that the most vibrant queer activism is one based not on identity politics and the politics of identity but on a fluid and ill-defined subjectivity, which demands public space for interaction but not for political action. This subjectivity is able to ask little of those who participate in it, while providing them with large rewards. It is also less bogged down in the personal and positional fighting that occurs between larger groups. No one is forced to agree with any principles; they merely participate or not in what are primarily social events. A certain amount of unpredictability and even unwillingness to work with others limits the number of persons local activists will reach, but it will not destroy these groups, since they are not dependent on an organization nor on an organizing identity. Instead, these indigenous initiatives will survive because they provide useful, if unreliable, services without the costs of a politically and/or economically marketable identity.

ACTIVISM WITHOUT IDENTITY

So it is that the sort of queer "politics" that were envisioned in Soviet Stone-wall have been superseded by a different sort of queer activism, or if not activism, activity. In this way, the local groups represent an alternative to identity politics and the politics of identity. This alternative might be called a politics without identity—a sort of coalitional and contingent politics en-visioned by many postidentity thinkers, or what Donna Haraway has called "affinity without identity." [124] A postidentity politics is one where per-sons without consistent or abiding identities come together for common projects in coalitions, which are always temporary and contingent. Political alliances are more like affairs than marriages. Activists are not required to make abiding commitments to others "like them"; they make merely short-term commitments to tasks or activities that they deem worthwhile. [125]

Postidentity politics does capture some of what is going on with queer activists in Russia. Certainly, queer activity seems to center around affinity not identity. Yet queer activism in Russia enters realms that postidentity politics does not begin to describe. [126] Rather than identity or even post-identity politics, the sort of queer organizations that are thriving can best be described as subjectivities.

Identities require subjects to behave in ways that are "identifiable." For instance, to "be" a "lesbian" requires continuously behaving in agreed upon ways. Once the rules of the game are violated (e.g., by sleeping with a man), one can no longer be a lesbian. Subjectivity is not nearly as strict a taskmistress as identity. A woman can desire women, can represent those desires verbally or mimetically (i.e., be a self-speaking subject), without taking on an identity based on those desires. She can go to a disco or begin a romance through a publication without "being" a lesbian.

Some would call subjectivity without identity a "closet," but that term seems as limited in its explanatory powers as it is in its imaginative scope. The women who go to discos or concerts or buy journals with woman-to-woman personals are not closeted—they risk personal harassment and exposure for their activities—by criminals intent on blackmail, by security forces intent on harassment, by medical professionals intent on "curing" them. In Russia, to publicly engage in lesboerotic desires, whether sym-bolically or literally, is not an act for those who lack courage. What subjects of homosexual desire do lack, however, are the need to publicly identify as well as an identity in common. Queers may call themselves all sorts of things, including straight. To insist that all those who sleep with persons of the same sex take on the same identity, or any identity, is to miss that what they really share is desire, a desire in part constructed on the absence of a common identity (e.g., a "natural" desiring an "active lesbian"). Those who share common desires can act in highly public ways without ever contemplating a common identity.

Indeed this subjectivity without identity is exactly the part of Russian queerdom that is thriving, just as surely as Western models of identity politics have stagnated. The next chapter describes that part of public queerness which, like the more indigenous organizations, is based on common subjectivities, not identities. Queer subjectivities bubble to the surface of the Russian public sphere in the form of discos, publishing houses, cruising strips, theaters, and even restaurants. Subjectivities produce a variety of texts, which can be studied for what they reveal about both queer subjectivities and queer subjects.

chapter 4

Queer Subjects and Subjectivities

FROM NOTIONS OF SUBCULTURE TO SUBJECTIVITY

Sexual otherness in Russia has not formed easily into the rigidity of identity. Instead, queerness is more a free-floating pick-up game than the codified rules and clearly defined players of identity. Identity demands the identifier to perform in ways that are consistent and coherent with its founding mythology that we *are* an identity, rather than that we act in identifiable ways. A man married to a woman is not allowed to call himself gay, a man married to a man is not to call himself straight. To do so is to exhibit "false consciousness." Their consciousness is false because it shows (sexual) identity to be less "true" than is believed.[1]

Yet even without the safety of true identity, queerness represents itself, signifies itself, in a system of signs that speak in both recognizable and unrecognizable tongues. In order to maintain the "reality" of heterosexuality, we must refuse to recognize that which undermines it. But even this act of purposeful ignorance acknowledges slippages in the identity structure.[2] Queer subjectivities utilize the dominant language for their own purposes in ways that are sometimes incomprehensible to others. Queers gather secretly in public places—secret because their queerness is unacknowledged. Sometimes queerness is seen. Queerness can speak loud enough to get the public's attention. A queer play is seen by a large number of people; a queer singer is all the rage. They are popular, even if being queer is not. In this way, queer exists as both subculture[3] and culture, particular and popular.

Consumers and producers rely on queer subjectivities—sets of signs, symbols, rituals, a style—which are readable as queer. Queer subjectivities, unlike queer subculture or identity, are not limited to a well-defined group of persons. Subjectivities do not attach themselves to individual bodies. Instead, individual bodies participate in creating and consuming queer subjectivities, at times speaking for themselves, at times for others. Queer subjectivities constitute that space of the human collectivity in which sexual otherness is represented by self-speaking subjects and dreamed and even desired by those who do not or cannot speak as queers.

LOCAL QUEER SUBJECTIVITIES

The very ephemeral quality of informal queer subjectivities means that not only are they difficult to spot, but once spotted, recorded, and disseminated, they are probably already gone. What follows are some local queer subjectivities I recorded between 1989 and 1994.

Queer Wining and Dining

In the 1980s, *Kafe Sadko*, located near the Bolshoi Theater, was the place to be queer—literally, the only public shelter in which queers could gather. It was not "obviously" queer. There were no signs on the door, no symbols or stigmata of the gay movement like pink triangles, skin-tight Levi's 501s, or motorcycle boots. Yet somehow the place was "known," not just among those who gathered there, but among many in Moscow's nonqueer population as well.[4] The only visible sign that this was a queer restaurant was the fact that its clientele was almost entirely male. During the winter of 1989–90 I went to *Kafe Sadko* several times. Each time I was the only woman in the restaurant (with the exception of the waitresses). I never found anyone there willing to speak about being homosexual, but I did discover men holding hands and rubbing each other's thighs and every so often kissing (in a manner distinct from the wet comradely kisses of Party members). There were usually about fifty or so men (mostly middle-aged) and a few very young boys (possibly sex workers from the nearby cruising strip in front of the Bolshoi). With privatization and gay discos, *Kafe Sadko* could not compete for the next generation of gay men and faded out of queer subjectivity, but while it existed *Kafe Sadko* was both clearly and quietly queer, a public expression of homosexual relations at a time when even private ones were forbidden.[5]

Other gathering places quickly took over from the *Kafe Sadko*. In Moscow the first openly and expressly gay bar and grill, the Underground,[6] began serving a queer clientele in the fall of 1993. The Underground was opened by Roman Kalinin, one of the first activists for gay rights in Russia.[7] The bar was located in the shadow of the Kremlin right next to a Western-owned pizzeria and from the outside the Underground appeared surprisingly aboveground.[8] Even in New York it is difficult to imagine a gay bar in so visible and acceptable a location. Of course, the entrance to the bar was very discreet and like its predecessor, the *Kafe Sadko*, the Underground did not publicly display any obvious signs of queerdom. Instead, nighttime customers would enter a black stairway and pay a relatively small entrance fee[9] and then make their way into the bar area, a small room about eight by four meters. The decor consisted of more black paint and colored lights, the drinks priced about the same as they were in New York,[10] and the music "techno pop" (i.e., synthesized dance music). Like the *Sadko*, the Underground's forty or fifty customers were almost all men.[11] Also like the *Sadko*, and unlike the discos, customers could stop by earlier in the day, for a sandwich and some conversation. The customers were, however, different from the *Sadko* crowd in their queer visibility—many sporting rainbow buttons, pink triangles, leather, shaved heads, and combat boots. There was also more sexualized physical interaction between the men in the bar than between their older counterparts at the *Sadko* (e.g., slow dancing and kissing).[12]

Another gathering place opened in Moscow in May 1994. The restaurant, *Petrovskii Dvornik* (Petrovskii Courtyard) openly billed itself as a restaurant "where gay customers will be waited on by gay waiters and gay performers will perform on the stage." The restaurant even had "gay" glasses, which sported men in bathing suits that disappeared with the presence of cold liquid.[13] Around the same time, a less openly queer establishment opened in St. Petersburg. *Kafe Kat* was located a block from Nevskii Prospekt (the architectural and tourist center). Like *Kafe Sadko*, *Kafe Kat* did not look obviously queer to the casual observer.[14] The decor was not obviously queer (reproduction art nouveau), but upon closer inspection the graphics on the wall were. The pencil drawings were of men with men and women with women. On the nights I went to the café, the host was the image of queer: a young man with platinum blond (i.e., dyed) hair cut in a short bob, khakis cut off at the calves, and a net tee shirt with nothing showing underneath but his chest, either too young or too waxed to grow hair.[15] There were often foreigners, who seemed not to know the "nature" of the café. In fact the café seemed partially geared toward foreigners, with a menu in English as well as Russian and prices that many Russians could hardly afford.[16] The encouragement of foreigners was not unique to the Kafe Kat. The Underground also (consciously) attracted a large contingent of foreigners — with vaguely American food, more emphasis on beer than vodka, and several employees who spoke some English. Unlike the Underground, however, the Kafe Kat was not attracting queer foreigners, just foreigners — more interested in a centrally located café open until 11 P.M. than the sexual practices of its owners, employees, and many of its Russian patrons. Instead, Kafe Kat was plotting its own course in the erratic Russian market — attracting both queers and foreigners (for very different reasons). But while Kafe Kat provided an openly queer atmosphere, it did not encourage openly queer behavior among patrons (e.g., no dancing, no tables out of view of others, and the toilets were single occupancy).[17]

Dancing to a Different Beat

By 1994 Russia's large cities were awash with discos and clubs, each with its own particular style and clientele. Some of the discos were aimed exclusively at the "nouveau richniki," those who could afford twenty-five-dollar cover charges and eight-dollar glasses of wine; still others were aimed at the "fashionable" youth (e.g., raves); and, of course, some discos were for queers. In both St. Petersburg and Moscow, there were three discos/bars in 1994.[18]

Near the center of Moscow were two discos for queers and their friends — Prem'era and Shans (Premiere and Chance). Both discos took place in theaters that had plenty of room for the three hundred or so revelers who gathered each weekend night.[19] The cost of the central discos was relatively high.[20] The language I heard most often was Russian, but there was always a large amount of English and German being spoken. The crowd seemed young (mostly under thirty), and the majority of disco patrons were men.[21] The third disco, MELZ (an acronym for Moscow Electric Light Factory) was located in a factory complex far from the center of town. MELZ offered lower prices (on entrance fees and drinks), and the crowd seemed to have more Russian, more women, and more age diversity.[22] In exchange for the more "democratic" atmosphere at MELZ, however, customers had to live with a far higher risk of violence and exposure. During the first half of 1994, several "gay bashing" incidents occurred near the entrance to MELZ.[23]

Whatever the costs of the discos, whether economic or bodily, the payoff seemed worth it to the hundreds, possibly thousands, who attended them every weekend night. The discos were an extremely unusual occurrence in Moscow. They were known to the public as "queer" places, and they were places where people could be publicly queer. One of the discos, Premier, consistently attracted some of the country's most famous pop stars. The (nongay) press often picked up the celebrity appearances.[24] In these public spaces queers publicly enacted queer desires. People dressed in ways that were visibly queer (e.g., men wore makeup and women's shoes; women wore no makeup and men's shoes).[25] Most of the dancing occurred between same-sex pairs. Many couples found the darkened rooms amenable to kissing and touching one another. The bathrooms were isolated and easily turned into places for public sex.[26] More importantly, like the restaurants, the discos offered a space to publicly act out queerness without requiring anyone to be a queer as part of the price of admission. Sexual otherness was a verb, a performance, a dance, rarely an identity.

Public Toilets and Pleshkas: Queer Sex in the Street

"Well, and then in Moscow I found out. At Bykovo airport I went into the toilet. It was all written up on the wall, look through such and such a gap, and a guy there signaled to me and gave me a blow-job through a hole in the partition."

"How did you find out about cruising in the city center?"

"Well, that guy told me . . ."

—Evgenii Kharitonov

Public toilets are one of the places where men can have completely anonymous, if not completely safe, sexual encounters with other men.[27] Public toilets near cruising areas are "known" as sites of gay male sexual encounters, both by the men who cruise them and the police who clear them. Unfortunately, men's toilets are not easily accessible to a woman field researcher. Dressed as a man, I tried entering two men's toilets near a cruising strip in Moscow. My "drag" was only successful as long as I did not have to pull down my pants.[28] One time I was intimidated out of the toilet by a police officer who asked me for "what" (not "whom") I was waiting (*Chego ty zhdesh'?*). Another time I saw no contact between anyone (perhaps my presence, as a nonurinating person, made the men too uncomfortable).[29]

Fortunately, one source of homoerotic desire in public bathrooms, graffiti, was accessible to me.[30] "I suck" (*sosu*), which does not have the English connotation of being bad at something, but rather refers only to oral sex, was the most popular graffito. Also, men who wanted to be fellated often wrote about their wares (e.g., "Who wants to suck off my big member?"). Some of the transactions were clearly of a more commercial nature: "I am looking for an 'active' [a man who penetrates but is not penetrated] man with an apartment. I love to put on makeup and wear women's underwear. I'm 34 years old. Your age doesn't matter. I will give it to you in any position. Write how we can meet. . . . I'm ready, Zhana."[31] Still others relied on humor to signify their homosexual desires: "Boys, don't be afraid of sex, a member in the mouth is sweeter than cakes" (this nearly rhymes in the original: "*Mal'chiki, ne boites' seksa, chlen vo rtu—poslasche keksa*").[32] As queer desires, much of the graffiti is meant to be all talk and no action.[33] Yet the fact that they exist alerts men, all men who use public toilets, that there is a potential for sexual interaction with other men in such locations. Even if a man knew of no other place in the city to engage in homosexual contacts, he would almost certainly know that it is possible, at least at a textual level, to do so in public rest rooms.

In addition to public rest rooms, large cities have cruising strips where men (and a few women) can go for sexual encounters.[34] In Moscow the most renowned cruising strip or *pleshka*[35] is in front of the Bolshoi Theater. Why the Bolshoi *pleshka* became so popular is unclear, but the fact that it is located in the center of town (easy access) as well as by two separate metro lines (easy escape) may have played a role. The Bolshoi, as the center of both opera and ballet, may have acted as a queer icon, drawing opera queens to its pink exterior with its statues of stallions in all their phallic glory,[36] but few of the men [37] I met at the *pleshka* came for the (high) culture. Instead, during the course of eight outings to the Bolshoi, I mostly met very young men from out of town who were looking for an older and richer man who could put them up for a few days. There were, of course, always older men scouting the possibilities.[38]

At the Bolshoi *pleshka* as well as all the others I "cruised" in both Moscow and St. Petersburg,[39] there were always a fair number of other people, families with children, elderly heterosexual couples. The "others" seemed not only uninterested but also unaware of the male-male cruising occurring around them. Not only does the *pleshka* remain an unacknowledged site of homoerotic desire, but the word has also taken on pejorative connotations for many queers. An editor of a gay magazine told a mainstream newspaper that public cruising strips had outlived their usefulness in the age of gay discos and bars. Those who continue to cruise are interested only in sex and the sex is often commercial, making cruising an "embarrassment" to the gay community.[40] Despite the refusal to acknowledge the *pleshka* by many nonqueers and the opprobrium for it by some queers, the *pleshka* continues to thrive. *Pleshka* is not merely a metaphor for anonymous sexual contacts but an actual physical location and located set of physical activities. Like other informal forms of queer culture, the *pleshka* does not require a queer identity or subculture. Instead, all of the young men I interviewed insisted that desiring another man did not make a person queer, and almost all of the young men were looking for a "natural" (straight) man. If a man desires sex with another man, there is a place in the heart of Russia's cities where public homosexual sex is both imagined and located, but rarely identified.

Queer Journals and Newspapers

Although newspapers and journals are among the major textual expressions of queer subjectivities, they are not as solid as books. They are less solid in the sense of "mainstream." Unlike books, journals and newspapers are not trying to sell at a national level to a general audience. Instead, they appear in smaller and more specific editions, something they are able to do because they are far easier and cheaper to produce than books. Anyone with access to a copying machine can create these sorts of texts. Many of them do not even rely on a typewriter, but use the far more democratic media of paper and pen. Yet the relative ease with which these texts can be produced means that they often remain hidden from view. They do not rely on large print runs or advertising, but they also are difficult to find and often only available to those "in the know." Journals and newspapers, unlike the far more visible books, are always in danger of disappearing into thin air, dropping from the public view without the public ever being aware they were there. In this sense, journals and newspapers are more like discos than books. What follows are the newspapers and journals I found mostly in the course of 1994, although a few date to 1990. I asked almost every queer I met to tell me what existed and then tried to obtain copies. Sometimes they were available at queer events (e.g., a conference), occasionally they were available at a store or newsstand,[41] but mostly the texts were sold informally, with no consistent or even obvious means of distribution, often by the editors or writers who produced them.

In February 1990 *Tema*, the first newspaper or journal solely by and about queers, appeared in Moscow.[42] Although other samizdat or unofficial[43] publications appeared prior to it contained some material for or by queers, *Tema* was the first queer publication. Its first editions, consisting of eight tabloid pages and cut-and-paste graphics, were both difficult to read (especially discreetly) and aesthetically primitive. The issue contained the newspaper's address, but all of the editors used pseudonyms.[44] As time went on, *Tema* adopted a magazine format and computer graphics. By 1991 *Tema* was officially registered. As it became more professional, *Tema* also become more politicized against the communist regime. The first issue of 1991 features a caricature of Leonid Brezhnev with Josef Stalin's face in place of a penis and the slogan "A condom will save you from any sort of infection" (i.e., with the potential infection seemingly emanating from the Stalin-phallus). The editorial, from the now fully named Roman Kalinin, continued the critique of "procommunist newspapers and People's Deputies." The issue had a more visible lesbian presence,[45] but the personal advertisements, as in previous issues, were almost entirely male, with only two of twenty-eight sent by women. The personals were probably indicative of a predominantly male readership, by then numbering twenty thousand.[46] During its last year of publication, *Tema* was twice as long (now sixteen pages) and more like a magazine than a newspaper. The focus was no longer overtly political, since the communists were by then the proverbial dead horse that no longer needed to be beaten into the ground. The publication had also transformed from a gay and lesbian publication to an exclusively gay male one. A 1992 issue features Tom of Finland graphics,[47] articles on openly gay pop singer Freddy Mercury, and the establishment of a cruising strip by one of *Tema's* editors. All the personal advertisements were from men as well. The only presence of a female reader or writer was a letter to the editor by Galina Alekseevna, a retired school teacher from Moscow who observed that homosexuality, a most "noxious" and "bourgeois" "infection," must be "burned off (Russian society) with a will of iron."[48] Apparently women were no longer part of *Tema's* world, except in the role of "straw men," easily knocked down as homophobic and communist (i.e., sentinels of the old, long-discredited system).

When *Tema* stopped publishing in early 1993, it did not leave a vacuum. Several other journals of queer subjectivity had already appeared. In October 1990, just nine months after *Tema's* first issue, RISK began publishing.[49] RISK, a much slicker publication than *Tema*, was a magazine, published on higher quality paper and with well-reproduced graphics. It contained articles on queer organizational events (e.g., conferences) and queer culture (e.g., gay singers and writers), as well as humor, personals, and "centerfold" pictures (i.e., masturbatory ones).[50] Like *Tema* nearly all of the articles and graphics appeared to be aimed at men.[51] The personals were also almost exclusively male.[52]

A similar publication, 1/10: *Gazeta dlia vsekh* (1/10: *The Paper for Everyone*),[53] began in November 1991. Although it was not as polished as RISK, 1/10 contained similar articles on gay culture and health. It did not publish centerfolds but was illustrated with sexually explicit (and generally original) homoerotic graphics. The male focus was maintained in the articles and personals. In fact, one of the only mentions of women was explicitly heterosexual, about a young woman from the provinces who had "trouble meeting a man for intimate purposes."[54] 1/10 maintained its overall tenor as a playfully erotic gay journal and changed little in its first three years of publication, continuing to print articles on queer politics alongside (male) homoerotic cartoons and information on safer sex practices (for men).[55]

The gay male subjectivity expressed in *Tema*, RISK, and 1/10 was repeated in other large-circulation journals and newspapers being sold in Moscow and St. Petersburg. *Ty* (*You*), an "illustrated journal for homosexuals and lesbians," did include articles on events of interest to men and women, but most of the articles and all of the images were by and about men. Even the large amount of AIDS information distributed by the journal because of its connection to the AIDS organization My i Vy (We and You) did not present any information on safe sex practices for women.[56] Another journal, Impul's, also attempted to include women, but was primarily for men. It did include an article on the causes of lesbianism ("injudicious upbringing and the patriarchal orientation of society") as well as announcements by two women's clubs.[57] Yet the overall tenor of the journal was by men and for men. Finally, a collection of "gay stories" put out under the rather apt title Other (Drugoi) gathered twenty-one new works of prose and poetry about queer loves, but only two of the entries were by women.[58]

The texts that were most likely to represent queer women were those with the smallest circulation. Unlike their larger and more commercial counterparts, which generally had print runs in the tens of thousands, the smaller publications circulated in the hundreds. One small journal, Probuzhdenie (Awakening), was specifically "for lesbians." [59] Two other publications, one a literary journal and the other a politically oriented newsletter, represented both male and female (homo)sexualities. The newsletter was put out by the Moscow organization Triangle,[60] while the literary journal, Gay, Slaviane!,[61] was put out by St. Petersburg's Tchaikovsky Fund.[62] All three publications were not only less circulated than such gay men's journals as RISK and 1/10, they were also clearly less interested in being widely distributed. Awakening remained opposed to attracting a male readership.[63] Neither Gay, Slaviane! nor Triangle's bulletin tried to popularize themselves with erotic photographs or gay horoscopes, as the men's journals did. All three publications had specific mandates—being relevant to lesbians, creating a queer literary magazine, and facilitating a queer movement—that were unrelated to the vagaries of the marketplace. The lack of commercialism and fiscal viability, however, also meant that these publications were subject to the vagaries of highly motivated, but unpaid, individuals. The handful of persons responsible for the publications that spoke to and for women had to juggle large egos and very little money with the demands of publishing in Russia. The result was a few publications that appeared erratically, were extremely difficult to find, and often disappeared with few people even knowing that they existed. If shouts of queer subjectivity have barely been heard above the din that is post-Soviet Russia, then queer women's voices have never been louder than a whisper.[64] Queer publications in Russia, like other queer subjectivities, are gendered, and they are gendered male. The phallic drift of public queerness says much about the gendered distribution of power.

Surprisingly enough, queerness was also drifting into popular culture. Queerness is consumed at a local level in the form of cruising strips, discos, and texts written by and for enthusiasts, but queerness is consumed throughout Russia as "true art." In the next section, I explore how queer has become popular in books and on stage.[65]

POPULAR QUEER SUBJECTIVITIES
Queer Books

The first queer subjectivities represented in Russian-language books happened long before the Soviets came to power. Some of those books survived or were revived by contemporary queers, who imbued them with an excess of significance, in part because they were the only literary signifiers of queerness. One of the most important of these artifacts of queer desire is Mikhail Kuzmin's Krylia (Wings).[66] Written in 1907, Wings was not easy to find in Soviet Russia, since it was only widely published a few years ago.[67] Despite the relatively limited supply, Kuzmin's homoerotic classic was read by a large number of queers. A St. Petersburg activist group used Kuzmin's title for its name.[68] Many queers also spoke of Wings as one of the few representations of homoerotic desire in pre-glasnost Russia.[69]

Another queer "classic" is a cycle of poems written by poet Marina Tsvetaeva to her lover Sophia Parnok.[70] Tsvetaeva is widely cited as a "great poet" (an honorific of no little significance in Russia), which makes her all the more valuable as a representative of lesbian desire.[71] Many Russian lesbians I met have memorized large passages of Tsvetaeva's poems.[72] The lesboerotic poems are romantic rather than sexual, but are clearly addressed to a female lover.[73] In addition to Kuzmin and Tsvetaeva, European writers "known" to be queer, such as Oscar Wilde, were also published under the Soviets.[74]

Once queers, rather than the state, began to decide what to publish, the range was not limited to those who lived a hundred years ago. In 1990 Aleksandr Shatalov founded Glagol Press, which concentrated on publishing works by or about queers. Unlike the magazines and journals, the books were aimed at a far larger audience—those interested in "good" literature, regardless of their sexual practices.[75] The first book Shatalov chose was the semiautobiographical account of Eduard Limonov's émigré years in 1970s Manhattan. Limonov's It's Me, Eddie chronicles the disintegration of Limonov's national and sexual identity as he moved from being a heterosexual Russian to being a bisexual émigré.[76]

In addition to It's Me, Eddie, Shatalov has published James Baldwin's Giovanni's Room, William Burrough's Naked Lunch, and Evgenii Kharitonov, a Russian writer famous before his death in 1981 as a theater director and after his death as a writer of intensely homoerotic prose.[77] Thus, besides bringing Western homoerotic and homosexual writings to a Russian readership, Shatalov was the first in Russia to publish two queer Russian writers.

Because Glagol Press was the first (conscious) source of homoerotic books, it had the onerous task of "representing" queer literature. Like any representation, Glagol's was at best a partial one. As a conscious representation, Glagol's was surprisingly particular. Glagol has yet to publish any women.[78] All of Glagol's books are of a time and generally a place quite separate from their present readership. Baldwin's Giovanni's Room was written in 1956 and takes place in Paris. Burrough's drug-hazed ramblings are also set in the 1950s, this time in the United States. Limonov's sexcapades are set in 1970s New York, and Kharitonov's two-volume works in mid-century Russia.[79]

Shatolov justifies his choices on "artistic" grounds,[80] which are, of course, always slippery.[81] Why James Baldwin and not David Leavitt? Why European and American writers and not South American or African? Clearly a lot more is going on here than the publication of the "best" works of art. Glagol's editions speak not just to Shatolov's preferences and prejudices, but his understanding of what will sell in the Russian market. All of the Glagol books tell similar stories, stories that make sense in Russian.

Baldwin, Burroughs, Kharitonov, and Limonov share neither a common language nor a common culture nor historical moment. Instead, what is present in all four authors is a recognizable (at least to a Russian reader) concept of queer male sexuality. This sexuality is neither bounded nor fixed. It is not an identity, but a practice. The characters are not "either gay or straight" but both, or neither. They are men who are sexual with both men and with women, not because they identify as "bisexual" but because their lives are bifurcated.

The split between the under- and overworlds, the hidden queerness and public normalcy, is most pronounced in *Giovanni's Room*. Baldwin's protagonist, David, is a young American in Paris. In the course of the book David has a variety of sexual experiences with women as well as two lovers to whom he is emotionally tied, one a woman, the second a man. In the course of his stay in Paris, David moves in with the man, Giovanni, only to abandon him for his female lover, Hella. David leaves Giovanni, and by implication homosexuality, not because he loves Hella more, but because he cannot continue to live "underground." After trying to reestablish his heterosexuality by having sex with a second woman, whom he literally finds repulsive, David convinces himself that he can still come out of the queer underground if only he will be "strong."

> What a long way, I thought, I've come—to be destroyed! Yet it was true, I recalled, turning away from the river down the long street home, I wanted children. I wanted to be inside again, with the light and safety, with my manhood unquestioned, watching my woman put my children to bed. . . . I wanted a woman to be for me a steady ground, like the earth itself, where I could always be renewed. It had been so once. . . . I could make it so again, I could make it real. It only demanded a short, hard strength for me to become myself again.[82]

The idiom of a dark and queer underground beneath a brighter aboveground is reversed in Burroughs, where the underground and those who live there—drug abusers, sex workers, homosexuals—are the only objects worthy of interest. Some homosexuals are part of the "straight" world in Burroughs. Yet even these "straight homosexuals" are attracted to the underworld. Describing a gay man on the subway, Burrough's narrator says: "Young, good looking, crew cut, Ivy League, advertising exec type fruit holds the door back for me. I am evidently his idea of a character.

You know the type comes on with bartenders and cab drivers . . . a real asshole."[83] For Burroughs, a homosexual, even the most respectable "asshole" is always in danger of slipping underground.

In Kharitonov, homosexuality means a complete and total separation from others, a loneliness bordering on pathology. In the disparate works he wrote throughout his life and originally titled *Under House Arrest*, Kharitonov describes homosexual desire and homosexuals as permanently on the outside. Kharitonov, writing in the 1970s, was the first Russian writer in nearly half a century to write openly about homosexuality, and he did so in a way that was far more filled with the details of sex than his predecessors. Yet Kharitonov's work is not about sexual liberation, but imprisonment. Kharitonov's work describes queer desires as not only inevitable, but inevitably sinful. Kharitonov was a devout Russian Orthodox Christian and insistently queer man,[84] which may explain the obsession with homosexuality as sin. His paradoxical relationship to his sexuality—as both sinful and inevitable, as both hidden and demanding to be recorded in great detail—speaks to the contradictions between his aboveground life as a highly successful theater director and his furtive, underground existence as a gay man in communist Russia.[85]

The above/under separation rings true to a Russian ear, where the metaphor for "coming out of the closet" is "coming out from underground."[86] Yet all Glagol's writers celebrate the underground, especially its darkness. Limonov's main character, Eddie, loves only one woman, his ex-wife. The rest of his female lovers are treated with a contempt bordering on misogyny. Limonov juxtaposes his passionless heterosexual encounters with his passionate homosexual ones. The homosexual encounters always occur with an air of danger and crossing borders not meant to be crossed. Limonov, the white Russian intellectual, relates his encounters with black and socially marginal American men in a manner that can only be described as radiant.[87]

The strict boundary between queer and normal lives, above- and undergrounds, exists to divide not persons but practices. None of the protagonists of the Glagol books is a divided person, but rather someone who continuously crosses over the queer/normal divide. Once on the queer side, the protagonists are not permanently "marked." Instead, they move about these sexual barriers as a pedestrian who must travel from a respectable neighborhood through a red-light district several times in the course of a day, a week, a lifetime. Consider Limonov's Eddie, who is both a man in love with a woman, and a man who sleeps with women, and a man who sleeps with men. He does not reveal a "truer" homosexual self to his female partners. Eddie doesn't feel compelled to announce his newfound sexual practices as part of a previously hidden but more "authentic" identity. In Baldwin, David's female lover discovers his queer practices, but at no point before this did he feel compelled to confess his homosexuality to her. Although the queer heroes never reveal themselves, at least willingly, to the hostile straight world in which they also reside, there seems little shame in heterosexuality (and perhaps some pride) in the queer spaces they inhabit.[88]

In the same way that "underground" is a powerful description of Russian queers, so is the fluidity of boundaries, the crossing back and forth between straight and queer worlds, without ever having to settle permanently in one location or another. The "compulsory heterosexuality" of the Soviet system demanded that one bore the label "married" in order to obtain scarce resources like housing and jobs. Socially it is a lot easier to explain that one is divorced or separated than never married.[89] That nearly everyone must participate, at least to some extent, in heterosexuality never stopped some from also participating in other sexualities. Since heterosexuality was mandatory, like military service, it did not threaten a person's status as "queer." Many of Russia's leading queer activists are or have been married to someone of the opposite sex.[90] Many young queers, even those active in political organizations, spoke of their desire to marry someone of the opposite sex. A twenty-one-year-old member of the Tchaikovsky Fund told me he had every intention of marrying a woman in a few years and having children. I asked him whether or not he would tell his hypothetical wife of his homosexual practices. "Absolutely not. I may continue to sleep with men, but I would never tell my wife that. Why should she know about that?"[91] This is the fluidity of boundaries and mandatory nature of heterosexuality that is reflected in Glagol's books. It is not "artistic" merit that Shatolov has defined, but queer subjectivities that mirror the lives of Russian queers.

Staging Queerness

Another major form of popular queer subjectivity, theater, also wraps itself in the cloak of artistic merit. Like queer literature, the queer theater is not for queers per se, but for those interested in "art." The art happens to represent queerness, but many of its queer producers and consumers seem to feel that is beside the point. Many queers I interviewed believed queer theater was important, not because it represented queerness per se, but for its representations of "true love." Typically queers argued that theater can transcend the banality of a particular sexuality: "This [referring to Roman Viktiuk's production of M. Butterfly"] is far more important than any political organization. This is about love, which is never heterosexual or homosexual." "Viktiuk's work does a lot more for us than [queer political activists] ever will."

Like queer books, queer theater is, despite its protests to the contrary, highly representative of Russian (male) homosexuality. In almost all the theatrical stagings of queerness, queer characters are not defined by a coherent and fixed (homo)sexual identity. Instead, the stories consider how men engage one another in love and lust without ever placing all such men under a common or even any sexuality.

Since 1989, Jean Genet's The Maids and David Hwang's M. Butterfly have been produced by one of Russia's premier theater personalities, Roman Viktiuk.[92] In Genet the male homoerotica is metamorphosed into the (never overtly) incestuous relationship between the two sisters/maids, Claire and Solange. There is no need to call the men playing the parts of the maids "gay," but there is no denying the sexual attraction they feel for each other and Madam/another man.[93] In M. Butterfly the homosexual relationship is literally played out, but one of the lovers is married to a woman, and the gender fluidity of both characters makes it difficult to affix a sexuality to either man. Whether consciously or unconsciously, Viktiuk chose plays (and audiences responded enthusiastically to them) that spoke to intense sexual and emotional attachments between men without ever trying to "identify" those men (especially since they were also women). In fact, Viktiuk explained the homosexuality of one of his productions as "Blind faith brings one man to fall in love with another, without ever considering what sex he is."[94]

Viktiuk has not only imported stories that make sense in Russian/Russia, he has also produced an indigenous tale of love and lust between men. The play was Rogatka (Slingshot), written by Nikolai Koliada, and its opening in the fall of 1993 constituted the first time in seventy years that Russian (as opposed to imported) queer subjectivity was seen on stage.[95] The play itself centers on the relationship between two men, or more exactly, a man and a boy. The man, confined to a wheelchair (perhaps to physically signify that he is bodily/sexually other), is quite clear about what he wants. In the first act he confides that he has never been with a woman. Later, the man compares his "love" for the boy with a female neighbor's animalistic "lust," which is no different from that of "rabbits or pigs."[96] The boy, however, is much less certain about his sexual feelings. The boy has failed to "perform" with his girlfriend and does indeed confess to being exactly the same as the man in all things. Yet when the boy and the man finally do have sex, the boy wakes up disgusted and angry with himself. He returns in the second act to blackmail the man. Eventually the man kills himself, and only then does the boy admit, in a conversation with his now deceased beloved, that he wishes to be with him.[97]

Slingshot is anything but subtle. The man and the boy sit and eat an imaginary/metaphorical apple, which turns out to be rotten. Dream sequences involve a large swing and an elevator shaft (rather like hotdogs chasing donuts). Worse, "The Show Must Go On," an English-language pop song, is played (loudly) in the background of the dream sequences. The overly melodramatic nature of the play did not seem to diminish audience enthusiasm. On the night I attended, Viktiuk was given a lengthy standing ovation by a crowded house. One of the reasons Viktiuk's belabored show was so popular could very well be the fact that Slingshot, like M. Butterfly and The Maids, is a story of ill-defined sexualities. The man speaks of dreaming that he is a bird, soaring into the sky, "neither male nor female." The boy, body hairless and a head of long hair falling loosely around his shoulders, also occupies an androgynous space. In the dream sequences, the now ambulatory man and the boy slash and jump their way through walls/borders. Finally, many of the dream sequences include the "lustful" female neighbor. The sex/love may be acted out between the two men, but a woman/heterosexuality is omnipresent.

Of course, this is a very particular (i.e., my own) reading of the play. Although I did interview the five persons with whom I attended the show, no one mentioned "sexuality without identity" as a reason for liking the show.[98] One person told me that *Ragadka* was "Russian, and if you're Russian you'll understand." Another said it was Viktiuk's staging that made the show that of a "genius." This person was not, however, able/willing to say what in particular she admired. Yet even if these and other viewers did not vocalize it, what made the play "Russian" and Viktiuk a "genius," at least in terms of presenting homosexuality to the public, was the absolute unwillingness to present homosexuals as a separate species/identity/lifestyle. Sexual love can happen between two men (any two men). No character in the play "is" gay, and the two lovers spend a fair amount of their time speaking about sexual relationships with women. The other obvious message of *Rogatka*, and Viktiuk's entire oeuvre, is that when sexual love does happen between two men, it often ends in tragedy. The tragedy, however, is not the love between the two men, but the denial of that love.

Viktiuk's plays, like Glagol's books, allow queer experiences and queers to represent themselves to a much larger public than the queer-specific magazines and journals, discos, or even bathrooms. The cost of obtaining a large audience is that queer representation seems to be limited to a trope of romantic (never sexual) love and to unimaginative and highly predictable tragic endings. Still, the rewards of popularly speaking of sexual otherness as "art" are many. First, the pesky imperative for "full" representation disappears. No one assumes that "great art" must also include women (and by shielding themselves in the metaphysical truth of art, popular queer subjectivity is free to completely ignore the particular and individual truths of queer women). Nor does "great art" include sexual identity, identity politics, or even just sex. No depictions of anonymous sex in a public toilet have pulled themselves up to the level of "art." Queer men who want sex without love are just as invisible as queer women are. Second, a particular political argument about queers is circulated among large numbers of persons, without those persons ever recognizing or rejecting it. Queer "artists" are arguing that "love" is the common denominator, the great leveler. "True love," whether between two men or a man and a woman, is universal and should be universally valued. This argument is obviously a useful one to many queers (and nonqueers) since it allows difference (as well as the violence directed at that difference) to become meaningless and therefore no longer threatening. That love leaves out a whole plethora of queer desires and practices is justified by its status as art and therefore above the mundane considerations of representation (while at the same time art is representing queerness as love).

The result is a world of queer subjectivities where men speak more often and louder than women, where queer is represented in some ways and not in others, where other forms of sexual otherness can only be found in a handful of easily erased texts—public bathrooms, cruising strips, texts written by and for enthusiasts. The result is also, however, the proliferation of some queer subjectivities among a much wider public. No longer confined underground, some queers can represent themselves in ways that are readable aboveground. In this way, queers, who had always been objects (of medical experts, laws, bashers, and a variety of persons or institutions willing to speak for them) have begun to speak for themselves. Perhaps even more importantly, queer subjectivities, at least a few of them, are now part of the "popular imagination."[99] By 1994, queers already occupied a large enough space in the Russian popular imagination that even their enemies could no longer ignore them. Those who would speak "about them" were being shouted down by queer subjectivities, not identities.

Queerness shifted from the monotonous monologue of objectification to a dialogic exchange between self and other. The shift from objectification to representation took place not because of a political movement, nor because of an attempt to represent queerness to other queers, but because a small portion of queer subjectivities managed to enter the gates of popular culture in the belly of the Trojan Horse known as true art and true love. That these representations of queerness are not the whole truth is inevitable, since not all queer voices would be heard by or comprehensible to the public. Instead, queer "reality" (at least as it exists in the popular imagination) is represented by those who can speak most loudly and comprehensibly to a public (both queer and straight) that believes in love and art, not identity and politics.

part III: intersections

chapter 5

Clothes Make the Man:

Gender Transgression and Public Queerness

Written on the body is a secret code only visible in certain lights; the accumulations of a lifetime gather there.

—Jeanette Winterson, Written on the Body, 1993

But you can't know. There's no way of telling someone's sexual orientation by looking at them.

—Comment to the author by a teacher of the methods of social science

I have been arguing that sexuality is a constantly shifting negotiation be-tween self and other, subject and object, expert and queer. The result is a cacophony of voices, some of which are louder than others. Those who speak in the first person hear not just those who speak about them, but eavesdrop on other conversations as well. The sense of self is not just cut in bas-relief against other, but against other selves. So it is that the language of sexuality makes itself comprehensible by speaking in other tongues. Queers are not just sexualized; they are gendered, classed, nationed, and ethnicized as well. In some cultural and historical contexts, sexuality does not necessarily intersect with these particular taxonomies, but sexuality will always collide with some other selves. No source of identity exists in a vacuum, a conversation unto itself, where no one is overheard and no one overhears. Sexuality speaks in the terms of other selves. In Russia queers utilize a whole range of self/other systems, but they are most reliant on notions of gender and nationality in their expressions of queerness. This chapter explores how queer sexuality relies on a system of gender (and how gender relies on a system of heterosexuality). The following chapter, "Patriots and Perverts," explores how queer sexualities and nationalism often reside in a single person.

Seven years ago I was *learning* how to do field research as part of a doctoral program in sociology. A short time later I found myself *doing* field research in Russia. As a student, I would conscientiously note not only the gender, age range, and race/ethnicity of the people with whom I spoke, but also their sexuality. My professor at the time found this unacceptable. He told me that I could not possibly know someone's desires from their outward appearance. As a student I never responded to him. As a researcher who is looking in part at just how we can and do "know," at how marking ourselves by our desires is one way of carving out space in the public sphere for those who desire queerly, I am ready to respond. Yes, yes I can tell. The telltale signs tell me someone's sexuality by looking at them. Sexuality is knowable, visible, written all over the physical and social body.

This is counterintuitive, or at least counter to the prevailing mythologies that not only make sexuality invisible, but make gender and sex (and race) visible by making them stable and "natural" (i.e., determined presocially). In a recent editorial, the *New York Times* referred to "gay Americans" as an "indistinguishable minority" because sexual identity, unlike race or gender, cannot be seen.[1] Indistinguishable from what? From heterosexuals? But if that is the case, then heterosexual desire must be visible, so glaringly visible that it obliterates nonheterosexual desire's signs. The press can call gays "invisible" only by ignoring that this invisibility is visibility as straight.

Yet nonheterosexual desires are not completely obscured by heterosexuality. Nonheterosexuality, queerness in all its forms, leaks into our field of vision from its confinement in the private and imaginary. There are "those people," the ones who refuse to not be noticed: men in tutus with fairy wings clipped to their shoulders and false eyelashes glued to their fluttering lids; women in suits with short hair and shorter fingernails; men and women in "uniforms," like cutoff 501 Levis, black motorcycle jackets open to reveal sparkling white T-shirts, combat boots, heads shaved and tattoos showing, or leather chaps and riding boots, crop in hand. Queer is not just an urban look. There are women in lavender clothes, Birkenstock sandals, and pinky rings in the most rural settings. There are everywhere men who always have a perfect haircut, fashionable clothes, and a certain way of say-ing their words and holding their bodies that makes them seem oh so light in their loafers. They, too, are recognizable, and not just to one another.

Each of us reveals, consciously and unconsciously, our desires. Our sup-posedly private sexuality is always enacted publicly, in ways that corre-spond to our sexual practices and in ways that do not. I can be queer in my practices and straight in my body. I can also be straight in my prac-tices and queer in my body. Some women who desire women wear high heels and A-line skirts. Some women who desire men shave their heads and wear women's symbols around their necks. Yet a lack of correspondence between practices and significations does not make sexuality unknowable. That we may not always display what we "really" are (i.e., what we really do) does not make the display itself untrue. Instead, those who break the rules occupy a liminal space known to most of us as the "unreal" (e.g., not a "real" man). When queer sexuality is seen, it is ignored (as in the *Times* editorial) or denied (as by my old professor), but always read. Sexuality is a codifiable system of signs, like gender or race, and we are all avid readers.

Gender and race, like sexuality, can also appear in ways that do not cor-respond with society's expectations. A person with a penis can put on drag, that is, choose a set of signs different from the "appropriate" ones. You and I read that person as she, or perhaps a he, but always a complex he. A person who is "really" African American we might read as "really" Euro-pean American or vice versa. Identities are never totalizing systems, since they can always be transgressed by identifying ourselves in unexpected or unallowed ways. That identities exist in a language of identifiable symbols is undeniable.

I want to explore how it is that sexuality is caught up in a bodily signify-ing system that very much mirrors gender. Gender is mirrored in sexuality in the sense that it returns a reflected image that is both more distorted and more true. And why is the reading of sexuality, unlike gender, always furtive, like the reading of pornography, under the sheets with a flashlight, hoping not to get caught?[2]

THE BOOK OF GENDER

Judith Butler tells us that gender is a performance that must be constantly enacted and reenacted in order to be successful. Gender is a tenuously constituted identity understandable from the outside through a "stylized repetition of acts." Gender "must be understood as the mundane way in which bodily gestures, movements, styles of various kinds constitute the illusion of an abiding gendered self."[3] Butler's definition of gender can be applied to other classificatory schemes, such as sexual or ethnic identity. Identities, or locations in the social world, are socially comprehensible because of this very repetition of the acts that signify them.

Literally and figuratively "acting out" our identity is what Pierre Bourdieu calls "habitus." For Bourdieu, habitus is "a system of acquired dispositions functioning on the practical level as categories of perception . . . or as classificatory principles as well as being the organizing principles of action." Habitus not only shapes the way we see the world and the way the world sees us, but it leads us to perform in certain ways and not in others.[4]

Both Bourdieu and Butler conceptualize identity as an act, but this act is not a choice. Neither is proposing some sort of "voluntarist account of gender," since such an account "presumes a subject, intact, prior to its gendering." A sense of self, a subjectivity, can exist only with regulatory regimes such as gender. In other words, there is no "I" choosing to put on gender as if it were clothing, since the "I" does not exist until it is already dressed in the fabric of a socialized (e.g., gendered or sexualized) self.[5]

Gender is not a choice then, but a practice, and in order to replicate itself gender must constantly be performed. How then do I practice gender? I have lived in Moscow and New York, Russian and English. I am readable in both places and languages as a woman, sometimes, and sometimes as a man or a boy. In Russian, "young man," "son," "brother," "girl," "sweetie," "woman," "What are you, a man or a woman?," "pederast," "dyke."[6] In English, "boy," "son," "lady," "girl," "lesbian," "dyke," "pervert." In both languages I "pervert" the language of gender: my hair is shaved, my face hairless; I wear my skirt and my combat boots, my lipstick and motorcycle jacket. I am not following the rules. My gendered body is a difficult text to read as "man" or "woman." Sometimes my body is written in a different, more accessible language. Sometimes I wear a suit and tie, wingtips, and a hat; I don't wear lipstick, and I even take off my earrings. Now I am clearly engendered as a man. The readers, in Russian and English, read my body and are happy that the text does not provoke them with difficult-to-pronounce terms.

There can be an unexpected failure in my expected gender performance. Sometimes I do not sit or stand or speak in the gender-appropriate ways. Then my "true" gender is seen and my transgression of the "proper" gender roles is punished: "pervert," "lesbian," "dyke." Perverting gender roles is, to both the Russian and the American reader, a sign of another sort of perversion—crossing the clearly marked boundaries of heterosexual desire. That a failed gender act comes to mean failed heterosexual desire in two separate symbolic systems reveals the way gender and sexuality are caught up with each other in both cultures.

The entanglement of gender and sexuality occurs in what Butler refers to as the "heterosexual matrix." In the heterosexual matrix, sex, sexuality, and gender depend on one another in order to be intelligible. The heterosexual matrix is a hegemonic system that "assumes that for bodies to cohere and make sense there must be a stable sex expressed through a stable gender . . . that is oppositionally and hierarchically defined through the compulsory practice of heterosexuality."[7] In other words, bodies are divided into male and female, genders into masculine and feminine, desires into a desire for the opposite. A vagina metonymically transforms into a woman who "naturally" desires a man, who is himself metonymically reduced to a penis. Sex implies gender; gender implies sexuality. Sexuality implicates gender; gender implicates sex. When my physical and performative self are a seamless whole (whether as a man or as a woman), my desire is unproblematic; it is heterosexual. But as soon as there is a slippage, a failed gender performance, a contradictory set of signifiers, the entire matrix is called into question. My perceived desires become as perverse as my gender performance (regardless of whether my practice of those desires is homo- or heterosexual).

In theory, then, homosexuality is a performance, comprehensible to the audience in part because it is a transgression of gender appropriate roles. In practice I collected these moments of gender transgression and (homo)sexual identification. I am presenting these moments of gender transgression as though they were fixed in time and space and around the single dimension of gender. In fact, these moments are much more complicated than gender transgression as homosexual enactment and the moments need to be dissected for other secrets about desire and the identities we build around it. For now, though, I am only looking at some points where transgressing the rules and roles of gender space is carving out space in the public sphere for queer desires.

Speaking Queerly

One of the most obvious and effective uses of gender transgression to signify queerness occurs in everyday speech. Because the Russian language requires gendering of all nouns/persons as well as all verbs in the past tense, it provides ample opportunity for using the "incorrect" gender. For example, a man speaking of another man might say that "she arrived at 2 A.M." ("*ona poshla . . .*"). Queer men use feminine forms of address to describe themselves, and/or other men like them. Vladimir Kozlovsky's compilation of Russian gay male slang is full of words and phrases that use "inappropriate" gender to speak of queer desires. Of 141 words that could describe a person, 105 of them used the "wrong" gender. For instance, a passive (male) homosexual could be called any of the following: *baba, gorizontalka, devka, zhenshchina, kozochka,* or *kurochka* (crone, horizontalka, wench, woman, nanny goat, or a young hen). A man who tried to pick up other men in a train station is a "station wench" (*vokzal'naia devka*), while such a man in a public toilet is a "bathroom wench" (*tualetnaia*) and one in a bathhouse is a "bania wench" (*bannaia*). A gay man who is also Jewish is pejoratively called a "kike" in its feminized form (*zhidovka*). Of the 36 words that used the "appropriate" gender, many were describing heterosexuals (e.g., *streit* or *streitovik* for a "straight" man).[8]

Although Kozlovsky's work is slightly dated and many of the terms are no longer part of current slang usage,[9] the "wrong" gender as signifier of queer sexuality remains a part of everyday speech among queers. Words like *devka, tetenka,* and *baba* (wench, auntie, and crone/hag) were an integral part of the queer male chatter to which I was privy. Speaking with feminine pronouns and feminine verb endings about men was so usual as to be unremarkable (e.g., "*Gde Pasha?*" "*Vot ona.*" Where's Paulie? There she is."). Describing a sexually active man as a female prostitute (*prostitutka*) or an older gay man as a grandmother (*babushka*) were as much a part of being queer as going to queer discos or cruising strips.

In contrast, most women I interviewed did not use "incorrect" words as part of everyday queerness. Still, many women who love women thought of themselves as men. Some of these men (women) used the term "transsexual" to describe themselves, many others spoke of a sense of always knowing that they were "really" men.[10] Some of these men (women) do use masculine forms to describe themselves (e.g., "*Ia poshel*" rather than "*Ia poshla*"). Also, many of these men (women) choose masculine names or nicknames: "Ira" becomes "Irik." Several men (women) who had neutral names (e.g., both Evgenii and Evgeniia shorten to Zhenia) cited this as evidence that their parents had recognized their masculine nature at birth. Also, in a highly gendered relationship, the active or butch partner can be called a male dog (*kobel*).[11]

The language of gender inversion/sexual "perversion" was not spoken loudly. It was only spoken among friends or in queer spaces, but it was enough a part of the public realm as to be understood by all who spoke it and heard it that using the "incorrect" gender was a powerful way of being publicly and "obviously" queer.

Plays on Gender

In the summer of 1994, Christopher Marlowe's *Edward II* played at a Moscow theater. This most queeny of kings was presumably enacted for what was not (or not only) a homosexual audience. By audience response to certain comedic and tragic moments, it seemed clear that all understood that Edward was, if not homosexual, then certainly homosocial as well as homoerotic. We laughed when he almost kissed his wife, Isabelle, and then pointed out how much better it was to shake hands. We were moved to tears when Edward's enemies kill his lover, Gaveston. Some of the signs that told us of Edward's queerness were his hair, longer and more elaborate than the other, presumably heterosexual, male characters; he was thinner and somehow more elegantly dressed; he spoke with a certain softness, almost a lisp; his body seemed to be in a perpetual curve, arms bent at elbows, wrists held limply. Not only did the Russian Edward embody femininity/homosexuality, but within Marlowe's written Edward is a loss of emotional control that textually marks him as feminine. The persecution of Edward is not for his sexual acts, but for his gender treason. It is the "Elizabethan concept of manliness that Edward transgresses not by loving a man but by his uneconomical emotional expenditure." [12] The act of enacting Marlowe's treasonous gender helped homosexuality to the public stage in Moscow.

Edward II is not the only play transgressing gender expectations to signify homosexuality. As I discussed in chapter 4, Jean Genet's The Maids is performed at some of the country's best-known theaters, including Moscow's Satirikon. [13] It has also been broadcast on television (May 1994). Thus Genet is playing to a mass audience, most of whom do not identify as homosexual. But this is the work of Genet, a work meant to celebrate subversion, including the subversion of gender and heterosexuality. The plot of The Maids seems to be about class not sexual perversions. Claire and Solange, the maids, desire Madam, and they desire her downfall. Their plot to imprison Madam's beloved, Monsieur, fails, resulting in Solange's suicide and Claire's punishment for her murder. Death is climax, orgasm. They want to take Madam, but they can only take themselves. The maids desire because they are debased, but part of their debasement is their desire—desire that is unspoken, violent, about power and its possible reversal through sexual acts, about sexual acts that occur between persons of the same sex. This is the homoerotic subtext, the parallel plot line, of The Maids. [14]

Viktiuk's production of Genet's The Maids begins with a disembodied voice, first in French then in Russian: "I believe the roles of the maids ought to be played only by men, specifically by men." The words, which are similar to statements made by Genet himself,[15] were made part of the production in order to convince a skeptical Soviet censor that men playing women was "art," not "perversion." [16] The Soviet censor sensed the connection between gender and sexual perversions/subversions. The audience senses it too. Some of the comments I recorded from the audience: "Yes, Viktiuk is a pederast, but so what? His work is beautiful. He is a genius." "Viktiuk may be gay, but he's not as rude as Genet. He understands beauty." The actor who played Monsieur, Sergei Zarubin, told me that the audience "knows," but Viktiuk does not "push the homosexuality of the play into their faces." Instead, he moves them with "beauty," since "beauty" transcends all differences.[17]

The audience "knows" and the censor "senses" the homosexual/homoerotic text within Viktiuk's production not because it is Genet (who is not widely known in Russia, since Viktiuk's 1989 production was the first production of his work). Instead, the unknowable is known because gender is subverted in ways that signify homosexual desire. Viktiuk's production of The Maids involves men in skirts, faces made up in white paint, with arched eyebrows, thick eyeliner, cheeks and lips startlingly red. The effect is not men passing as women, especially since the actors wear no shirts, their muscular, flat, and hairy chests embodying them as male. Instead it is men NOT passing as women that makes this work so homoerotically charged. Men who wear skirts and make-up and ribbons in their hair are men who pervert the gender system. Men who pervert gender are themselves perverts. They are men who desire each other (as women desiring women, who are really men desiring men). In Viktiuk's version, the characters dance as men, on a stage full of distorting mirrors (reflecting their distorted gender?). The choreography is (homo)sexually charged, rough and sweaty and physically exhausting: men dancing erotically in skirts, using skirts to entice and provoke each other.

Viktiuk also directed a production of M. Butterfly which has been playing to enthusiastic audiences in Moscow and St. Petersburg since 1989. M. Butterfly begins with Réné Gallimard, a French diplomat, in a small room, a cage or jail cell. The cage is the cage of Réné's fixed notions of gender. Réné is . . . " 'seduced,' 'deluded,' and 'imprisoned' by clinging . . . to an essentialist notion of identity. For him, cliched images of gender, race, and geography unproblematically occupy the inner space of identity, enabling . . . Song [a Chinese spy] . . . to seduce through the play of inner truth and outer appearance." [18] Gender is what traps and limits Réné, since his desire for the appropriate gender, the highly feminine Song, is also desire for the inappropriate sex (i.e. the male one).[19] Réné's desire so subverts his place in the world, as French colonizer of the Asian other, as male dominator of the submissive female, that he becomes that which he was supposed to take (i.e., he becomes both Asian and female).

In M. Butterfly becoming the other, crossing boundaries not meant to be crossed, implies homosexual desire. That Réné and Song are lovers and they are both men no longer implies but rather describes homosexual desire. She is a he, and we, the audience, are privy to this information even if it is a knowledge that Réné refuses to "know." The audience in Moscow does "know." Song, as a man, propositions another man. A small section of the audience cheers when the man refuses the male Song's desire. Apparently it is not the physical attraction between two male bodies that disgusts these viewers, but two male genders. Song's desire for a man produces delight if she is in a dress, disgust if he is in trousers. Perhaps gender is, as Wayne Kostenbaum suggests, "just a matter of developing a knack for the right accessories" and heterosexuality (and homosexuality) a fetishization of those accessories.[20] When Réné fetishizes the appropriate (read heterosexually oppositional) gender signs (Song's submissiveness, binding dress, painted face), his desire does not arouse disgust. Song's desire for a man as a man is revolting to the audience who "know" that like genders should not attract and that crossing the boundary of gender appropriate desire is literally revolting, a revolt against enforced heterosexuality and the invisibility of homosexual desire.

Cruising

As I discussed in chapter 4, most large urban areas in Russia have cruising strips, areas of the city where men can engage in (homo)sexual encounters. Moscow has several of them, one near the Bolshoi, another near the Kitai Gorod metro station, yet another along Gogolivskii Boulevard. I spent time at these places, sometimes engendered as a man, sometimes as a woman. At these points of homosexual desire's enactment, the men recognized each other and were recognizable. Many of the men wore their hair long, in "feminine" ways. Sometimes it was visibly dyed or permed. Often lashes were elongated with mascara, cheeks accented with rouge. There were also men who had their hair cut sharply and neatly, often a single earring, tight Levis, and cowboy boots. Their concern with style (a stereotypically female concern) and the style with which they concern themselves (i.e., a gay uniform of sorts) made them "look" queer. Then there were the men who "look" straight, but the way they looked at other men, the way they did not avert their eyes when caught in the act of looking (desiring) marked them, at least momentarily, as visibly gay.

I have cruised dressed in dresses. Interestingly enough, even in dresses I was often "read" as male, although admittedly a gay one. From some of the boys at the cruising strip, the pleshka, I received winks and smiles. From some of the passersby I heard pederast, a pejorative term that, like "faggot" in English, is meant to reside in a male body. Of the seventeen boys and men I spoke to at the pleshka, all of them insisted that all the men who come there come for sex with other men. A, a red-headed, freckled twenty-two-year-old who was often my "pleshka guide," explained that "there's only ever one reason to come to the pleshka. You look into their eyes, you ask them to light your cigarette, you can see if someone is one of us [nash chelovek]."[21] Homoerotic desire is visible at the pleshkas, written all over the men's faces and bodies, most often in the form of gender transgression.

The Dance of Gender

There are regularly occurring discos in Moscow and St. Petersburg that cater to a primarily gay male clientele. Once I showed up at the St. Petersburg Café Caprice and was told the disco for "my kind" had been rescheduled for the next night due to a faulty sound system. How did the man at the door know "my kind"? How did he know I was there for the queer disco and not a drink at the straight bar (which was open)? I was wearing combat boots and jeans and a motorcycle jacket. I had short hair and no makeup on. Did he think I was a man or a woman, a manly woman or a womanly man?

The discos themselves were populated with people, mostly "men," blurring gender lines. At Chance, a Moscow disco, on any given Saturday night there were several hundred people inside, about 80 percent of them appearing to me as men.[22] Many of these men were inappropriately engendered. Some of the men wore dainty slippers on their feet, shoes of suede with decorative buckles and low heels. Some of them wore earrings, or makeup, particularly lipstick and mascara. Some men wore skirts. A much larger

proportion of the crowd inside than outside wears black. "Black is the preferred color" of gays, I was told more than once. "We prefer something
leather, rocker-like, sufficiently aggressive." [23]

In addition to the discos, there were groups of women in both cities
who organize social evenings that occur before the discos begin. At a typical meeting of a Moscow women's club, twelve out of eighteen women had
short hair. Fourteen of the women had on men's suit jackets. One woman
said that "short hair, not dyed, in pants and one earring in her ear—this
is an active lesbian, who as a rule has masculine habits, knowing about
car mechanics, repair of electronics, knowing how to do things with her
hands." A woman who knows how to do stereotypically male activities apparently also knows how to engage in "male" desire, desire for a woman.[24]

Fashion Statements

On Monday nights, one of the most expensive clubs in Moscow, Manhattan Express, often had fashion shows. Some of the designers and performance artists who staged these shows are openly gay. Both their designs
and their staging revealed more than avant-garde fashion. L staged a show
full of unisex clothing and pretty young boys backing each other up against
Greco-Roman columns (a reference to Greek love?). The four times I attended such showings, I was part of a sizable contingent of people who,
like myself, were part of the openly queer Moscow community and were invited by the designers. We were given free entrance (admission was about
fifteen dollars), but we also gave the club a certain queer elegance. One
man, head shaved, often wore combat boots and a long kilt (unlike in
New York, even the most masculine of kilts results in waves of shock on
Moscow's streets). Several women wore men's suits, suspenders, ties, hair
cropped close to their heads. We stood out from the crowd of nouveau richniki in their business suits and designer dresses, sitting at their private
tables, viewing the exhibit and exhibition of queers.

I know other designers. V is thirty-four and from Siberia. He grew up on
a farm, and came to Moscow for the first time in 1994. But his clothes tell
another tale. V wears stylish bell-bottom jeans, beautiful cropped turtle-
necks, and flowered vests. He learned to make all these clothes himself. He
watched any fashion news he could in Siberia and spent a lot of time in pur-

suit of Western fashion magazines. From photographic images of (female) models, he sewed his wardrobe and created his publicly queer self. His brother tried to kill him when he found V studying these images in order to imitate them.[25] The brother told V that he was better off in a grave than being a faggot. V was a boy trying to dress like the girls. His brother knew what that meant.

The Song of Gender

In Moscow, on a blustery day in March 1994, the first gay tea dance was held. At the bar sat a man known for his unique blend of pop music and contemporary dance. The man, Boris Moiseev, first found fame while performing with Russian pop culture icon Alla Pugachova.[26] In 1991, after little success launching his solo career in Russia (in part because of persistent rumors that he had died of AIDS), Moiseev decided to "come out" in the press.[27]

Moiseev's image in the press often played on gender subversion in order to signify sexual "perversion," specifically homosexuality. A journalist asked what sort of toys he loved in childhood, Moiseev answered "I played with dolls. And even now I have my favorite dolls at home."[28] Moiseev told the reporter that his mother described him from birth as a "girl with balls." Later in the same article, Moiseev claimed it is his act of wearing a dress that turns his audience (male) on, forces them to stand erect (the double entendre works in English or Russian).[29]

Moiseev spoke aloud in the press his (homo)sexual identity, but his homosexual desires were already loudly stated in his work. Moiseev's performances are permeated with the homoerotic, particularly the homoerotic signified by inappropriate gender signs. A video of his song "Egoist" was often shown on the musical video program 2 × 2, that is, to many people who do not identify on the basis of their homosexual desires. The video, which has two versions, plays with gender in decidedly queer ways. The first version has Moiseev, unshaven but wearing a lot of lipstick and eye makeup, his hair bleached blond, singing alongside two female dancers. The dancers bump and grind on each other, the lesboerotica far from subtle. They wear transparent black shirts with pieces of black tape across their nipples (an apparent reference to pornography and its censorship). In the second version, a little girl gives another girl flowers. Later a woman wearing a suit and a mustache appears. Moiseev lies in a bed in golden underwear, face made up, a prince, a princess. Another Moiseev video is from his show in honor of Freddy Mercury.[30] The video begins with about twenty men in black tailcoats dancing together to a waltz. Here it is not the dancers' outward appearance that subverts gender and makes homosexual desire visible, but the inappropriate performance of gender (i.e., men twirling men in their arms). Men in formal clothes are not queer, unless they act that way.[31]

It is not just Moiseev I encountered in Moscow's gay bars—I have often seen another famous pop singer. This man, Sergei Penkin, was not loudly stating his sexuality in the press. In fact, as late as May of 1994, Penkin was denying his own homosexuality. In an article that begins with the question "Gay or not gay?" Penkin argues that if he were gay, which he is not, then he would not have been received by such high-level officials, which he has been. The author of the article, however, is unconvinced by such circular logic. Instead he tells us that Penkin's clothes, or more specifically, his "long, red gloves with fake diamonds and fur around his neck" "speak louder than words." The reader is left to read homosexuality into Penkin's inappropriate use of gendered clothing.[32]

Penkin's gender perversion and subversion is his public image.[33] He appears in his videos wearing women's dresses and wigs, and the front of his *Holiday* CD features him in lace, pearls, silver lame, a diamond brooch, and eye makeup. In the liner notes to the CD, Penkin admits that "[m]any . . . consider my image . . . shocking, they see in it some sort of . . . scandal. But I try to be just as I am, my main principle is naturalness."[34] Penkin may consider his image "natural" ("natural" is slang for heterosexual), but many people, including his interviewer, read queerness in his lace and pearls.

The Morality Police is a two-woman band. The women, Angela and Frida, have been described as "propagandizing all that is hidden and forbidden. Sadomasochism, lingerie, love among women . . . ."[35] Indeed, their stage act seems to do all of these things. Dressed in black leather, fishnet stockings, and dog collars, the two young women might be mistaken for stars of a pornographic film if they were not visible above the neck. Their heads, completely bereft of any hair, confront the viewer with a different sort of fantasy.[36]

It is the gender "inappropriateness" of the women, signaled most abruptly by their shaved heads but also by the physical play between them that makes them "visible" as queers, as well as visible to queers. The group is in extremely high demand at queer discos, and they themselves described their fans as "gay male."[37] These singers do not "admit" to being queer, probably because (privately) they are (also) straight. For them, lesboerotica is an "act."[38] Although the singers have insisted that "[b]isexuals are closest to us in spirit because they are not predetermined and they're original" and that a "[p]erson shouldn't place himself within some sort of limits, he should be exactly who he wants to be," they themselves have also been quite clear that their lovers are always male.[39]

The Morality Police are not the only women who act out lesboerotica on stage only to insist publicly that they do not engage in such desires off stage. The two "lesbians" who sing back-up for Moiseev, Lusia and Tania,[40] also insist that theirs is an act for the (male) audience. When the two "lesbians" were interviewed by the Russian-language *Penthouse*, they were asked what they felt about men's attraction to lesbianism or its enactment on stage. Tania answered that if lesbianism is "truly beautiful and truly arouses them [men], then it has a right to exist." Tania also made it clear that she has a husband and that he never "criticizes the lesbianism on stage" because he understands it is just an act.[41]

That men pop stars are *being* queer while women are only *playing* queer speaks to a different sort of intersection of gender and sexuality. Women have less of a voice in the public sphere, have less space in which to act out their sexual otherness. But the point here is that both men and women, whether being or just "acting" queer, transgress gender as a way of saying aloud desires that were previously unspoken.

TALKING BACK

I am claiming that one of the ways in which homosexual identity becomes public is through publicly breaking gender rules. But do they, the objects of my expert gaze, really "know" what I "know"? Are queers in Moscow and St. Petersburg knowingly making their (homo)sexuality visible by inappropriately engendering themselves? Between May and September I surveyed sixty-six persons who were in publicly queer space and visible to me as queer. In response to the question "Does a particular style of dress or color or type of clothing exist which signifies homosexuality? A hairstyle or jewelry?," twenty-six persons gave examples of such signs, and most of them named acts of gender inversion. Of nine women who felt they could read someone's sexuality, seven named inappropriate gender acts (e.g., a woman wearing men's clothes, short hair, no makeup, standing firmly with feet slightly apart) as signaling homosexual desire. Ten of the seventeen men put down gender subversion (e.g., femininity, speaking in a high, womanly voice, being soft and emotional, wearing earrings and cosmetics).[42]

Yet most people either said that no visible signs exist or that they themselves do not know of any such signs.[43] But these were people I asked specifically because they were in some way readable to me as "queer." How is it that the very people I claim are creating public queerness deny that they are doing so? In fact, the lack of correspondence between my interpretation and theirs is not surprising. I have been describing gender transgressions in ways that do not make sense to the very people about whom I am speaking. But I speak about, not for. I am trying to get to the bottom of why reading sexuality, unlike gender, is so furtive, even among the very people creating some of the strongest public images of queer desires.

Ignorance Is Bliss

August: K tells us that there have been several murders of gay men this year. Many of the men say they're too scared to go out at night. He says it's the third murder this year and that the police think it's a single person, a serial killer who may have already killed six gay men in St. Petersburg.

September: P, wearing a skirt, was severely beaten at the pleshka in front of the Bolshoi. The men who beat him used brass knuckles. They made a hole in his face.

—Field notes, Aug.–Sept., 1994

I recognize "sexual minorities" and they recognize each other. But they are "known" to those who are not "in the know" as well. Dozens of queer men and women have told me that they have been harassed by groups of young men. These men, known as *remontniki* or fixers, seek out the visibly queer and attack them (for their visibility). Many queer discos ask patrons not to leave in the middle of the night, but to wait until 6 A.M. when the metro reopens (and the *remontniki* have gone to bed). Not only do the fixers know who queers are, but the *militsia* does as well. Several queer men have told me that the police stop them and demand identification only when they are wearing things or acting in ways that say they are queer.[44]

It is only through the most purposeful acts of ignorance that we can and do ignore what is right before our eyes. Sexuality, like gender, is signified; it is marked and marked off in a myriad of ways that are readable to the reader. Although the reader can only read sexuality if s/he is a knowing reader, if s/he understands the language of desire, an "unknowing" reader, one who cannot see what is so plainly visible, is also caught up in this knowledge/power system. It is not, as Foucault would have it, knowledge alone that creates regimes of power, but ignorances as well. As Eve Sedgwick points out, "[I]gnorances, when they are the ignorances of a particular knowledge, are . . . far from being pieces of the originary dark, are produced by and correspond to particular knowledges and circulate as part of particular regimes of truth." Ignorance is even more powerful when it is an ignorance of sexuality, the most meaning-intensive of human activities.[45]

Ignorance of sexuality is part of a matrix of power relationships, Butler's heterosexual matrix. Knowledge of the "realness" of gender requires an *ignorance* of sexuality.[46] We must ignore sexuality, particularly sexuality signified by gender transgressions, to make gender real. When sexuality makes itself known by undermining the "realness" of gender, then to acknowledge sexuality is to acknowledge gender as a performance, a verb, not a noun. Our bodies and our minds cannot be disciplined by gender if we recognize breaks in its reality. When we write sexuality on our body, we must do so with invisible ink.

Even among queers, desires' signs often remain unacknowledged. Those Russians who desire queerly (and those who do not) use a fixed and dichotomous gender to create stable sexual identities. If being queer is breaking gender rules, and being straight is replicating them, gender itself is fixed, codifiable, a standard measure against which we can stand up (or not). To admit that gender is a performance threatens the very dichotomies around which straights and queers alike structure their desires. Girls may like girls or girls may like boys, but that there are girls and boys cannot be questioned. Gender must be seen as a noun, a thing, real, stable, and unchanging. Otherwise, queers and straights alike will disappear. Within the complex of rules that constitute gender, some Russians are managing to create public space for those who desire queerly. Some of those who desire queerly are perpetuating gender by transgressing it.

chapter 6

Patriots and Perverts: The Intersection of National and Sexual Identities

Ignatyev-Ignatyev . . . spouting long, ranting monologues of ultrarightist propaganda . . . was clearly in love with him. As time went on, the hysterics increased: Ignatyev-Ignatyev would throw himself at Luchnikov's feet and make homosexual confessions. . . . What was really behind it all—politics or glands?
—A description of one of several nationalist homosexuals in Vassily Aksenov's The Island of the Crimea, 1985

In the same way that sexuality employs a language of gender, it also speaks in the idiom of nation. Nationality/ism admittedly circulates differently in the United States than in Russia.[1] Nationalisms are as varied and as various as sex/gender systems.[2] National Identity, which like sexual identity was born a mere century ago, has proven very flexible. It is what Benedict Anderson calls "modular," "capable of being transplanted, with varying degrees of self-consciousness, to a great variety of social terrains, to merge and be merged with a correspondingly wide variety of political and ideological constellations."[3] Nationness is not only different among nations,[4] but it also performs differently within a nation. "Being" Russian, like "being" a man, depends not only upon geographical and cultural boundaries, but lines of class, gender, ethnicity, education, and of course, sexuality.

Despite differences between them, nation—like gender or sexuality—is a site of self-performance in both Russian and English. In part, nationalism is internationally and intranationally comprehensible because it relies on gender and sexual identities in a myriad of ways.[5] First, all three systems operate only insofar as we believe they are part of some prediscursive realm of "nature." One is born that way—a man, a citizen, a heterosexual. All three "natural" identities also employ binary oppositions to make sense. One is naturally a man, a citizen, a heterosexual because one is *not* a woman, a foreigner, a homosexual. Finally, the modern person is highly predicated on economies of gender, sexuality, and nation. Who we are relies on knowing what we are.

The ruling triumvirate of nation, gender, and sexuality do not, however, play with one another as equals. National identity and its logical conclusion, nationalism, are almost always engendered as "male" while the nation itself is generally "female."[6] The relationship between nation and sexuality, no doubt building upon the gendered nature of nation, works somewhat differently. The citizen may always be a he, but he is not necessarily a heterosexual. Indeed, national and nationalistic identities are often admittedly homosocial and ashamedly homosexual: "Typically represented as a passionate brotherhood, the nation finds itself compelled to distinguish its 'proper' homosociality from more explicitly sexualized male-male relations, a compulsion that requires the identification, isolation, and containment of male homosexuality."[7] Yet if nations generally try to hide the homosexual underbelly of national identity, they do not always do so. Public queerness in Russia often legitimizes itself through nationalism, and even more surprisingly, Russian nationalism is sometimes visibly, recognizably queer.

QUEERLY NATIONALIST

My brother is part of a neofascist punk band, and of course they're all gay and they're all for Zhirinovskii. I thought that homosexuals were always connected with fascism.

—Young Moscow woman to author, 1994

For centuries, we are told, Russia has been besieged by those trying to turn it into the West—westernizers—and those trying to turn the West away— Slavophiles. Tsars imported European modes of dress, languages, architecture, and more. Factions of the powerful classes resisted by asserting the superiority and inviolability of Mother Russia. Leonid Brezhnev offered Pepsi to the people; Aleksandr Solzhenitsyn drank kvass. Many persons from the West who live in Russia are in fact Slavophiles. Many persons from Russia are in fact westernizers. Both currents pulse and have pulsed through life in Russia, and ultimately both come from a single source—nation and the creation of self.

Nationalist queers not only identify as having both a nationality and a sexuality but also believe in the superiority of their national/sexual systems. There are westernizing and Russianizing queers, but they play out both their nationness and sexuality differently. The westernizers rely on a conceptualization of fixed sexual identities resting on their imaginings of an eternal hetero/homo split. In the mid-1980s the westernizers met little resistance since many people in Russia still believed that the West knew the way to a better life for them. The faith in "America" resulted not only in the economics of "shock therapy" but in the politics of "fixed identity." It was not so much an ambush as a surrender. The westernizing queers came armed with a wealth of economic, political, and cultural capital. They had faxes, computers, experience in the politics of identity, and the faith that there is one path to sexual freedom—their own. The Russian nationalist queers, on the other hand, occupied a less stable space of power. As I have argued throughout this work, in Russia sexual practices have not translated into a fixed identity as much as more free-floating subjectivities. National position is equally fluid. Russians are both dominant vis-à-vis certain groups, while dominated by others.[8] If Western nationalism comes at the cost of Russianness, Russian nationalism comes at the cost of other Others—Chechens and Uzbeks, Romanis and Ukrainians—who are removed from the circle of the Russian queer self. On the other hand, the Russians have very few resources with which to resist complete homogenization by the westernizers. As I discussed in chapters 1 and 2, there is no history of identity politics; there is not even a stable notion of sexualized self around which to organize. There are no broad collectivities of persons clamoring for representation—feminists, gays and lesbians, ethnic/racial minorities. There are certainly few computers and faxes, no organizational know-how, nor faith that they will successfully carve out their rights from a "reasonable" state. The westernizers enact their identities with the pomp and circumstance of opera while the Russian nationalists are more like graffiti artists, working with the limited materials and resources available to them.

Cultural Imperialism and Western Identity Activists

My own national identity never seems obvious to me in New York. After all, as a U.S. citizen I am the standard. I no more need to identify on the basis of my nationality than a heterosexual needs to identify his/her sexuality. In Moscow I "am" American. Even if I myself am not thinking how "American" I am and how "Russian" the people around me are, I am constantly surrounded by national identities.

> Young gay American living and working in Moscow to author: The Russians are subhuman. They have a long way to go to become civilized like us.

> Russian lesbian to author: I hate you Americans. You and your McDonald's. Before you occupied us, things worked here. The streets were cleaned of snow, things weren't like this.

These comments, of course, are easily dismissed. No reasonable person would say such things, at least not aloud. Nationalisms, however, are usually less obvious and more insidious. Like cancers, nationalisms can grow and multiply without our ever noticing them.

When I arrived in Moscow in January of 1994, I was particularly concerned with not "being" American (or Russian). At the same time, I had spent enough time living in Russia to know that I could not totally disregard the influence of the nationality I embody. When I was younger I had told Russian friends that they must identify as "lesbians." Generally they laughed at me, but sometimes they took me — or the national system I represented — seriously. Once someone listened to what I told her and almost died. The Russian friend, married to a man, decided to follow my advice and come out to her family. Her husband raped her and almost killed her. Her mother told her she deserved it, and so did the police.

My first lesson in the power of "cultural imperialism" — and surely it was U.S. culture that made my imperious words so powerful — made me much more cautious. Subsequently, I stopped telling and began asking what, if any, labels people chose to affix to themselves. Once, in 1989, I asked Evegeniia Debrianskaia[9] if she was a lesbian. "No, Laurie, you're a lesbian. . . . I'm not heterosexual, no. Nor am I bisexual, but I'm not a lesbian. I don't want to be what I do in bed."[10] A year later Debrianskaia helped to found the first organization of queers in Russia. The organization, the Moscow Association of Sexual Minorities, quickly became the Moscow Association of Gays and Lesbians, and Debrianskaia began calling herself a lesbian. I expressed surprise at the shifts in self-naming. Debrianskaia told me that certain activists in the United States had told her to change the name since "sexual minorities" included all sorts of sexual "deviants," like transvestites, transsexuals, and pedophiles. I responded with outrage telling her that the Russians should not listen to such "colonizing idiots." "What do I care what I call myself? If the Germans and Americans will give us faxes and computers if I'm a lesbian, then I'm a lesbian," she told me.[11] Debrianskaia's comment was aphoristic. She had told me that relationships of power go both ways and that Russians are not just the victims of American colonizing tendencies, but the beneficiaries as well. How Russians are appropriated by Westerners, and how Russians reappropriate those appropriations for their own purposes is where Western and Russian nationalisms collide.

WESTERNIZERS

I have told others how to live while being ignorant and insensitive to their lives. Worse, the new, colonial-like position of Russia vis-à-vis the United States has made my words more powerful than the speaker. I speak as an embodiment of America—whether I want to or not. Unfortunately, I am not alone. There are many persons from the United States who are actively trying to influence the meaning of queer sexual practices in Russia. These importers of fixed sexual identities are true believers in the ahistorical, acultural "nature" of sexuality. They firmly believe that sexualities comprise only the hetero- and homosexual. One is either one, or the other, or both—but never neither or something else. The importers rely on sexuality as central not only to the self, but to civilization—to a space of individual freedoms and individuals. The believers are trying to convert Russians, transform them into "lesbians," "gays," and even "bisexuals."

Some Russians become westernizers themselves. They see the West as offering them the necessary tools and skills to build their own lives and identities. They embrace the West as other Russians embraced European languages, fashions, and cuisine—all the while adding their own linguistic, stylistic, and culinary flourishes.[12] The following stories of westernizing queers from both the West and Russia illustrate how nation and sex become entangled in a complex set of relations of colonization and resistance.

Importing Fixed Identities

Glupye Golubki   A major importer of fixed sexual identity comes in the form of a dove, a *golubka.* Golubka is a Moscow organization for democratic initiatives. For the past several years, with the initiative of LesBiGay activists from the United States, Golubka has sponsored annual three-day workshops for "lesbians, gays, and bisexuals" in Moscow and St. Petersburg. In August of 1994 I called to ask to participate in one such workshop. A man answered the phone and asked me if I were "lesbian or bisexual" (*lesbianka ili beseksualka*). I asked if those were my only choices—whether I could be transsexual, or consider myself a gay man trapped in a lesbian's body, or not identify on the basis of my sexual practices at all. *Rozovaia* (pink), or "one of us" (*nash chelovek*), belonging to the "sexual minority," or even "transsexual" were all terms I have come across in my research, but very few Russian women I knew described themselves as lesbian, and almost none as a *biseksualka.*[13] The man, a Russian-speaker from Australia, was confused by my question. He explained to me that the seminar had limited space and was only open to those who identified as lesbian, bisexual, or gay.[14] A similar limitation was written into the flyer announcing Golubka's "Practical Seminar for the Gathering of Strengths for Gays, Lesbians, and Bisexuals." The flyer invited only members of these three groups and in particular encouraged "movement activists" to attend in order to explore several issues, including, "What basic conflicts [exist] in the gay/lesbian community of this country, and what steps can be taken to solve these conflicts . . ., learning the principles of working in groups and leadership, including how to effectively lead meetings, making decisions on a democratic basis."[15]

Three American activists, two gay men and a bisexual woman, ran the seminar. None of the organizers spoke Russian and they were thus unaware of the comments coming from the audience. For instance, one of the organizers told the crowd that he was from Philadelphia and then in the singsong voice of a kindergarten teacher asked whether anyone had ever seen the movie *Philadelphia*. P yelled out "No, of course not, after all we're Russians." P, like many of the audience members, had recently returned from New York City and the twenty-fifth Stonewall Celebration and had seen the movie there. The organizers also chastised participants for whispering among themselves as a sign of not "respecting others" (the irony was apparently lost on them). At another point, the organizers asked the participants to say something about themselves. Nearly everyone ignored this request and said something like "Either people here know me and already know everything about me, or they don't, in which case we'll save it for when we do know each other." The organizers kept urging the Russians to "open up." They seemed completely unaware that Russia is not a culture permeated with public self-confession. Russia is, after all, a post-Soviet country, a country where public self-confession could and often did result in state intervention.

At a certain point in the seminar, audience responses became more caustic. When the first break rolled around, at least half the Russians were running for the door. I admit that I was among them. I knew that a good field researcher would stick it out till the bitter end, but I did not have that sort of stamina. At first I thought it was the fact that I had to listen to everything twice, first in English then in Russian. After speaking with other participants, I realized that I was not the only one baffled by the appearance of these Americans, so optimistic that they could make the world a better place if only everyone obeyed the rules: be on time, do not leave cigarette butts on the ground, do not drink, and fit into our notions of sexuality.

> I catch up to a friend and ask her for a ride. She's fuming "kinder garten" she screams. "How dare they come here to be our so-called teachers when they'll leave tomorrow and we stay and who knows what will be tomorrow—who'll be in power, anything could happen, and they encourage people to say they're lesbians. That's irresponsible, and unconscionable." I nod.[16]

My friend's anger mirrored many other reactions to the Golubki seminar—which quickly became known as the *glupyi* or "stupid" seminar. Iuri Ereev of the Tchaikovsky Fund found the seminar redundant at best, since most of the people who attended were already activists who "didn't need to be told the importance of sexual orientation." I asked Ereev whether he thought these sorts of ideas, about sexuality, could be translated from the American context into the Russian one. "Of course, they don't really understand a lot of things. For instance, it's done so strictly—much more like a lecture and not a dialogue. They don't allow enough participation from the Russians, not enough back and forth." In St. Petersburg, as in Moscow, the attendance dropped off sharply after the first day. In a later interview, Ereev became even more agitated about the American organizers. They had, according to Ereev, made a woman very emotional, "hysterical," by getting her to speak about things "best left unsaid." The woman was eventually removed from the seminar and given a sedative by a doctor. "What is the point of talking about such things here? We aren't like Americans, we can't go and talk to a therapist every week." Ereev was also angry that a man who had attended the seminar decided to "come out" as gay. "He lives in a provincial town outside the city. He's married and has two children. When the hospital he works at finds out, he will be fired—and what can he do? He's registered there, he can't just move to Petersburg. This isn't San Francisco or Amsterdam." [17] Several other leaders of sexual minorities echoed Ereev. The organizers were at best ignorant of Russian culture, at worst, willfully so. Debrianskaia, who was consulted by the seminar organizers, said later that she was really "far too polite to them. They really don't belong here. They come here without understanding anything. Their ideas are so banal, and they base everything on sexual orientation." [18]

A few days after the seminar in Moscow I spoke to two of the organizers, Alma Beck and Adam Behrman. [19] I interviewed them to indict them. I had already judged them as imperialistic missionaries. Not surprisingly, I shaped the interview to reinforce that assumption. The first seminar was held in November 1992. I asked the organizers whether they had consulted with any Russian queers before that point.

> Behrman: I of course talked to Julie Dorf and the IGLHRC people before I came [International Gay and Lesbian Human Rights Commission—a San Francisco–based group with no active Russian members].
> . . . Before we did our first workshop we did spend four or five days beforehand meeting with [local activists]. . . . Post-training information exchange exists to make things better each time. . . . Part of our com-

mitment is to empowerment. . . . We're so clueless sometimes. We try really hard but. . . . There are so many things about this we just don't understand. Last year there were fifty people in Moscow on the first day, twenty on the second. . . . This year we only had twenty-two people in Petersburg. . . . In Moscow 50 percent don't come back usually. . . . Beck: This year [their third year] we learned that the reason there are so many women on the first night is they have nowhere else to meet. . . . It would be ideal if everyone who comes on Friday would understand what they've gotten themselves into and be ready to stay. . . . By Saturday the participants are so into it they're teary-eyed thanking us [!].

In an attempt to discuss the imposition of a fixed sexual identity on the fluid space of sexuality in Russia, I posed several questions to the seminar organizers. I asked to what extent the organizers assume that gay/lesbian/or bisexual are the only identities available. Beck, paraphrasing an "African American Jewish bisexual activist," said she too longed for the day when such labels were unnecessary, "but in a state of oppression [labels] allow us to identify our allies." The seminar was for "creating a safe space for people to take on their identities. . . . A lot of people here have been so oppressed and are so pained and unable to take on terms like gay, lesbian, bi." Her partner added that the seminar is not meant to encourage people to come out as much as teach them to "feel connections" with others. They both agree, however, that one of the advantages to creating safe space and focusing at the "level of feelings" where any—and only— feelings are "valid" is that coming out to one another becomes possible.

The seminar organizers are not as insensitive as my rendering of them. They are aware of charges of "cultural imperialism," but they believe— with the faith of any missionary—that what they are doing is worthwhile. One insisted that "the role of the outsider can really be a positive one," and the benefits of being an outsider far outweigh the risks of doing nothing. They noted how one Westerner who attended the seminar said: "If you knew how impossible what you're doing here was, you wouldn't be doing it, but I'm really glad that you are here doing it." They repeated over and over again that they are "culturally clueless," but innocently so. Their goals are "pure" of any colonizing impurities. They merely wish to "develop increasing self-respect, develop confidence in self and others, develop unity

while appreciating diversity, and help create a strong gay/lesbian/bi movement during times of social change." [20]

I was not convinced. The seminar organizers spoke with the authority
of America—American culture, history, politics. I was frightened by their
evangelicalism, but others disagree. One Russian friend told me: "You can
take this anti-imperialism stance too far, to the point where it becomes
patronizing." [21] An American friend pointed out that you cannot import
identity, "It's not like they're selling it out of a kiosk, like a Snickers bar." [22]
Of course, the Russians will not necessarily be destroyed in the campaign
to identify. Some of them will resist; others will convert while simultaneously incorporating their own beliefs and practices, a vibrant Santería
within a moribund Catholicism. One recent convert is Valeriia Kurskaia.
Kurskaia [23] felt transformed by the first seminar in 1992. "After that seminar, I began to understand people better and I learned how to listen, maybe
even be helpful." In the 1994 seminar, Kurskaia participated in the post-
seminar training sessions. The sessions left her feeling hopeful about her
goals for a lesboerotic movement. "I don't know what's happened to me,
but something has definitely changed from this seminar. I feel like I want to
do something worthwhile. I have the motivation to do something." When
asked what she would like to do, Kurskaia mentioned the projects she
was already working on, such as the acquaintance service and the monthly
meetings, as well as her dream to set up a center.

Kurskaia may be a believer, but she maintains a core of beliefs untouched
by her newfound religion. Despite what she perceived as pressure from the
seminar organizers to come out, Kurskaia refuses to be too public about
her sexual practices.

> I'm still married [to a man]. I would not exactly call it fictive, because
> it was a real marriage—in the sense that it was necessary. In the 1970s
> and even still today you have to be married for society—you have to try
> it if only for one day. That's what's demanded of you—that you try it
> and get that stamp on your passport. You have to make up stories about
> children—either you're unable to have any children or they're living in
> the country because of their health. . . . I would never try to register
> the group officially because there's nothing official recognition would
> give us. In fact, if anything it would just increase the unhealthy curi-

osity of men. . . . My mother doesn't know anything about me, but I'm not afraid of blackmail because I'm not embarrassed of who I am. Of course, I'm not going to go scream it in the streets.

When asked whether there were parts of the seminar that did not make sense in the Russian context, Kurskaia nodded her head emphatically.

Yes, things are more open in the West and it makes sense to be out to everyone, but this is Russia. . . . I tried to take anything I could from the experience that was useful. We're good at that here. We've learned to find what's useful and ignore the rest.

Kurskaia concludes her description of the seminar with a moral. At the end of the training session, an American woman asked a question about "Russian culture." "One of the boys at the seminar got very angry and answered: 'Yes, that's right, we wear our fur hats and dance with bears and drink vodka.' . . . Of course she didn't have to judge a person by nationality, but he didn't have to be so hard on her either." [24]

Celebrating Fixed Identities: Festivals and Parades

Soviet Stonewall   New Year 1990 heralded the beginning of queer sexual politics in Russia. The Moscow Association was formed; St. Petersburg's Tchaikovsky Fund was soon to follow. In the United States another organization was forming, the International Gay and Lesbian Human Rights Commission, IGLHRC. IGLHRC was the brainchild of Jim Toevs and Julie Dorf, a San Francisco resident who often traveled to the Soviet Union as a guide/interpreter. Dorf brought in several people, including Masha Gessen—who was just beginning to reacquaint herself with the homeland she had left as a child. Dorf and Gessen dreamed of a "Soviet Stonewall" and actually made it happen with very little help from Russia.[25] Soviet Stonewall occurred in July and August of 1991 and brought together about seventy persons from the United States and tens of thousands of persons from the Soviet Union. In Moscow, Stonewall was a combination of seminars conducted by the Americans on subjects ranging from AIDS to coming out, a gay/lesbian film festival, and press events—such as a "kiss-in" in front of the Bolshoi Theater. In St. Petersburg, both the seminars and the film festival took place, albeit with far fewer numbers.[26] IGLHRC chose Roman Kalinin as their Russian counterpart, in part because Kalinin was already attempting to create a Western-style movement in Russia. Kalinin was also able to handle many of the logistics for his U.S.-based partners. In Moscow over twenty thousand tickets to the film festival were sold, in St. Petersburg more than a thousand people without tickets showed up. At the Moscow conference, Kalinin introduced Dorf as the "mother of the gay and lesbian movement in Russia." Years later, Gessen called the description of Dorf "accurate" if "dangerous." "Dorf played an incredibly important role in encouraging both the gay and the feminist movement here." Gessen also pointed out that the "Russians don't have the luxury of being the first gay/lesbian movement." [27]

But if Russians cannot be the first movement, they should at least be able to create their own. The attitude of many of the Western activists attending the conference was that of rich volunteers visiting the slums—deeply suspicious and patronizing. One reporter in the U.S. gay press wrote that some of the Westerners "wondered about the propriety of spending energy on an 'advanced' issue like gay/lesbian rights in the midst of the squalor of the daily lives of Soviet citizens. But they [the Westerners] observed the pure joy in the eyes and faces of the Soviet gays and lesbians gathered for the first time—and remembered that freedom is as fundamental as anything." [28]

The "deprivation" of the Russians is shown in a section of the article entitled "Shoddy Shambles," which quotes longtime gay activist Harry Hay as saying, "I am hopelessly sad when I look at this workers' state and realize what a shoddy piece of work it is," along with a long list of what is unavailable in this "Third World" country. The "joy" of the "natives" due to the arrival of the Westerners is shown in quotes from Soviet gays thanking the Americans. "We have much new information on what it is to be gay. . . . It is very difficult to speak of what your visit means to us," gushed one young man. Kalinin added that the Americans have "infected us with the will to be free. . . . Thank you. We owe you for the fact that when we started coming out, we were not alone." [29] The poetics of the reporter mirror many themes of colonial literature—the noble few bringing the poor and ignorant masses "pure joy" in the freedom of becoming just like them.[30]

There was obviously a different story that could have been told about Soviet Stonewall. Many Russian activists I interviewed during and immediately after Stonewall cringed at the assumption that Russians had a lot to learn from the Americans. Many Moscow-based activists expressed a certain amount of anger that Dorf and not the Russian activists had been credited with getting the movement started and the fact that a single Russian, Kalinin, came to represent all the various activists who had already emerged. Several times that summer in Moscow, people suggested to me that Kalinin was chosen because he was quite young, still a student, who could easily be manipulated to do what the Americans wanted him to do.[31]

Yet if many Russian activists were understandably angry about the way IGLHRC orchestrated the supposedly Soviet Stonewall, many others were extremely pleased. One Siberian activist told me that the events in St. Petersburg had literally "changed her life." "Imagine, I came to Leningrad for the first time. I knew nothing about the festival. . . . There I was with all these other lesbians, and for the first time we were saying that word— "lesbian"—and it was with pride, not shame."[32] Gessen justified the role of the Americans as that of a catalyst, "unleashing" a movement that was already forming on its own. Gessen admitted that what the American-made Soviet Stonewall did was to import ideas about a strong and stable identity and community, but that the ideas are being used differently than the festival organizers had intended. "Even McDonald's is transformed (in Russia)." Instead of offering cookie-cutter identities, Gessen argued that the 1991 events could never impose a "Western binary model" onto Russian sexuality, since sexuality in Russia is too fluid to be "trapped."[33] In many ways, Gessen seems to be right. In a survey of sixty-six Moscow and St. Petersburg "public" queers, of the ones who mentioned an event as shaping their sense of their own sexuality, many of them mentioned the Soviet Stonewall. However, most of the respondents (forty-five of the sixty-six) did not feel that this or any other "social event" had shaped their sense of self.[34] Despite the absurdly colonizing impulses of many of the Western participants, Soviet Stonewall was ultimately a Russian event—if for no other reason than the Westerners were outnumbered by about three hundred to one. Like hamburgers, sexual models are consumed differently in Russia than in the United States.[35]

The Train from Berlin to St. Petersburg and Back

"Don't you think that it's too early to show these films in Russia? We have no freedom of relationships, we have no basis with which we can understand this."

—*Gay Russian audience member to gay German filmmaker, 1994*

Another gay/lesbian film festival occurred in Petersburg in May of 1994. This time the Truth of gay/lesbian culture was brought to the Russians via Germany.[36] In April one of the festival organizers, Mahita Lein, told me she was organizing the festival "for the Russians." Lein also mentioned that the only Russian organizer of the festival was no longer involved.[37] Thus none of the films was imported at the request of the Russians.

I attended the festival, "The Boundaries of Love—Another View," the following month.[38] According to the festival's program, the organizers claimed their goal was not to show international lesbian-gay filmmaking, but rather "the varied forms around the given theme [lesbian/gay]."[39] The films ranged from dated pieces of propaganda like *It Is Not the Homosexual Who Is Perverted, But the Society in Which He Lives* to more artistic endeavors, such as Fassbinder's *Kiril* and Ulriche Ottinger's *Johanna d'Arc of Mongolia*. The festival also included several avant-garde and other marginal forms of film and video, such as Hans Schierl's *Red Ears* and lesbian safe-sex videos. After each film there was often a "discussion session." In addition to attending the discussion sessions, I interviewed many of the people milling around in the lobby and café for their responses.

Generally, reactions were mixed, although some films seemed unanimously controversial. One controversial film, *Prince in Helland*, juxtaposes beautiful cinematography with a fast-moving plot to depict the relationship between two men, one a heroin addict, the other a political activist, and the assorted group of oddballs and misfits with whom they live. Most Russians responded that they did not like the image of gay men the film portrayed. "The film showed homosexuals as pederasts, drug addicts, antisocial—these are all stereotypes we have to fight against" was a typical response. My friend P was surprised that I liked the film. I tried to explain that in the West, many queers feel it is more important to not imitate heterosexual "normalcy" than to be homogenized as "just like everyone else." P was horrified. "But that's just what we want, to be accepted as just like everyone else."

Once, one of the organizers and an audience member debated the gender implications of a video on transgendered persons. The video documented the lives of a male-to-female transsexual as well as a woman who passed as a man. After the video the male organizer asked a male audience member if he would like to be a woman. Russian: "That's not my particular problem." German: "It's everyone's problem because we have to think about our gender roles. Russia is a highly patriarchal society and the gender roles here are too rigid." At this point Mahita Lein added, "I have seen a very primitive idea among some lesbians here that they are really men," to which a Russian woman responded that she was glad to be a woman. The last remark elicited loud applause from the audience and organizers alike, although they appeared to be clapping for different reasons. The impulse to remake "primitive Russians" in their own image was all too obvious among many of the festival organizers. They applauded what they believed was "victory." I spoke to the Russian woman later that week about her comment. "People are different," she told me. I asked if she meant Russians are different from Germans. "No, people in general are different. Russians are different— we're not all identical." The woman was speaking against sameness, while many of the German participants cheered it.

At the end of the festival, a video on safe sex for women, *You've Been Called*, was shown. The festival programs described the video as "for women only." This quickly became a point of controversy, with several members of the audience describing a women-only policy as discriminatory. Lein explained that the video was meant to facilitate discussion on AIDS and it is easier to discuss HIV transmission between women among women. At one point the discussion became heated. One of the German participants—perhaps in an effort to decrease the hostility—told a particularly disturbed male audience member that the Germans "came here to hear your thinking on sexuality and find ways to unite." The man answered: "Thank you so much for coming, but we don't have enough in common to work together." In the end, men were allowed to attend.

The video shows the hypothetical transmission of HIV in a group of lesbians not practicing safer sex. It ends with a "doctor" showing two women practicing safe sex techniques while using dildos as well as "fisting." The women are trendy in a way rarely seen in Russia. One has a shaved head, the other has blond dreads. They are tattooed and unshaven. I viewed the video with a group of lesbians from St. Petersburg. Many of them walked out before the end. "This is funny . . . no, it's disgusting. Those women are revolting," said M. At the end of the screening a group of women associated with Sappho Peter all stood up and left, but not before one of them told the filmmaker: "It's not enough to make a lesbian film, but you should have a more sophisticated, artistic approach." One man shouted: "Safe sex is not new here, nor is it unknown among lesbians. But the aesthetic here is so low, no one will understand such a thing when you show ugly women with poor figures." In response, many of the Western women in the audience booed and hissed him. Lein pointed out that this video was not made for men and then asked him to leave, adding that men like him were the reason she wanted the session to be limited to women, but most of the Russian women had already left.[40]

Besides the actual films imported by the Germans, there were several other points of interpretive breakdowns. For instance, while I was escorting one of the German filmmakers to an apartment, she asked about the festival's attendance. I told her that there were usually about 100–150 people per night, with slightly more than half of them men. From my interviews, most of the people I had spoken to identified themselves as "not personally connected to the theme" (i.e., not homosexual). M asked why there were not more gays and lesbians at the festival. She felt they should be "grateful for what we've done for them. They should be coming. They should appreciate this film festival that we've put together for them." I tried to explain to her that few persons in Russia would identify as "gay," especially to an unknown interviewer. M was not convinced that what I was saying was true. "Well, they should come out then," she answered.

Another misunderstanding occurred when several of the festival organizers and a few interpreters (including myself) went to a disco.[41] When we arrived and were asked to pay the door charge of eight thousand roubles (about ten dollars at that time and consistent with most of the city's discos), some of the Germans reacted with anger. One German kept saying: "But we're here doing this for them. We shouldn't have to pay." Some of the people who live in Russia, including two German interpreters, explained that the men who run the bar are businessmen, not gay activists. Furthermore, because they run a gay bar, both the local police and the local mafia demand more money from them for "protection." Eventually, the door charge was waived.[42]

Many Russians returned the Germans' colonizing gaze with looks of their own. One evening, an all-night women's disco was held. That evening, I spoke to one of the Russians providing a lot of the logistical support for the festival. The woman, V, was in her mid-twenties. V confided that she was fed up with her German guests and their "capricious ways." I asked V why she was doing so much work for the festival and whether it had to do with her own sexuality. She replied: "I am not myself a lesbian. I slept with a woman once and thought maybe I was—so I joined the Fund [Tchaikovsky], but it's not what I want sexually. I continue to work with the fund because I would like to emigrate to Germany. After putting up with all of [the German organizers'] capriciousness, you can be sure that I'm going to Berlin and staying with them, just for a couple of weeks, maybe a month, until I find a man there to marry." [43] At the disco were about fifty women, at least half of them Russian. Many of the women I recognized from either Sappho Peter or the Tchaikovsky Fund. I interviewed some of the women I did not recognize. One of them volunteered that she runs an acquaintance service for women. [44] In 1993 she placed an advertisement for women who want to meet women in a weekly circular. She has been introducing women to each other ever since, including the couple at the table with us. I spoke to one of the women in the couple. They were both in their mid-twenties and had been together for a year. One of them worked in a factory, the other in a kiosk. The one who worked in a kiosk seemed relieved that I was not German. "I hate Germans," she said. "My sister emigrated to Germany, and I will never forgive her for abandoning her motherland." After a few shots of vodka, the woman began to complain not just about Germans, but Jews as well. "I'm tired of them coming here thinking they're better than we are. . . . The Slavic peoples will save the world, we must, it's our duty. . . . Zhirinovskii is right about that, even though he himself is a kike [zhid]." I asked the other women at the table if they agreed with their friend. One laughed and said why not, the other said there was nothing with which she disagreed. Ironically, these remarks were made within earshot of the festival organizers, who undoubtedly had not come to Russia to engender this sort of national identity among queers.

SLAVOPHILES

The organizers of the German film festival, of the America-run Soviet Stonewall, and of the Golubka consciousness-raising seminars are all examples of queers who are westernizers. These national/sexual identities originate in the West, but are firmly rooted in Russian soil. Clearly the queers who try to westernize Russia help to create a backlash, an anti-Western response. But that is not all that is going on. Russian nationalist queers are responding to many things—not just their Western counterparts. Nationalism as a source of self is highly popular in Russia, as the electoral success of Vladimir Zhirinovskii and other nationalist politicians indicates. Nationalist newspapers and parties are all readily available and acceptable ways of enacting oneself in Russia. Furthermore, even "democratic" politicians such as Boris Yeltsin are known to participate in the rhetoric of nation, a rhetoric further reinforced by the Russian Orthodox Church and a multitude of spiritual leaders. Nationness and even nationalism is a language formed not only in the matrix of colonizing relations between the West and Russia, but within Russian society itself, a multi-ethnic society in which a notion of self is inseparable from a stable and coherent nation.

The fact that certain queer activists, then, are themselves Russian nationalists is not terribly surprising. They are crafting their sexual selves against the West and within Russia. In Russia some queer leaders are coming out as nationalist—a sense of nation based on the superiority of Russia and Russianness and the inferiority/separateness of others. There are two leaders in particular, Evgeniia Debrianskaia and Yaroslav Mogutin, who are the embodiment of nationalist queers. They are not the only nationalist queers, but they are surely some of the most outspoken.[45]

Nationalist Queers

Debrianskaia   At the founding of Triangle in August 1993, Evgeniia Debrianskaia did something she had never done when she cofounded the Moscow Association of Sexual Minorities four years earlier—she excluded Westerners. The year before, Debrianskaia told me she wanted to have a conference for Russian sexual minorities. The Soviet Stonewall of 1991 was, according to Debrianskaia, an "American affair." Thus no conference for and by Russian queers had been held.[46] In 1993 Debrianskaia called for all-Russian and only Russian participation. Even Gessen was originally asked not to take the stage because of her "foreignness" (i.e., because of the thirteen years she spent living in the United States).[47] Debrianskaia's fixation on Russianness is not limited to maintaining a "Russian" queer movement.

Debrianskaia has spoken openly of her admiration for the nationalist politician Vladimir Zhirinovskii. In February of 1994 she told me that Zhirinovskii was "intelligent," not at all like his clownish public image. Debrianskaia described her relationship with the nationalist "patriotic" movement as a personal one. At first I assumed she was referring to the fact that her youngest son's father, Aleksandr Dugin, is a very prominent member of the Vasilev branch of Pamiat', probably the most powerful nationalist/neofascist group in Moscow.[48] What Debrianskaia meant, however, was not the familial relation to Pamiat', but that she personally finds it attractive—philosophically, intellectually, and spiritually—and not something she allied herself with for political reasons (i.e., future or present positioning within the ever anachronistic power structure of Moscow). Dugin and a leader of a Muslim movement, Gaidar Zhamal, are for Debrianskaia "mentors," and they fulfill her "image of what a real man is, what a real man should be. They are the center around which a philosophical group has formed, and I'm a part of that circle. I've never met such sharp minds. . . . Sasha and Gaidar are spiritual leaders. They're behind the scenes, not political leaders. . . . They taught me to read Nietzsche, Goethe . . . in new ways, in ways that opened up some part of me that I didn't know existed."

In August of 1994 Debrianskaia was considering leaving the politics of sexuality, but said she would continue to "take up the patriotic position" ("Ia sama stoiu no patrioticheskuiu pozitsiiu"). The reasons for allying herself with the quasifascist leaders of Pamiat' while simultaneously distancing herself from the gay/lesbian organization Triangle were again quite personal: "Among homosexuals I never met any soul mates. The only thing we have in common is sexuality, but that's not enough. In every way besides sexuality these people are alien to me, we have no common way of thinking. I will always be for gay and lesbian rights but the patriotic movement is what draws me. . . . I'm not really interested in the future of homosexuals here."[49]

Unlike me, Debrianskaia did not see any connection between the "patriotic" and "sexual minorities" movements in Russia. "No, the gay movement is an entirely Western influence. Masha Gessen and Julie Dorf bring
their ideas here but you cannot unite people just by their sexual actions."
Western influence is something Debrianskaia called "cultural death."

> The truth is that the fate of Russia is different from other countries. It is
> very difficult, impossible, to accept Russia as one among many nations.
> Russia has a metaphysical responsibility for saving the entire world. It
> has a mission. To move away from this conception is not possible. It
> is only through suffering that we will be able to do this. Among lesbi-
> ans I have not met this conception, but I have certainly met it among
> gay men. I really can't stand the old crones. There are very few lesbi-
> ans who have any effect on me, although there are a few "naturals"
> [heterosexual women]. . . . I can't stand the lesbians here. I don't want
> to hear [Gessen] go on about the "gay movement" in America. I am
> not impressed. I've been to America and I understand its soul. [Ges-
> sen] doesn't understand that people are much freer here than in the
> West because here we spit on any rules, we break them whenever we
> want. This is exactly what freedom is. It's not having responsibility, but
> the freedom to break any rule. . . . The totalitarian regime gave people
> a plasticity that couldn't exist in a democratic regime. People had to
> learn to bend themselves and the rules.[50]

Debrianskaia is not hostile toward the West per se, but westernizing. "The
West is fabulous, but so is Russia. And the West is not Russia. . . . Oscar
Wilde said any influence, any influence at all, is immoral because the person influenced is always hearing the echo of music that wasn't written
for him."[51]

Of course, Debrianskaia is a radical queer activist, a former dissident, a
founder of the first protopolitical party, the Democratic Union. She could
not be in complete agreement with the politics of "patriotism." The nationalists "have a concept of the radicalization of society which I don't like,
because I know what a radicalized society is. I don't want to live in such
a society anymore. I'm tired of such a society. I want to live in a middle-
of-the-road society." Debrianskaia, like many of the queer leaders who expressed sympathy for nationalist politics, simultaneously admitted that if

a quasi-fascist such as Zhirinovskii does come to power, open queers like herself will be the first to go. "Look at Roehm," Debrianskaia once told me. "He was Hitler's best friend and helped him get to power, and Hitler killed him because he was a fag." [52]

Mogutin   In August 1994 I confronted Yaroslav Mogutin about rumors that he was not only a nationalist, but also a fascist. I had heard that Mogutin was associated with certain nationalist politicians, including Zhirinovskii and Limonov. I also knew that Mogutin had made a career of "shocking" his readers and I was curious to find out whether his nationalism/fascism was more than publicity seeking. During the interview, Mogutin expressed bitterness at the "so-called democratic" press for not supporting him during a state prosecution for his article "Dirty Peckers." [53] Nationalist papers such as *Den'* and *Zavtra* had been "very supportive . . . [since] they understood that this was a question of free speech, not homosexuality. . . . Basically the democratic press is very homophobic. . . . The oppositional [i.e., nationalist] press is much more willing to accept sexual minorities."

Mogutin was also willing to support ultranationalist politicians like Zhirinovskii. "Zhirinovskii was the only politician who said before the elections that he was willing to support sexual pluralism; he said this in many of his television appearances." Of course, Mogutin also admitted being "shocked" by Zhirinovskii's electoral success, and although Zhirinovskii had asked him to work as his press secretary, Mogutin had turned him down.[54] Like Debrianskaia, Mogutin expressed doubts that a nationalistic regime would protect queers. Regardless of Zhirinovskii's verbal support for homosexuals, Mogutin described Zhirinovskii as a "cynic, a total cynic, and if he comes to power there is little doubt that a Terror will follow, even worse than that which took place under the Soviets." [55]

Mogutin was less willing to distance himself from Eduard Limonov, whose ultranationalist politics are not considerably different from Zhirinovskii's. He described Limonov as a "good friend" and insisted that Limonov's National Bolshevik Party is not fascist. "Those who compare Limonov to Nazis are wrong to do so. He's arguing for the protection of the National Majority, but that doesn't necessarily mean discrimination against other peoples." I asked Mogutin whether Jews were part of that national majority, to which he answered, "Of course not, they're not Russians." I asked whether Limonov, who has written a book highly critical of Zhirinov-skii in part because of Zhirinovskii's "hidden Jewishness," is anti-Semitic.

> . . . . I think Limonov's main point here is not anti-Semitic but to say that Zhirinovskii should be criticized not for being Jewish but for trying to hide it. . . . This anti-Semitic label has been affixed to Limonov, but I don't see a single moment when there's any anti-Semitism. In fact, his first wife was a Jew. . . . He's very proud of his first wife. And there are many moments in his books that are the opposite of anti-Semitism. For example, he writes, 'I'm a talented non-Jew' — it's a paradox that a man who thinks so highly of Jews would be called an anti-Semite when it's just the opposite.

By seeing the world through a prism of Russianness and Otherness (in this case, Jewishness), Mogutin is able to defend nationalist politicians like Limonov. Mogutin's willingness to align himself with nationalistic press and politicians ended up being much deeper and having greater conse-quences than even he imagined. In March 1995, Mogutin was forced to flee Russia because of state prosecution for a vehemently nationalist article. The article, "The Chechen Knot: 13 Theses" was published in *Novyi vzgliad* in January 1995.[56] On 14 and 21 February, the Presidential Commission on Disputes in the Mass Media met to consider Mogutin's writings. The com-mission had previously criticized Mogutin's work, particularly his openly gay articles (see chapter 1), and had issued a statement to all the licensed press in Russia warning editors not to publish the work of this "corrupter of public morals, a propagandist of psychopathology, sexual perversions and brutal violence . . . including the use of profane language."[57] At the 21 February meeting, the commission accused Mogutin of "the incitement of racial and national enmities, propagandizing violence and hatred be-tween peoples." The commission recommended prosecution of Mogutin under Article 74 of the Criminal Code (subject to seven years' imprison-ment) and *Novyi vzgliad*'s license to publish was rescinded.[58] On 25 Febru-ary, the decision to prosecute was announced on the official evening news program *Vremia*. Several articles followed in the mainstream press, praising the government decision and denouncing Mogutin.[59] In March, a criminal case was opened in the Moscow City Prosecutor's Office against Mogutin, and he decided, on his lawyer's advice, to flee the country.

Mogutin left Moscow for New York with the knowledge and support of the U.S. Embassy.[60] The embassy granted Mogutin a visa because the issues surrounding Mogutin's article and prosecution are complicated by two facts: the state prosecution of Mogutin seemed to be a continuation of previous prosecution for his open homosexuality, and Mogutin himself has denied the nationalist/racist tone of the article. The article itself supports the war in Chechnya with statements that are not only nationalistic, but racist as well. Thesis number six proclaims that "[a] War for Chechnya Is a War for Russia. Chechnya is a part of Russia, it always was, it is, and it will be Russian territory." In the article, Mogutin argues that Chechnya is Russian territory in part because "½ of its population is Russian." The article not only defends Russian "interests" in Chechnya, but paints a picture of the Chechen "enemy," a nationality—not a group of human beings. With the finesse of the Raj in British India, Mogutin proclaimed that Chechnya "became civilized thanks to Russians, the conditions in which one can live as a human being did not exist there before the Russians. This is a half-wild, barbarian nation."[61]

Mogutin's article fanned the flames of Russian nationalism at the height of his country's genocidal war in Chechnya. Yet many people in the West have serious doubts that this is the reason Mogutin was chosen for prosecution. Several prominent human rights and gay rights organizations have rallied to Mogutin's support, including Lambda Legal Defense, IGLHRC, Helsinki Watch, New York PEN, and the Committee to Project Journalists.[62] Although some organizations want to describe Mogutin's prosecution as an issue of freedom of speech, many other observers argue that this is a case of state prosecution of a journalist for being gay, not for being a nationalist.[63] The case for the persecution of a homosexual rather than the prosecution of a nationalist rests on several pieces of evidence. First, the Russian government was itself executing the war in Chechnya. Their eagerness to prosecute Mogutin cannot be traced to an ethical commitment to the people of Chechnya. Second, Mogutin's article is one of many nationalist points of view published in Moscow on the very same day. Neither the government nor the "liberal" press chose to attack the well-entrenched and highly connected nationalist publications, but focused instead on an already marginal figure with no ties to any of the "patriotic" parties and politicians and with very little public support (in large part because of his open homosexuality). Indeed, much of the press coverage was openly homophobic, calling Mogutin a "mama's boy" and suggesting it was too bad the "earring-wearing Mogutin" hadn't been killed, instead of the more popular, heterosexual D. Kholodov (who was killed by a letter bomb while working on a report on corruption in the military).[64] Mogutin, then, did not write anything unusual for the Russian press, but the reaction was predicated on homophobia, a homophobia built upon the state's previous prosecution of Mogutin for writing an article that was "too gay."

These facts alone make labeling Mogutin a simple bigot a difficult task. But the task is even more complicated once Mogutin's postpublication words are considered. According to Mogutin, the article was meant to represent the "voice of the people." Mogutin claimed that he never meant it to be his own thoughts on the war, but the thoughts, the "theses," he could hear on the streets of Moscow. Furthermore, Mogutin expressed disdain of the "liberal" press's refusal to acknowledge the deep-seated hatred many Russians express toward Chechens, a hatred that allowed the war to begin in the first place.[65]

Queer Nationalists

Nationalist queers are disturbing, but they also make perfect sense. Queers —from both the West and Russia—rely on national and even nationalist identities in order to enact their own sense of sexualized selves. Nation, like gender, is a familiar language with which to speak unspeakably queer desires. Yet if nationalist queers are comprehensible, queer nationalists are not. Still some Russian nationalists—secure in their "masculinity"—publicly sexualize themselves as queer.

Limonov   Eduard Limonov emigrated to New York in the 1970s and remained in the West until 1991 when he returned to Moscow. Limonov had achieved a certain amount of fame in the West as a writer—Random House published his book *It's Me, Eddie* in 1983.[66] He was not, however, well known in Russia. Then, in 1990, Alexander Shatalov and his assistant, Yaroslav Mogutin, decided to publish *It's Me, Eddie* in its original Russian. Limonov was the first book Shatalov's Glagol Press published, and it was a huge success. Since 1990 Glagol has published three editions of *It's Me,*

Eddie, as well as several other works by Limonov. *It's Me, Eddie* has sold more than two million copies for Glagol.[67] Since Glagol's success with *It's Me, Eddie*, other publishers have also put out their own editions.[68]

Shatalov described Limonov as an "amazing writer . . . [who] has already established himself as one of our great writers with *It's Me, Eddie* and he thus has reserved a place in history." In *It's Me, Eddie*, Limonov certainly "amazes" his readers. The tenor of the semiautobiographical text is shocking. Through the course of the story the hero, Eddie, goes from being a dissident writer in Moscow—a relatively respectable profession during the Brezhnev years—married to a beautiful woman to being an unemployed, heavy-drinking bisexual in New York City. The transfiguration of Eddie is the result of bearing the pain of loss—loss of his wife, his profession, his native language, his homeland. In the course of his descent into the hell of 1970s America, Eddie also finds much of what he needs—sex, friendship, adventure.

Limonov's language and landscape in *It's Me, Eddie* are both unusually harsh. Everything that occurs has a feeling of "dirtiness" about it. For instance, Limonov's first sexual encounter with a man occurs in a vacant parking lot. The lover is described as young, smelling of "some kind of acrid alcohol" and "a criminal for sure." After wrestling each other to the ground, Eddie begs the man to make love to him, in large part because the lover is "black all over" and Eddie has heard of the "legendary tool" of black men.[69] Later Eddie has a sexual escapade with another black man, this one a homeless person whom the protagonist describes as the "lowest of the low." The "foreplay" to their lovemaking consists of Eddie waiting for this "lowest person . . . dressed in dirty rags. . . . There's no one worse or less than he . . . everyone chases him away, and he's obviously panhandling. . . . Nevertheless, I have to wait for him, the lowest filth from the New York sidewalks, I have to be with him."[70]

The story of Eddie, despite its exotic setting, is not that unfamiliar to a reader of Russian literature. Eddie is in a tailspin, recklessly becoming lower than the lowest (*padenie*). Rather than despairing, however, the hero experiences true joy, moments of great insight, and inner peace when he is suffering the most humiliating of circumstances.[71] Yet Limonov's Eddie "descends" by having anonymous homosexual encounters on the streets of New York—a path to redemption that must have startled most

Russian readers since the Soviet regime had never allowed such overtly (homo)sexual scenes to be published.[72] Eddie's homosexuality, however, comes as part of the overall despair into which he is sinking, a despair deepened by dead-end jobs, large quantities of alcohol, and an increasingly reckless and violent existence. Eddie, like a Russian Jean Genet, finds beauty in society's outcasts and so has little choice but to ally himself with the most marginal members of society—criminals, homeless persons, political dissidents, and, of course, homosexuals. By creating an entire aesthetic of the excluded, Limonov lures his readers into accepting the homosexuality of Eddie as a "natural" part of the already familiar fall/redemption.

Yet if millions of readers in Russia accepted Eddie's homosexuality because of its use of the familiar plot of descent/redemption, not all Russians have been willing to accept Limonov's nationalist politics. Shatalov ended his association with his star author in part because Limonov's politics have "prevented him from writing anything worthwhile." Shatalov did not see Limonov's political activities as threatening, but merely the result of an arrested adolescence. "[L]ike a teenager [Limonov] has always wanted to be antiestablishment. The patriotic movements are against the establishment. . . . [Limonov's] politics come from his insecurities, his lack of confidence in himself. . . . He's always looking for approval from other men."[73]

Since his return to Russia in 1991 Limonov has indeed bounced from group to group, leader to leader. Like his character Eddie, Limonov appears to be searching for a "brotherhood of raw masculine revolutionaries, to whom in love and devotion I could give over my soul."[74] During the attempted coup known as the October Events Limonov was in the Parliament building fighting against the "illegitimate" Yeltsin government.[75] Limonov has fought with the Serbs in the former Yugoslavia and against Moldovan nationalists.[76] For a time Limonov even allied himself with Vladimir Zhirinovskii, an alliance that ended with the publication of Limonov's bitter diatribe against Zhirinovskii as someone incapable of leading the Russian people to greatness because of his own mediocrity. In his book *Limonov against Zhirinovskii*, Limonov insists that Zhirinovskii is not only "obviously" a Jew because of "his manner of speaking, his quarrelsomeness," but also calls him an "American-type" politician—"provincial and Jewish." Jewishness is Zhirinovskii's "weak spot." The problem with

Zhirinovskii according to Limonov is that his Jewishness is combined with a lack of patriotism to the motherland.[77] The truth, Limonov tells us, is that "Zhirinovskii isn't a nationalist, but a democrat!"—an insult perhaps unfathomable to the American reader, but roughly translatable as "Zhirinovskii works for the West, not Russia."[78] More recently Limonov made a Red-Brown alliance with radical communists and nationalists. According to Limonov their Red-Brown alliance will create a new Iron Curtain to keep Western businesses from Russia.[79] Limonov along with ultranationalist Aleksandr Dugin, formed the National-Bolshevik Party, whose very name invokes Nazism.[80] Not surprisingly, Limonov's party adopted the Nazi flag, with a hammer and sickle in place of the swastika as his symbol.[81]

Perhaps even more surprising than Limonov divorcing himself from the "too liberal" Zhirinovskii is Limonov's distancing himself from Eddie. Limonov has claimed that if he came to power he would ban his own novel. Limonov has consistently refused to speak out on behalf of the rights of sexual minorities and now claims the gay sex in his novel was not autobiographical.[82] Although Limonov's refusal to support gay rights has disappointed many of his queer supporters, it seems to have done little to change the association of this supernationalist with homosexuality. Limonov is generally referred to in the press as "bisexual" and It's Me, Eddie is described as autobiographical. Within queer circles in Moscow, I have met many men who support Limonov's nationalism while insisting that Limonov is himself gay. Shatalov and other "friends" of Limonov's laughed when I asked whether Limonov was in fact exclusively heterosexual. When I pressed them to tell me, they all said that he was in fact gay, not even bisexual. "Limonov worships men. All his favorite writers are men—all of them. He spends his time only with men." Whatever his private sexual practices, Limonov's public association with Eddie and queer sexuality exists simultaneously with his neofascist politics—a single body of queer nationalism.

Zhirinovskii   Vladimir Zhirinovskii surprised the world when he won nearly a quarter of the vote in the 1993 parliamentary elections—more than any other candidate. Although his public presentation of self is clownish, his political platform is not. Zhirinovskii speaks of reunifying the now disparate parts of Imperial/Soviet Russia—including Finland and Alaska. He has threatened Germany and Japan with atomic weapons. Worse, Zhirinovskii

has promised to execute a hundred thousand prisoners as soon as he becomes president.[83]

Even more surprising than Zhirinovskii's political popularity is his peculiar brand of queer nationalism. Zhirinovskii and his Liberal Democratic
Party (LDP)—which is of course anything but liberal or democratic—have
consistently defended the rights of "sexual minorities." Before the parliamentary elections in December 1993, Zhirinovskii spoke on Russian television about the rights of such minorities.[84] According to Vlad Ortanov, a
publisher of the gay journal RISK, in the spring of 1994 the Liberal Democratic Party attempted to create a parliamentary faction to represent the
interests of "sexual minorities." Although the request was turned down on
a technicality (the LDP did not have sufficient numbers of sexual minorities to create a faction), the fact remains that the nationalist-fascistic party
of Zhirinovskii has been the lone voice among Russia's politicians for the
rights of queers.[85]

Many queer leaders link Zhirinovskii's public willingness to support
queer rights to his private sexual practices. Rumors abound that Zhirinovskii prefers young boys to the blond women who so often mill around
his public events.[86] In June 1994 the New Republic published a short piece
about Zhirinovskii's supporters in New York. In the article the supporters are asked whether Zhirinovskii is gay. "He's never been very interested
in women. . . . And he's always got those good-looking guards around
him." [87] Later the male author is asked if he would like to sleep with Zhirinovskii himself, a liaison that was apparently simple enough to arrange.[88]
In Russia, earlier that year, a photograph of Zhirinovskii and a young man
in a sauna had also appeared in the Russian press.[89] The photograph was
countered in the LDP's official newspaper with a series of "candid" shots
of Zhirinovskii with women and the caption "They say that Zhirinovskii
is indifferent to women. Oh, really?" [90] Around the same time as Zhirinovskii's pictorial enactment of heterosexuality, two stories appeared in
the bulletin of Triangle (the Association of Gays, Lesbians, and Bisexuals)
about his homosexuality.

The articles in Triangle's bulletin were the first published texts that explicitly questioned whether Zhirinovskii was heterosexual. The first interview in the bulletin asked Zhirinovskii to describe his official positions
on several issues relevant to the "gay community." Zhirinovskii reiterated

the LDP's stand against any state interference in the "private life of the citizen." "Individually, there are those who are wrapped up in Eastern religions, those who stand on their head all day in the pose of some yogi, there are those who have a particular sexual orientation. Why interfere in their private lives?" When the journalist pointed out that Zhirinovskii is the only Russian politician to address homosexuals, he answered: "Well, the American president himself addressed this. But of our [politicians] I'm the first, huh? Well, that's good. And note my, as they say, progressive worldview." Finally the journalist asked him whether the charge made by former ally Limonov that Zhirinovskii liked young boys was true. "In what sense?" Zhirinovskii asked, seemingly confused. "In the sexual sense," the reporter replied. "Well, that's him. For him, this is a continuation of his books. He has already written about this in that book of his, what's it called, I, Eddie? [It's Me, Eddie]. . . . Well, it's his theme. It's desirable for him to write that, otherwise he wouldn't be able to." The journalist interrupted Zhirinovskii's rather confused response to ask him whether it is true or not, to which Zhirinovskii replied that of course it is not true that he's a pederast.

Unfortunately for Zhirinovskii, the second interview in the bulletin reveals a bit more about his sexual practices than his "official" statements by exploring a night in the life of the "Genius Populist at Home":

> V.V. [Vladimir Vol'fovich Zhirinovskii] was lying on the sofa. Near him a young girl sat on a stool and read aloud from a children's Bible.
>
> Besides myself—a Western journalist—there were two young boys in the room. V.V. called one of them to him.
>
> "Vitalik, sit on my legs, I'm cold."
>
> Vitalik, gangly and pimply, as sometimes happens in adolescence, immediately went and sat down at the feet of the "chief." The girl continued to read. Vitalik took the feet of V.V. onto his own knees.
>
> "I'm still cold," V.V. complained after a few minutes and turned to the second boy.
>
> "Dog, come here. Lie down here on the sofa, this way, so that your feet are there where mine are, and your head here."
>
> "Well that's somehow not very comfortable," "Dog" answered with embarrassment.
>
> "Don't worry about it. I'll be comfortable then."

On a previous evening [Zhirinovskii] had introduced me to Serezha ["Dog"], one of his volunteers whom he had sent to fight in the former Yugoslavia.

"How old are you?" I had asked Serezha.

With a smile Serezha had turned the question over to [Zhirinovskii] — "In truth, how old am I?"

[Zhirinovskii] grinned: "Eighteen."

After that first and short interview, the same girl came to read the Bible, after which [Zhirinovskii] and Serezha undressed to their underwear and Serezha began to give V.V. a massage.

"I'm definitely not that sort" [Serezha] reassured me after a couple of hours.

"Everyone else here is a faggot."

This time, with great embarrassment, Serezha walked over to the couch on which V.V. was lying and sat on the edge. V.V. ordered him to lie alongside him. Lowering his eyes, Serezha lay down with his head on V.V.'s shoulders. The "chief" stroked his head with his left hand — his right one lay on the hand of Vitalik who — for his own part, was lying on V.V.'s knees.

Judging by the expression on his face, Vitalik was very jealous of V.V.'s attention to Serezha, but then, on the next morning when I woke up, I discovered Serezha downstairs . . . and Vitalik I found upstairs, in V.V.'s bed.

The journalist admits a certain fascination with Zhirinovskii.

If I had the right to vote in Russia, it's completely possible that I would vote for him. There are moments when life seems completely unreal, and all who take life seriously seem so boring. Zhirinovskii lives as though his actions have no consequences. . . . And therefore, despite everything, I liked V.V. very much. Perhaps he needs another press secretary.[91]

The expression of queer admiration for nationalist politicians is not unique to the Triangle reporter. Many men claim to have slept with both Limonov and Zhirinovskii.[92] Even if their claims of sexual conquest are untrue, the very fact that so many queers would make them reveals a level of respect and admiration and certainly desire for leaders who espouse policies that are highly racist and discriminatory. Queer nationalists are powerful symbols to many of Russia's queers, and some of those queers, like Mogutin and Debrianskaia, are nationalist themselves.

OTHER HISTORIES OF THE UNION OF PATRIOTS AND PERVERTS

The intersection of nationalism and queer sexuality disturbs our sense of the world. For queers to be nationalists and nationalists to be queers, history must have fallen through the looking glass. We know the history in the United States—queers are marginalized and therefore ally with other marginalized groups.[93] Women, queers, persons of color go together like love and marriage. Nationalistic/fascistic politicians cannot be queer, since they seek to eliminate all otherness, including sexual otherness. Yet once on the other side of the looking glass, we realize there are other histories circulating—histories of gay Nazis and gays in Nazi Germany undisturbed by rising fascism. Russia is not the first place where queers and nationalists got into bed together. The marriage of queers and Nazism in Germany is a chilling historical precedent for post-Soviet Russia.

Despite their ultimate extermination, in the beginning many gay men joined the ranks of the Nazi Party. Although some gay leaders worked against the party, many actively supported it. One homosexual survivor of Nazi persecution said later that "[w]hen the Nazis took over we didn't think it would be as terrible as it actually became. . . . I just didn't give politics and Nazis too much thought."[94] The historian Frank Rector points out that conscious connection between Nazism and homoerotica: "As Hitler intended, the masculine vigor, adventure, thrust, vitality, and virile camaraderie of the Party were to many gays an irresistible attraction, just as it was for heterosexual males."[95] According to Rector, "[T]hat gays without number rushed wildly into the Nazi fold only later to end up dancing at the end of a rope merely illustrates that gays can be as stupid as anyone else (and as immoral)."[96] Of course, it was not just their "stupidity" or "immorality" that motivated gay men to ally themselves with the Nazis, but their sense of self-preservation. Many gay men believed that Hitler's New Order would bring about gay emancipation.[97] Although Adolf Hitler was himself rabidly homophobic, like any good politician he was not above using queers to gain power. Hitler used gays as a group and individual gays in order to gain power. When they were no longer necessary, Hitler merely systematically murdered gay men—individually and en masse.

One of the reasons Hitler could so easily welcome gays into the Nazi fold while simultaneously spewing homophobia was his close association with Ernst Roehm, an openly gay man. As the commander in chief of the Nazis' largest military organization, the SA, Roehm led an openly gay lifestyle. Roehm went to gay bars and bathhouses in Berlin, he suffered a highly publicized legal case for "pederasty," and surrounded himself with other open homosexuals, such as his occasional lover Edmund Heines.[98] In short, Roehm was publicly known as gay. With the second most powerful man in the Nazi regime openly gay, many homosexuals believed they were safe with the Nazis.

The safety of pro-Nazi gays did come at a cost—those gays who did not support the Nazi regime were in danger from the beginning.[99] Even during the Weimar Republic, Nazi harassment had forced some gay groups to disband.[100] Yet as long as Hitler needed Roehm and the SA, pro-Nazi gays did indeed seem safe.[101] In response to criticisms about Roehm's homosexuality, Hitler released a statement in February 1925 insisting the SA was "not an institute for the moral education of genteel young ladies, but a formation of seasoned fighters. . . . His private life cannot be an object of scrutiny unless it conflicts with the basic principles of National Socialist Ideology."[102] Hitler, however, did not need open homosexuals forever, not even Roehm. In June and July 1934, Hitler turned against Roehm and symbolically began the campaign to exterminate all homosexuals. During the Night of the Long Knives, as the purge of the SA came to be known, more than five thousand were killed,[103] including Hitler's loyal friend and ally, Roehm.[104] Of course there were many reasons Hitler decided to destroy Roehm and the SA, including the fact that Roehm was calling for a second revolution, which could very easily have swept Hitler out of power.[105] Whatever the motivations, the stated justification for Hitler's policy of mass murder was the "cleansing" of "homosexual pigs."[106] According to Richard Plant, Roehm "had made it easy for Hitler to act out against him by so flagrantly flaunting his homosexuality. His unapologetic behavior had provided a convenient peg on which Hitler could hang a multitude of sins." [107]

The murder of Roehm also killed all hope that gays would be untouched by the Nazis. Exactly one year later antisodomy laws were passed. [108] By 1935 nine other "perverted" acts were illegal, including same-sex kissing and fantasies. [109] One German homosexual wrote to his friend: "Have you heard about the Roehm murders? With that it all started, the rounding up, the closing of bars. . . . [C]ontact with Ferdi is lost but I'm afraid his SA uniform is no protection with Roehm gone." [110] After the Night of the Long Knives no queers, not even Nazi ones, were safe in fascist Germany.

Rector claims that such an ending to the alliance of queers and fascists was inevitable. "Open homosexuality and fascism are not compatible, at least not for very long. One or the other must eventually go." [111] Yet universal laws, other than gravity, are extremely rare. Fascism and queer sexualities may make the perfect couple—they certainly are compatible in post-Soviet Russia. The Red-Brown coalition in Russia is the flame that draws those critical of the system—including many queer activists. Eventually the queers may be scorched by nationalism, but for now it provides a place from which to criticize not only the Russian state, but also the Western nationalists who have come to conquer them. Queers in Russia, unlike queers in Weimar Germany, do not have the liberty of being the first to organize around sexual identity. They are trapped between the rock of Western imperialism and the hard place of the Russian state. Nationalism may be a literal dead end for them, but for many Russian queers it seems the only way out.

That patriots and perverts have been caught in the proverbial (and often literal) bed together is not the story I wanted to tell. Outing neofascist politicians like Zhirinovskii and Limonov is as liberating as claiming the SA as "our people." Outing queer heroes like Debrianskaia and Mogutin as nationalists is the surprise ending to a narrative that has told of their heroic deeds. Debrianskaia began queer activism in Russia. Mogutin forced the subject of homosexuality into the mass media. Both of them have risked their friends, families, livelihoods, and even lives to create public spaces for queer sexualities.

But queerness and nationalism, for better or for worse, are married in the public imaginings of the two. There is no divorce in sight. The marriage was in part born of frustration with westernizers. Attempting to make Russian sexualities over in Western drag has alienated some, even while it has been useful to others. At another level, nationalism is a compelling site of identity formation for a lot of Russians—not just Russian queers. Nationalism provides a sense of self against an outside other—the West, but it also bounds and protects a sense of self against an internal Other. Like Nazi Germany's nationalism, Russianness is also defined against the enemy within. The Jew, the Chechen, the Armenian, the Roma all provide negative space against which the image of Russian can be seen. Nationalism is also the last place from which to protest the system. Nationalist press and leaders have been the only ones to support the rights of sexual minorities, and they have done so from a position of opposition. Attacking the establishment in post-Soviet Russia means working against the "liberal democracy" of shock therapy, mafia run amok, and the suffering of the majority while a small minority reap unimaginable awards. Anti-American and anti-Yeltsin sentiments appeal to marginalized groups—including queers—in a Russia gone to the wolves of capitalism and crime.

Nationality, even more so than sexuality, is a meta-identity, one which everyone is required to have and to hold. All who identify on the basis of sexuality must also identify as part of a nation—but the reverse is far from true. In the process of ennationing themselves, some queers have also become nationalist—as a way to protest the Russian status quo and Western imperialism, as well as protect their national selves from the taint of internal otherness. Queers in Russia, like queers in Nazi Germany, are caught up in the same identifying imperatives as everyone else. One New York paper asked whether Mogutin was a "Rebel or Racist?"[112] The answer is that Mogutin, Debrianskaia, and all the nationalist queers are both—and perhaps neither. Looking for a way to create space in the center for the margins, they have sold their souls to an ideology of hate.

Yet perhaps they had no choice. For in the "democratic" Russia, queerness is dangerous. The "democratic" government has turned a blind eye to violence against queers. Worse, the "democratic" government has kept queers in a state of fear, refusing to acknowledge their rights and even attacking them with brute force. In February of 1998, the government's antinarcotics squad came busting into a queer disco armed with billy clubs and machine guns. After senselessly beating many of the dancing queers, the troops arrested nearly a third of the patrons. Some of those arrested were forced to go to a hospital and give blood and urine samples. Many fear that the blood samples will be used to determine their HIV status. If positive, they will undoubtedly face further state intervention into their desires. They will be forced to reveal the names of all of their lovers, who will themselves be tested. They will be legally prohibited from having any sexual intercourse again.[113] They will live in constant fear of arrest, forced institutionalization, and their own deaths in a country where anti-AIDS drugs are as chimerical as democracy. This was not the first time the "new" Russian government attacked queers, nor will it be the last.[114] When queers in Russia turn to the nationalist opposition for respite from "democratic" persecution, they are making one of the few choices that make sense in their through-the-looking-glass state. Their future is not sealed. There will not necessarily be a Night of the Long Knives in Russia. Then again, history just may repeat itself.

part IV: sex

conclusion

Sex is fucking, everything else is gender.

—*Kate Bornstein, 1993*

Last night I had a dream. I was crossing a border and I knew I was in trouble because I didn't have the right documents or I had forged a document and so when I walked up to the young Russian guard I was extremely nervous, but he just waved me through. I was ecstatic to have crossed the border, but when I was about ten feet into the new territory he called me back. He smiled and said (in Russian) "There's a problem with your passport, but don't worry, I can fix it." Then he took my (Russian) passport and crossed out the "Zh" (for woman) and wrote in an "M" (for man). Then he winked and we both laughed and I walked through for a second time, feeling freer and happier than I ever had in my life.

—*Field notes, September 1994*

Toward the end of my fieldwork, I had a powerful dream. In the dream I was able to cross borders because I was both behaving and misbehaving according to the rules of the game (the game, of course, being the disciplinary regimes of gender, nationality, and sexuality). I was passing as a man and a Russian, but I was also a woman and an American. A year later the dream seems more and more like a vision of what this work could be. We cannot escape from the inevitable borders and boundaries of sexuality, gender, nation, but we can also not avoid the fact that these disciplines are constantly being called into question by those who act "inappropriately." In transgression of rules (whether or not we ourselves are the transgressors) lies a sense of freedom. Like the young border guard in my dream, we do not have to break the rules ourselves to acknowledge the carnivalesque release of subversive acts. I want to conclude this work, then, by breaking the rules, by blurring the very boundaries I have worked so hard to create: self/other; straight/queer; Russian/Western; researcher/subject.

The boundaries had a purpose—to render a theory and story of self comprehensible and meaningful to the reader and to the author. The story has gone something like this: Whenever we speak about ourselves we rely on terms and languages created in the complex negotiation between self and other. This negotiation begins with speech acts about the other, from a position of power and authority, but the other, once formed, is always potentially speaking back. The power differential between the authorities of otherness and the self-speaking subjects shapes how loudly "I" can speak, but power does not prevent us from forming an "I." The self can and will speak, even if only in an inaudible whisper.

In the United States, speaking about ourselves relies on a fixed and abiding subject position. We are a gender, a nationality, a sexuality. In recent years academics and activists alike have attacked this "metaphysics of substance" for turning a time-bound set of practices into a permanent state of being. Despite these criticisms, the imperative to "be" (a gender, a nationality/ethnicity, a sexuality) is stronger than ever as the process of self-identifying becomes not only mandatory, but increasingly detailed.

The "metaphysics of substance" circulates differently in Russian economies of sexuality, for several reasons. First, there is no history of political/social movements based on sexual identity in Russia. Second, queer practices did not solidify into the homosexual person as quickly or as easily in Russia as they did in the West. When "the homosexual" was finally born (during Stalin's reign), s/he was still not a stable entity. For men, homosexual behavior was criminal and worthy of punishment. But, with the exception of capital punishment, legal intervention implies rehabilitation of the criminal individual. Men who slept with men were no more a species than bank robbers are a species. Even if the stigma of the crime was permanently marked on the bodies of those punished, the repetition of queer practices, like robbing the bank, was expected to cease. Women who desired women were not marked as criminal, but as diseased. Disease, like criminality, offers an end in sight—the Cure. Women were not put into a stable sexuality, but ensnared by a trajectory of illness, an illness that was supposed to get better (even if it never did).

So it was that until the 1980s the meaning of queer others resided in a

Law and a Cure that attempted to erase the very categories of sexual otherness that the Law and the Cure had created. It is not surprising that when those who had been caught in the trap of queer otherness began to return the experts' gaze that the result was subjectivity, not identity. Queers tended to look for expressions of sexual otherness that did not require an individual body on which to reside. These subjectivities were much more ambiguous than identities. Unlike identities, subjectivities did not require actual persons to feel "represented," nor did they require individuals to practice "being queer" in certain ways. Instead, individuals could behave in ways that were both queer and straight without having the existence of "queer subjectivities" threatened. Men could be married to women and still sleep with men. Women could have children with men and still have female lovers. Individual practices did not threaten to topple queerness itself.

Subjectivities were able to move queer selves out of the shadows. Queerness as spoken by queers began to take up space in the public sphere, and talk of the queer other could no longer determine the meaning of queer sexual practices in Russia. One of the most powerful ways queerness went public was by transgressing gender. The intersection of queerness and gender transgression reinforced an oppositional system of gender and desire (the heterosexual matrix). It also illustrated how sexuality operates in conjunction with other systems of the self, including national selves.

National identities came into play most forcefully at the point where queer subjectivities failed—identity politics. Queer subjectivities could provide no promises of relief from the wounds inflicted by the body politic onto queer bodies. Subjectivities do not work to change antisodomy laws nor psychiatric diagnoses nor gay bashing. Because of the weaknesses of subjectivity, some queers did coalesce into fixed identity groups. Unlike subjectivity, identity tries to represent queer interests (and repress practices that do not fit easily into its definition of self). Identity politics demanded far more than subjectivities, especially in a country where there had never been a clearly identified other. Persons who did not fit into the "gay/lesbian/bisexual" model of self were excluded, desires and sexual practices that were not "homosexual" were made secret, and private life, a much coveted commodity in a formerly communist state, was forced "out" into the open. Identity politics and the queers who created them found themselves caught between a strong indigenous impulse against identifying and imported pressures to identity. Being between the proverbial devil and the deep blue sea of foreign identities and domestic subjectivities, identity politics floundered but was then revived by the hopes and dreams (or perhaps the schemes) of Western activists. This collision of national cultures has resulted in a thriving exchange of queer nationalisms that may be as much a harbinger of things to come as anything else in the Russian landscape of queer sexualities.

The story of the production and performance of queerness in Russia, then, could only be told by imposing a series of (false) divisions. Self had to be separated from the other, Russia from the West, queer from straight, public from private, men from women. Yet these divisions were authored by me, not by the complex social space about which I've been speaking. Even from my limited vantage point, I have been able to see far more that does not fall within the bifocal view of my series of oppositions. Yet the oppositions protected not only me (from telling a tale far too tangled) but also queers in Russia. By telling you about public queerness, I have avoided exposing the private life of queers to the prying eyes of a still present security apparatus. By focusing on the discursive realm of queerness, I have avoided exposing the sexual practices of queers to a prurient public. But what I have avoided speaking about is far more central to the self than I have let on. The missing piece of this story is sex — queer sex and the bodies that engage and/or desire to engage in it. It is queer sex, after all, that sets the entire discursive regime of sexual otherness in motion. It is practices of desire, not fashion statements or linguistic constructions, that engage experts and spectators and participants alike.

But how do we get to the sexualized body without violating the borders that have offered protection? One answer might be to break down other divisions, particularly the division between "truth" and "fiction." Thus far I have veiled this text in the language of social science. I have presented the reader with evidence — field notes, newspapers, journals, interviews, surveys. Thus what I have been saying is part of the realm of (pseudo)scientific Truth. Yet I have already admitted that the divisions are false. The only way to glimpse through them is by telling you about the (homo)sexualized body and desire outside of the prurient (and dangerous) public sphere, and the only way to unveil the private is through the screen of fiction.[1]

Blurring the boundary between truth and fiction subverts, or perhaps perverts, the already shaky foundation upon which academic writing rests. Presenting fiction as truth is a risky enterprise, one that is just as likely to result in delegitimizing the entire text as it is in opening up to view a previously unspoken part of the Truth of queerness in Russia. By ending this story of sexual otherness in Russia with pieces of fiction, I risk losing my place as an "expert" of queerness in Russia. But I am not the first scholar to find the line between truth and fiction, scientist and storyteller, observer and observed, a difficult one to see. Trinh Minh-Ha has long interspersed her cultural critique with her own verse and stills from her films.[2] Eve Sedgwick forges similar frontiers in her 1986 essay "A Poem Is Being Written." By juxtaposing her own poetry from over twenty years of her life with her scholarly analyses of the poems, Sedgwick is able to explore notions of the female body and its (hidden) potential for anal eroticism.[3]

Interspersing (my own) fiction with (my own) academic text, then, is not completely outside the realm of what is imaginable within the confines of the university. My hope is that presenting you with admitted fictions will actually provide a fuller, if not truer, account of sexual otherness in Russia. Consider the following scene:

In Moscow nothing moves in a straight line. The streets spread out from the center only to turn back upon themselves. The result is knots, not intersections. Pedestrians are constantly darting into courtyards, maneuvering their way around mountains of burning garbage, barking dogs, screaming children. Muscovites do this not because these circuitous routes get them to where they are going more quickly, but because the back ways are not direct. That's how I ended up here, in this darkened room in a stranger's apartment, nursing a hangover and sore ribs with a bottle of vodka. Logically I know that I should get up, maybe go see a doctor, at least find my way home, take a bath, get some food. But then again, nothing ever moves in a linear fashion in Moscow, not even my brain. . . .

(After losing my way, I asked a passing babushka for directions to the metro. She sent me the back way, of course, but I slipped on the ice long before I ever found the metro.)

I'm not very brave about pain, which may explain why I fainted. The next thing I knew there was a young man in a thick coat and an even thicker accent looming over me. He smiled and told me that I looked terrible. Then he helped me stand up and insisted I come to his apartment, just across the courtyard. I tried to tell him I was fine, that I could make it back to my apartment, but the fact that my legs had abandoned all good sense and begun to buckle didn't help to convince him or me. . . . There was nothing to do but smile at this nice young serial killer and accept his offer of hospitality.

Once inside his apartment, he helped me to take off my boots and coat and then led me to his one room. He laid me gently on the divan and went into the kitchen to make tea. His room didn't look like the room of a maniac. There were neither instruments of torture nor pleasure hanging on the walls. I could detect no smells of death and decay seeping up from the floorboards, only the odor of laundry soap and drying woolen clothes coming from the bathroom. No, this was not the apartment of a serial killer. It was too cozy. There was even a cat, Mysha, who after a few minutes of feigned indifference, positioned himself in my lap and began to purr. On the walls hung the requisite contrasting patterns of any truly Russian home. Green wallpaper with yellow daisies ran into a ging-ham pattern in a lighter shade of green, over which was hung a rather large kilim. . . . I would have continued evaluating the apartment's furnishings, try-ing to glean clues of my hero's inner life from his interior decorating, but before I even had a chance to examine a rather kitschy collection of clay toys he came to the doorway. He was carrying a tray laden with tea, bread, chocolate, and that ur-healer of all that ails us, vodka.

It was then that I realized that my hero had transformed himself. He had taken off his thick coat and his fur hat and without them he really was quite beautiful. He was also a she. I smiled at this woman before me, taking in her black hair and even blacker eyes, low cheek bones and full red lips, long limbs and even longer eyelashes, and yes, breasts, big, beautiful breasts. I wanted to bury my head in them, to let them comfort me and then slowly arouse me. I laughed and startled both of us out of our reveries.

During tea we exchanged all the necessary information. Her name was Mu-khabad, which in Russian was Liuba, meaning love. She was from Uzbekhistan, and had come to Moscow to work for a foreign oil company. She liked Moscow, but hadn't made many friends yet. Then she smiled and slowly stretched out the words to make sure I felt the full impact of what she was saying. "It's difficult to meet our kind of people." That's when I understood that we would make love on that narrow divan of hers, thrown into each other's arms by my own clumsi-ness, or perhaps it was something more profound, like Fate, or Sexual Despera-tion. We both knew how difficult it was to find others like us, other women who wanted to be with women. When it happened, the story was always the same. Girl meets girl, girls throw all caution to the wind, girls have whirlwind romance, girl hates girl, girl leaves girl. We too would have to follow that well-worn path.

Sometimes I longed for something less emotionally draining. I wanted to be a man and have sex with other men in a public toilet, fucking my brains out with someone I'd never seen before and would never see again. Or go to a prostitute, giving her money for meaningful, meaningless sex. But that's not how it ever worked with the women I met. We had to fall in love to make love and then fall out of love to survive. Usually the whole process didn't take more than a few months, although once I was with someone for two years. . . .

On her narrow divan I kissed her and then she me. . . . Then we kissed again, this time more violently, allowing the sexual tension in our bodies to envelop us in an urgency that passed for passion. We began to remove our layers of clothes. There's no alluring way to remove three pairs of socks and two pairs of long underwear, but my beautiful Uzbek had already turned off the light. Without the slightest bit of grace we ripped off our clothes as quickly as possible and climbed under the blankets of her bed. Naked, we felt shy again. She hugged me to her body, lean but strong. Without saying a word to each other we had established our roles. She would be active. I would be passive. It had all been decided in less than a minute, by her pulling me toward her and my moving willingly. I was slightly disappointed. I had already fantasized about taking her. . . . But now I had to play by the rules. My disappointment faded after a few seconds. Submitting to her would be my pleasure. She had a certain unpredictability, no, I should just say what it was, a violence, right below the surface of her control and the thought of that violence exploding on me made me want to get down on my knees before her.

That's why I'm still here, lying on her bed, drinking her vodka. My Amazon from Uzbekistan was powerful and violent, taking me again and again. Even after I had fallen asleep, even after hours of fucking me, she was still going. Her need consumed her but it wasn't me she needed, but the space of a night with a woman, any woman. I know it wasn't me she needed because she kept insisting over and over again that I was a "natural," a straight woman. I tried to tell her that I liked to make love to women, but she slapped me. Then before I had time to respond she had rolled me onto my stomach and was taking my ass. She had to hit me because I had broken the rules. For her to be an active lesbian, I not only had to submit my body, but my desires as well. She wanted to take a woman who was attractive to and attracted to men, not some pervert like herself. I understood her because I used to be her, but then I met Sasha. . . .

This scene speaks to several different levels of queer sexualities in Russia. Within the imaginary private, sex, and not just talk of it, happens. The way sex happens is obviously not the same for everyone since even the narrator and her lover have different ideas about what might happen between them, but that their sex happens within societal boundaries is clear. The discipline of binary gender and sexuality (*aktivnaia/passivnaia*, lesbian/natural) structures their desire for each other as well as the bodily acts they perform (although not necessarily the bodily acts that the narrator imagines). Within this discipline, however, is not just repression, but release. Liuba releases her desire, built within the constraints of opposition, onto the narrator, who in turn finds release within the confines of her roles as passive and heterosexual. Gender and sexuality are not the only disciplines in bed with these women. Nation, too, rears its head. The narrator, whose nationality is unclear, not only fetishizes the gender of Liuba (i.e., she is only attracted to Liuba when Liuba is engendered as female; engendered as a male, Liuba inspires mistrust and fear), but her nationality as well. The narrator eroticizes Liuba's "exotic" Otherness — her dark hair, her black eyes, her "full" red lips.[4] Liuba is eroticized and exoticized as an "Amazon," not an "ordinary" Russian woman.

At the same time that disciplines of self and other structure and facilitate the erotic exchange between these two women, they also make the narrator feel loss, loss of other possibilities. Because the narrator is aware of the loss, she longs to transgress the disciplinary boundaries of her sexuality and gender. In the next scene, the narrator is able to do that, to some extent, although she is always entering another disciplinary matrix, without ever fully exiting the first.

Sasha, beautiful Sasha. Actually Sasha's rather ugly, but I think of him as beautiful. His forehead protrudes over his eyes, contorting his face into a permanent scowl. And then there's the scar along his left cheek, left there by a lover in prison who wanted to show Sasha the dangers of betrayal. But he's got the most beautiful eyes, the color of ice in winter — so pale that they're almost transparent, until you see him laugh and his eyes suddenly become a layer of steel. And when he laughs, that's when I love him best.

He was laughing last month when I told him about my night at the *pleshka*. Sasha and I had started out together, going down to the *pleshka*, looking for boys. Sasha thought it would be funny to disguise me as a man, which isn't that hard since my body is anything but womanly. There we were, my Sasha and me, only it wasn't me, or it wasn't the usual me. . . . I looked like Sasha's brother, or lover. . . . Sasha said I looked scrumptious as a man. I just felt like a fraud. . . .

As we walked in front of the Bolshoi in the fading twilight of an October afternoon, I could feel the stares of the men penetrating my façade. I whispered to Sasha that they could tell, but he just laughed and pushed me into a man. The man was older, in his late fifties, wearing an Italian suit and a smirk on his face; until I ran into him that is. He had been leaning, in studied casualness, against the fountain, one leg up on the rim, and when I crashed into him he almost fell into the water. I mumbled an apology and turned to run across the street to the metro, run home, tail between my legs, horrified at the thought of getting caught. Then I felt his hand on my arm. He was dragging me across the square. I looked at Sasha, pleading for help, but he was busy with his own affairs. "Where are we going?" I asked, hoping to slow down his progress. I was afraid he was a cop, taking me into the station for being a fag. How would I explain that to my mother?

He never did answer, just kept dragging me after him. First through the underground passage, then up the slight incline of the Kitai Gorod walls, finally into a dark passageway. He ordered me onto my knees and pulled out his cock. I wasn't sure I wanted this, but then again I wasn't sure who I was anymore. I looked up into his face; he looked mean enough to hit me. There was nothing to do but give him what he wanted. He kept telling me how much I liked sucking men off, and after a few minutes I knew he was telling the truth. I was a queer-boy, kneeling before a man, enjoying my new self, especially when he started moaning about what a good little boy I was. That's exactly what he said, little boy. I would have laughed if I hadn't been so afraid. After he came, he bent down and looked at my face. I flinched when I realized he might kiss me. I didn't want him to do anything gentle. I was afraid I might cry. But he didn't kiss me, he just asked how old I was. Before I could make up an answer, he smiled and said: "You're so young. You can't be more than seventeen. You don't even have a beard yet. What a good little boy." He reached down and pulled me to my feet, then he stuck some bills in my pocket. He told me he wanted to take me to a restaurant, but couldn't because he was supposed to meet his wife. I nodded. I'm not sure why I didn't give him the money back. Maybe I was too far inside myself by then. In the course of a few hours I had become a boy and a fag and a prostitute. I wasn't sure who I would be the next day and I might need the cash. . . .

In this passage, the narrator attempts to escape the confines of a binary gender by moving from female to male. Yet the female is still there, a more embedded discipline always in danger of seeping through her/his performance as male. The sexual exchange, although very different from the encounter with Liuba, is similarly predicated on the opposition between "active" and "passive" (the possibility of the narrator penetrating the man is not part of either partner's imaginative landscape). As with the female/female encounter, the male/male sexual attraction is also predicated on the separation of natural from pervert, except this time it is the "active" partner (i.e., the man) who is "straight," while the "passive" partner (i.e., the narrator) is the one who "likes it" (i.e., is the "real" queer). Although there are no universal rules of desire, the straight/queer dichotomy is an important way in which all of us, straights and queers alike, speak about sexual desires. Sometimes desire is for another queer; sometimes it's for a straight person.

The final dichotomy here is between adult and pubescent. This is another difference that can create and structure sexual exchanges. Many of the stories of sex that I was told (as well as the stories I wrote with my own body) utilized differences in age (woman/girl; man/boy; woman/boy; man/girl) to construct passion. My friend S could only sleep with "girls." Women, she said, couldn't give themselves to her, not totally; they always held something back. Another friend, Y, usually slept with women, but occasionally she liked to sleep with young boys. I asked Y whether she thinks of herself as a "lesbian" (her term) when she's sleeping with boys. "Why not? I'm still me, I'll still be with women. . . . I just like to be with boys sometimes, they're so sweet when they're that age." Y wasn't the only friend who likes young boys. A male friend in his fifties, E, who once served time in prison for having sexual relations with underage boys, has a boyfriend who is still in high school. I spent an afternoon with the boy once. We talked about the computer games he liked to play and what a waste of time school was. He likes being with E, even though E is a bit "too serious" at times.

These anecdotes are not meant to be evidence of how Russian queers are caught in desiring difference (as though the rest of us were "free" from such divisions). Instead, they're meant as illustrations of some of the ways queerness happens outside of the public realm, and some of the public differences upon which private queerness is built. Within the public realm, within discursive regimes, it is relatively easy to separate talk of the queer other from talk of a queer self. In the messy, bodily space of sex, queerness and heterosexuality are often enmeshed in a single act performed by a single body. To be queer bodily is not necessarily to speak (privately or publicly) as a queer. To be straight bodily is not necessarily to desire that way.[5] But the supposedly private realm of queerness also reveals how ephemeral the division between self and other is. A woman is a boy and has sex with a man — is the body straight or queer, male or female, adult or pubescent? A lesbian desires a woman only if that woman performs as though she were attracted to men — does that make the desirer both a lesbian and a man? Is the desired straight when she becomes what her female lover desires? A husband meets his wife after having sex with a boy. Which is his "true" self?

Sexualities, like the individual bodies on which they reside, are not trapped in the limitations of a binary opposition like straight/gay, male/female, but find pleasure (and frustration) in a maze of intersecting boundaries. It is not just gender or sexuality differences that move us to the bedroom, but differences in age, nationality, race, class, and religious background. More important, there is no escaping the divisions that structure our sexual selves. Our narrator can be a girl who becomes a boy who wants a girl whom she thought was a boy, but s/he is still entangled in gender. A woman can desire a woman "just like her," they can both identify as "lesbians" or "Americans" or "intellectuals," but that desire for sameness is still structured on a system of differences (i.e., women are different from men, straights from lesbians, Russians from Americans, intellectuals from the not terribly bright). The existence of heterosexuality also relies on a series of differences. Gender is the most primal difference for straight desires, but it, too, is permeated with other differences, in nationality, in age, in class, even in sexuality (e.g., the attraction of a man to a lesbian).

Differences (and similarities), then, are what structure our sexual selves. We can slip between queer others and queer selves, between first- and third-person narratives, but we cannot make the boundary disappear completely. If this exploration in the messiness of our sexual selves tells us anything, it is that all of ourselves are caught up in this grid of blurry boundaries. Our national identity and our gender are just as implicated by the complex relationship between self and other as sexuality. Self/other is a shifting matrix of differences and similarities, full of as many possibilities and combinations as a body engaged in sex. Boundaries get crossed and then crisscrossed. Although the divisions remain, their clarity is under constant attack. Within any set of oppositions rests the possibility not of escape, but of transgression, of blurring the borders and betraying our selves by taking on a different self. A mask is pulled off but underneath is only another mask.

This conclusion is merely another mask—making the private public has only opened up all the divisions of this work to the endless possibilities of creative desires. Self becomes other, straight becomes queer, male becomes female. The story of self-formation becomes as entangled as bodies during sex. The only conclusion that can be drawn is that sex and the self are a story that can be told only in bits and pieces. Either in the highly idiomatic and individual forms of fictional or personal narratives or in the highly partial idiom of academic writing, which cuts the sexualized self off from the body as easily as it limits the field of vision to the public and the discursive. I conclude this work on queerness in Russia the only way that I can—with both the revelation of and revelry in the messiness of our sexualized selves.

postscript

The primary research for this book ended in 1994. I have tried to update the book where I can, but I have not been back to Russia since that time. On my last night in Moscow, I went out to a queer disco with some friends. Suddenly I found myself sobbing. I realized that I was never coming back, not really, not to live there. My partner and I were going to have children, and we both knew we wouldn't be raising our family anywhere but New York. My friends laughed at me. "Don't be ridiculous, you'll be back over the summer," cried Ksiusha. After all, I had always come over the summer, for years and years and years. But I didn't come back that summer. I was too pregnant. The next summer I had a baby. The following summer we were already trying to get pregnant again. This summer, another baby is here. Sure, we keep in touch with phone calls and E-mails. Our family and friends make it to New York occasionally, and soon we'll get to Moscow for a visit. But as my thirties caught up with me, it became more and more difficult to keep a foot in both places. I felt roots growing under me, keeping me here, making me miss there less and less.

Maybe, when the children are older, the roots will loosen, and I'll once again find myself as much a resident of Moscow as of New York. Maybe then I'll write another book on queer in Russia. Until then, it will have to stand as a story about sex, self, and the other that is as rooted in a particular time and place as any other story. This book describes a moment, a dazzling, spectacular moment in Russia when queerness began to speak about itself after decades of being whispered about by others. That moment remains as overburdened with significance as it ever was. From it we can learn much about notions of self and stability, sex and gender and nation. But like all moments, it has ended. Someone recently informed me that "gay and lesbian" are becoming stable identities in Russia. It may be that this person is correct, that sexuality in Russia is stabilizing into a fixed and bifurcated identity that mirrors Western notions of sexuality. Or it may be that the long tradition of not identifying on the basis of sexual practices continues. This still seems the more likely scenario to me. After all, even if a core group of activists in large cities begin to assume a coherent and stable identity, there is still a long cultural tradition of not doing so. It will take those activists at least a lifetime to have an impact on those traditions. Men married to women will still go to the baths and have sex with other men. "Heterosexual" women will still be intimate with their girlfriends. And queers of various stripes will still experience a full range of desires and those desires will not be easily controlled and divided into "straight" or "gay." But if I am wrong and sexuality in Russia has become "just like us," then this book is an even more important document of what was and what might have been. This is a record, perhaps a fantasy, of a world of multiple desires and flexible identities that was not yet colonized by Western notions of sex and its meaning. I will leave it to future scholars to decide whether that world has disappeared forever. I look forward to their stories about queerness in Russia.

notes

PREFACE

1   The antisodomy statute, Article 121.1 was repealed in July 1993.
2   Based on field research by the author among self-identifying "sexual minorities" in Moscow and St. Petersburg. Note that not all who engage in nonnormative sexual practices identify themselves as "sexual minorities." In fact, the term is rarely used to describe the individual. Nor does this study consider all people who engage in nonnormative sexual practices but do not identify on the basis of those practices. Such persons are not (could not be) considered since they are not part of any public meaning of sexuality.
3   I am grateful to Yaroslav Mogutin for pointing this out to me.
4   Eve Kosofsky Sedgwick speaks to the way in which queer is true when spoken in the first person when she says, "A hypothesis worth making explicit: that there are important senses in which 'queer' can signify only *when attached to the first person. One possible corollary: that what it takes—all it takes*—to make the description 'queer' a true one is the impulsion to use it in the first person." *Tendencies* (Durham, N.C.: Duke University Press, 1993), p. 9.
5   "Iron closet" is David Tuller's clever retooling of the "Iron Curtain." Dave Tuller, *Cracks in the Iron Closet: Travels in Gay and Lesbian Russia* (Boston: Faber & Faber, 1996).
6   See Chapter 1, "The Law."
7   Telling you about the theory behind this work is not only intellectual masturbation (although it is certainly that as well). I took theory very seriously when I was writing this book, apparently far more seriously than I knew. Imagine my embarrassment when reading Tuller's work on gays and lesbians in Russia, when I noticed a passage about a "queer studies scholar" who "exclaimed, without apparent irony: 'That's so Foucault!' " While I have no memory of ever using an exclamation point, I believe I was the scholar who had no ironic distance vis-à-vis Foucault and other theorists. See Tuller, p. 138.
8   Central to the task at hand is the word "subject," and it is a lie. "Subject" is a noun; it acts as though it is tangible, real. I am skeptical of a subject; I want to shake it up, to see not the thing, but the practice of the thing. "Subject" here is the enactment and reenactment of complex negotiations in the social world. The epistemological foundations of this work, then, interrogate any claims to "be," any claims to an "I." The interrogation occurs somewhere between constructivist

and postmodern epistemic camps. I am specifically rejecting an essentialist or unified understanding of sexuality.

9   Enacting *ourselves* happens not at the level of choice, but in a realm of habits and patterns. Thus subjects do not begin to speak because of some conscious choice of identity, but as part of a set of patterned behaviors that developed in response to power in the social world. Pierre Bourdieu calls these habits and patterns "habitus." See Pierre Bourdieu, *In Other Words: Essays towards a Reflexive Sociology* (Stanford: Stanford University Press, 1990), especially pp. 11–13. Also see Bourdieu, *Distinction: A Social Critique of the Judgement of Taste* (Cambridge, Mass.: Harvard University Press, 1984), pp. 170–72. In fact, "habitus" as a system of acquired but unalterable dispositions was a concept first explored by Marcel Maus in his 1934 article "Techniques of the Body," reprinted in *Economy and Society* 2, no. 1 (February 1973), pp. 70–88.

10   This is similar to Clifford Geertz's Weberian understanding of culture as "webs of significance." Geertz wants to "interpret," to find the local meanings of these webs of significance. See Clifford Geertz, *The Interpretation of Cultures* (New York: Basic Books, 1973), p. 5. For Geertz's insistence on the way in which cultures must be read in their own locations, see *Local Knowledge* (New York: Basic Books, 1983).

11   This is similar to James Clifford's critique of Clifford Geertz's use of synecdoche as the preferred trope, creating a whole culture out of a particular cultural enactment, for instance, basing a discussion of Balinese culture on a cockfight. James Clifford, *The Predicament of Culture: Twentieth-Century Ethnography, Literature, and Art* (Cambridge, Mass.: Harvard University Press, 1988). Mikhail Bakhtin first explored texts as having more than one meaning by coining the term "heteroglossia." See Bakhtin, *The Dialogic Imagination* (Austin: University of Texas Press, 1981). There are, of course, many cultural theorists who see reading and meaning as contingent and precarious. For example, see Janice Radway, *Reading the Romance: Women, Patriarchy, and Popular Literature* (Chapel Hill: University of North Carolina Press, 1991), and Dick Hebdige, *Subculture: The Meaning of Style* (London: Routledge, 1979) and *Hiding in the Light* (London: Routledge, 1988).

12   The "public sphere" is a (mis)appropriation of Jürgen Habermas. See Habermas, *The Structural Transformation of the Public Sphere*, trans. T. Burger and F. Lawrence (Cambridge, Mass.: MIT Press, 1989). I say "misappropriation" of Habermas because he never meant for the "public sphere" to be used as a Weberian ideal type. Instead, Habermas theorized the public sphere as both historically and culturally specific. Ibid., pp. 18–28, 169–72.

Although not an ideal type, Habermas's public sphere is clearly an idealized version of history. For interesting critiques, see Geoff Eley, "Nations, Publics, and Political Cultures: Placing Habermas in the Nineteenth Century," and Michael Warner, "The Mass Public and the Mass Subject," both in Craig Calhoun, ed., *Habermas and the Public Sphere* (Cambridge, Mass.: MIT Press, 1992).

Despite its limitations, the notion of the public sphere does provide a way to distinguish between public and private queerness. I am employing the public sphere in order to create an imaginary space of narrative. It is in the public sphere that stories and sets of stories are told and retold, discourses are created and recreated. The stories are told in academic and popular publications, in cultural events (e.g., plays) and symbolic systems (e.g., style). Where Habermas described the public sphere as a café conversation where all speakers speak at the same volume and are equally heard, then I would describe it as a busy street corner, where billboards, newspaper sellers, a car radio, a police officer, and a street philosopher all compete to be heard. Not everyone gets to be heard, not everyone is a self-speaking subject, but we are all a captive audience, created and confined by what is being said. In my version, it is not rational debate that takes place, but exchanges of power. The philosopher begins to scream; the police siren is turned on; the radio is turned up; the billboard flashes neon. It is in this web of stories that the meaning of sex is negotiated among those with the power to speak.

13   I take this point up again in chapters 2, 4, and 5. For now it is sufficient to point out the obvious: the visibility and voice of a public subject are contingent on social power, and power is not randomly distributed, but divided by gender, class, and other taxonomies.

14   Michel Foucault gives us a clue to how Russian queers entered the public discourse on the meaning of sexual practices. According to Foucault, "objectifying practices" engender subjectivity. Publicly speaking *about* the Other simultaneously creates the possibility of publicly speaking *as* the Other. See Michel Foucault, *Discipline and Punish*, trans. Alan Sheridan (New York: Random House, 1979) and *The History of Sexuality*, vol. 1: *An Introduction*, trans. Robert Hurley (New York: Vintage, 1980).

15   Alexander Shatalov, an openly gay publisher, wrote an article that he himself described as "homophobic" since it spoke of "those" homosexuals. Author's interview, July 1994. The two women of the band The Morality Police are known for their leather attire, shaved heads, and lesboerotic displays on stage; in interviews, however, they describe themselves as heterosexual. See my discussion of the band in chapter 5.

16   Most of this work was derived, to some extent, from Michel Foucault's *History of Sexuality*. In terms of the legal construction of homosexuality in the West, Ed Cohen's *Talk on the Wilde Side* (New York: Routledge, 1993) is highly informative. Judith Butler's *Gender Trouble* (New York: Routledge, 1990) provides an in-depth exploration of the psychiatric underpinnings of the sexual and gender "other."

17   The quotation marks around "participant observation" signal the conflicts over the meaning of the term as well as my own separation from the tradition. Participant observation includes many traditions, from the Chicago School's letting the facts "speak for themselves" to the literary accounts of should-be novelists. For a good summary of fieldwork styles, see John Van Maanen, *Tales of the Field: On Writing Ethnography* (Chicago: University of Chicago Press, 1988), p. 73. Unlike most field-workers, I am not trying to understand "others, close or distant." I am skeptical of the metaphysics of sexuality, the claims to be a Russian queer. I too could make that claim, I too am queer in Russia. But I do not want to tell you about them/us. Instead, I am trying to understand an abstract notion (i.e., the Self) in a concrete setting (i.e., the discursive realm in and around sexual otherness in Rus-

sia). I participate in Russian queerness, but I am observing neither the culture nor the natives, but claims to be one or the other.

18 In all, I interviewed fourteen leaders of organizations/groups in St. Petersburg and Moscow, as well as three leaders from Siberia (Krasnoiarsk and Novosibirsk). Some of the leaders I interviewed several times over the course of several years. I also interviewed seven writers, one publisher, three editors, six actors/directors, and an artist.

19 I distributed 183 questionnaires, 90 of which I received back; 70 of these 90 were completed by queers who were in "public" spaces.

20 Unfortunately, finding written materials was more difficult, since before 1987 no professional articles were published in public-circulation journals. Instead, nearly all such information is written in the form of closed publications (*zakrytaia dissertatsiia*), which are geographically decentralized, each such publication being available only within a particular medical/psychiatric institute and generally not available to anyone from the outside. Information based on my interviews with sexologists Igor Kon (July 1994) and Dmitri Isaev (August 1994), as well as I, a (gay) professor of library sciences in Moscow (July 1994).

1 THE EXPERT GAZE 1: THE LAW

1 Michel Foucault. *The History of Sexuality*, vol. 1: *An Introduction*, trans. Robert Hurley (New York: Vintage Books, 1978), pp. 33–35.

2 Describing turn-of-the-century England, Ed Cohen locates the transformation of homosexual desire into homosexual self within a web of class and gender relationships. State regulation of sex was the result of campaigns to control (middle-class) male sexuality and protect (working-class) female virtue. A man who could not "control" his sexual desires, one who succumbed to masturbation, prostitution, and/or homosexuality, was not really a man. In 1885, the legal injunction against "unnatural" acts was rewritten so that the site of indecency was no longer the acts but the actors. Men who desired other men were now "grossly indecent." Ed Cohen, *Talk on the Wilde Side* (New York: Routledge, 1993); see esp. "Marking Social Dis-Ease."

3 Simon Karlinsky argues that homosexuality in Russia was both "widespread and tolerated in all strata of Russian society" prior to the westernizing influence of Peter the Great. Karlinsky also points out that the code only pertained to soldiers on active duty and was never actually enforced (a fact possibly attributable to Peter's own homosexual relationships). Simon Karlinsky, "Russia's Gay Literature and Culture: The Impact of the October Revolution," in Martin Bauml Duberman et al., eds. *Hidden from History: Reclaiming the Gay and Lesbian Past* (New York: NAL Books, 1989), pp. 348–49.

4 Ibid., p. 349.

5 Laura Engelstein, *The Keys to Happiness: Sex and the Search for Modernity in Fin-de-Siècle Russia* (Ithaca, N.Y.: Cornell University Press, 1992), p. 59.

6   Ibid., pp. 75, 84, 94.

7   Karlinsky, pp. 350–56.

8   Even the popularity of filmmaker Sergei Eisenstein could not protect him from the need to arrange a marriage with a friend. Eisenstein never actually lived with his wife and continued his homosexual relationships. Karlinsky, pp. 360–61.

9   There are numerous histories that deal with the politicization of daily life under Stalin, as well as a number of very informative biographies and novels. For instance, see Nadezhda Mandelstam's memoir, *Hope against Hope* (New York: Atheneum, 1970), or Sheila Fitzpatrick's *The Russian Revolution: 1917–1932* (Oxford: Oxford University Press, 1982), pp. 129–53, and Donald W. Treadgold's *Twentieth-Century Russia* (Boulder, Colo.: Westview Press, 1981), pp. 237–74, 321–30. It is disappointing to note that none of the histories deals with the politicization of homosexuality.

10 Without entering into the endless and seemingly fruitless debate over whether Stalinist Russia was indeed "totalitarian," it seems worth noting that both Nazi Germany and Stalinist Russia politicized homosexuality for the first time. Homosexuality was made both more powerful and more punished than ever before. Some of the history of homosexuals in Nazi Germany is discussed in chapter 6, "Patriots and Perverts."

11 Legal scholar Valery Chalidze writes of the political nature of homosexual acts in the Soviet Union. If in the West homosexuality is/was seen as a threat to the "family," in Soviet Russia it was seen as a direct threat to the government. As quoted in Vladimir Kozlovsky, *Argo Russkoi Gomoseksyal'noi Subkul'tury: Source Materials* (Benson, Vt.: Chalidze Publications, 1986).

12 Masha Gessen, *The Rights of Lesbians and Gay Men in the Russian Federation* (San Francisco: IGLHRC, 1994), p. 8.

13 Author's translation (all translations are author's unless otherwise noted). Maksim Gorky, "Proletarskii gumanizm" ("Proletarian Humanism"), *Sobranie sochinenii* 27 (1933–36; Moscow: Gosudarstvennoe literaturnoe izdatel'stvo, 1953), p. 238. It is worth noting that Gorky spends the rest of the essay criticizing the "fascist" countries (i.e., Western Europe) for their anti-Semitic and racist policies and praising the goal of racial and ethnic harmony in the Soviet Union.

14 Ibid., p. 241. Perhaps Gorky's hysteria can be explained by a rumor, which I often encountered in Moscow, that Gorky's own son was gay.

15 B. A. Vvedenski, ed., *Bol'shaia Sovetskaia entsiklopediia* (Moscow: Gosudarstvennoe nauchnoe izdatel'stvo, 1952), p. 35.

16 *Bol'shaia Sovetskaia entsiklopediia* (Moskva: Izdatel'stvo "Sovetskaia entsiklopediia", 1974), vol. 7, p. 56; vol. 17, p. 83.

17 Igor Kon, "Sexual Minorities," in Igor Kon and James Riordan, eds., *Sex and Russian Society* (Bloomington: Indiana University Press, 1993). The Soviet censors went to absurd lengths to erase homosexuality from all publications, even narrowly distributed academic ones. Kon relates how in 1974 he submitted an article to a journal of ancient history on friendship in ancient Greece. Kon was forced to replace the word "pederasty" with the euphemism "those specific relationships."

18   I am using "juridical complex" here to signify a continuum of institutions and practices that intersected with the law against male homosexuality. In particular, I am considering how the legislative bodies and political figures employed the law through a system of arrests, trials, prisons/labor camps, and through paralegal means, such as blackmail and intimidation.

19   *Ugolovnyi kodeks* RSFSR (Moscow: Iuridicheskaia Literatura, 1987), p. 77. Only the first article was removed; Article 121.2, homosexual sex with a minor, remains a crime—regardless of the age of the "criminal." Olga Zhuk, who was on the first fact-finding commission on homosexuals in Soviet prisons, describes one young man who was sentenced to eight years for having sex with his boyfriend. The young man was nineteen at the time, the boyfriend a year and a half his junior. Olga Zhuk, "The First Report: Iablonevka" (in Russian) in *Gay, Slaviane!*, no. 1 (1993), p. 68.

20   There are no exact figures of the number of men sentenced under Article 121, in part because the article prohibits both consensual homosexual relations between men and homosexual rape. According to Ministry of Justice numbers, about 500 men were sentenced annually under Article 121 between 1989 and 1992. Gessen, p. 10.

21   *Verkhovnyi Sud SSSR* (Sekretnaia Chast'), Fond no. 9492, Opis no. 6c, Delo no. 69. Documents were given to me by David Tuller.

22   The category of *opushcheny* includes more than those sentenced under Article 121. Any man who violates the strict unwritten rules of prison camp life can become "degraded." For instance, someone who works as an informant for the prison administration or steals from his fellow prisoners can be degraded. Once part of the degraded caste, these men are subject to rapes, beatings, even death. They typically are assigned the most filthy tasks, forced to sleep on the concrete floor, not given any food except at the whim of their cellmates. Many of these men, regardless of their sexual orientations, prostitute themselves for food, a cot, even physical protection from others. P. Masal'skii speaks of prostitution as the only way he would have survived his imprisonment under Article 121. Interviews with P. Masal'skii, Y. Ereev, G. Trifonov, and four other men who have served time under the antisodomy statutes.

23   The term *opushcheny* seems to be going out of vogue. Instead, *obizheny* seems to be more popular among prisoners. *Obizheny* indicates those who have been insulted (as opposed to degraded). Whether or not this semantic shift indicates a shift in the lived meaning of the terms is unclear.

24   As quoted in Olga Zhuk, p. 66. Author's interviews with men who were sentenced under Articles 121.1 and 121.2 revealed other reasons, including losing at cards or just being "too pretty to be left alone."

25   D. D. Isaev, "Homosexual Contacts in Places of Interment and the Problem of AIDS" (in Russian), unpublished copy of paper given to author by Isaev, August 1994. Results from this study were also published by Isaev in A. D. Borokhov, D. D. Isaev, and A. V. Toliarov, "Sociopsychological Factors of Homosexual Behavior among Prisoners" (in Russian), *Sotsiologicheskie issledovaniia*, no. 6 (1990).

26   A "passive" (*pasivnyi*) homosexual is the receptive partner. It goes without say-
     ing that this sociosexual hierarchy in the prisons relies on the larger sociosexual
     hierarchy of gender. A "passive" homosexual is in the position of "woman" — not
     necessarily actual women, but "woman" is the opposite of a real "man."

27   Interview with V, July 1994.

28   Interview with E, September 1994.

29   Consider the fact that since Article 121.1's repeal in 1993, several new laws have
     been written that could be used to prosecute both men and women for homo-
     sexuality. For example, Article 132 of the new Criminal Code allows prosecution
     for sodomy or lesbianism (or any other sexual act) that takes advantage of the vic-
     tim's "helpless position." These laws were written and adopted without the input
     of any advocates for the rights of "sexual minorities."

30   Gennadi Trifonov, "Open Letter" (in Russian) published in Kozlovsky, p. 180.

31   Interview with Masal'skii, August 1994.

32   Interviews with Ereev, April, July, August 1994.

33   Interview with Kukharskii, August 1994. Kukharskii claims to have ended his
     prosecution by revealing the homosexuality of the prosecutor, who was not only
     gay, but hoped to obtain Kukharskii's relatively large and centrally located apart-
     ment. Although this may seem absurd to the American reader, such things were
     not unheard of under the Soviet housing system.

34   This is especially true since many men were sentenced under a variety of laws, in-
     cluding hooliganism and corrupting the morals of a minor for even having sex in
     the same household as a minor. Thus the repeal of Article 121.1 did not necessarily
     free many of the men sentenced for homosexual acts. Also, the responsibility for
     actually implementing the repeal fell to prison administrators, who are the very
     persons "who maintain the prison caste systems with homosexuals at the bot-
     tom." Gessen, p. 28.

35   Interviews with M. Gessen of IGLHRC, February 1994.

36   This is the version of the code passed by the Russian Parliament in 1993 as re-
     printed in *Kommentarii k ugolovnemu kodeksu Rossiiskoi Federatsii* (Moscow: Verdikty,
     1994), p. 226.

37   Gessen, p. 28.

38   As printed in *Rossiiskie vesti*, no. 110 (1031), 15 June 1996, p. 1.

39   See Article 115, *Ugolovnoe pravo Rossii Osobennaia chast'* (Moscow: Iurist, 1993), pp.
     128–32.

40   "Kommitet po okhrane zdorov'ia: proekt," 24 May 1994. Although the proposal
     has not yet received the parliamentary majority necessary to pass it into law, it
     seems likely that some version of the law will pass with such a provision in tact.
     Interview with J. Stachowik, director of Moscow's AIDS-Infoshare, January 1995.

41   The article against "hooliganism," Article 206 of the Criminal Code, was one of
     the Soviets' favorite tools of harassment of political dissidents.

42   As of May 1994, *Eshche* has a circulation of 190,000 at the relatively high cost of
     1,500 rubles. " 'Eshche': It's Not Yet Evening, but They're Already Sitting (Behind
     Bars)" (in Russian), *Komsomol'skaia pravda*, 17 May 1994, p. 3.

43   Vadim Trukhachev, "The Passions Surrounding the Paper '*Eshche*' " (in Russian), *Megapolis Xpress*, nos. 10–11, March 1994, p. 6.

44   Interviews with M. Gessen and Y. Mogutin in February 1994.

45   Interview with Y. Mogutin, February 1994. Apparently Kostin's unjust imprisonment was all the more harrowing because of a chronic health condition that requires a strict diet. At several times during his imprisonment, Mogutin and other friends and colleagues were concerned that Kostin would not survive his imprisonment long enough to stand trial. This was a sentiment echoed by Kostin's lawyer. See *Komsomol'skaia pravda*, 17 May 1994.

46   According to an op-ed piece in *Novoe vremia*, Kostin was still being held in Butyrskii prison in Moscow a year later. The writer Zufar Gareev and his wife were both being charged under Article 228 for the "distribution of pornography" for having had copies of *Eshche* in their apartment. Also, the editor, Vladimir Linderman, was charged in absentia (he's a resident of Riga). The piece ends by asking why Russia's journalists have been so quiet about this case. *Novoe vremia*, no. 49 (December 1994), p. 5. Correspondence with M. Gessen, February 1995, and conversation with Gessen, March 1995, provided me with an update on the situation.

47   For instance, see *Miss X* or *Krasnaia shliapochka*. Even the very middle-of-the-road *Nezavisimaia gazeta* described *Eshche* as a publication that could hardly be called "radical." Kris Khokli, "A Tabloid Makes the World a Happier Place" (in Russian), *Nezavisimaia gazeta*, 18 June 1991, p. 7.

48   " 'Eshche': It's Not Evening, but They're Sitting," *Komsomol'skaia pravda*, p. 3.

49   Aleksander Podrabin, "Commentary" (in Russian), *Ekspress-khronika*, 11 February 1994.

50   Maria Vil'mis, "Pornography" (in Russian), *Ekspress-khronika*, 1 April 1994, p. 4.

51   Author's interview with Y. Mogutin, February 1994. Mogutin told me it was specifically the argument between the bureaucrat from the Ministry of Internal Affairs (MVD) and Kostin that resulted in the editor's arrest. Mogutin also pointed out that the very same troops brought into Moscow to quell the coup are being used in this "fight against porn." The conflict at the round table was also mentioned in various press accounts. See *Komsomol'skaia pravda*, 17 May 1994, p. 3; Evgenii Komov, "The Publisher of '*Eshche*' is Arrested" (in Russian), *Segodnia*, 8 February 1994.

52   *Komsomol'skaia pravda*, 17 May 1994, p. 3.

53   In fact, *Eshche* did publish several articles by or about queers, including excerpts from the writing of Evgenii Kharitonov and articles by gay journalist Yaroslav Mogutin.

54   The sentiment was shared, at least at the time, by major queer voices, including P. Masal'skii, Y. Mogutin, and E. Debrianskaia. I heard it almost every time I had a conversation with a queer in Moscow during February. Interestingly enough, members of my decidedly straight Russian family also shared their suspicions that *Eshche* was singled out of all the other erotic publications because of its queer-friendly orientation.

55   Emphasis added. From a draft of a report by Masha Gessen, "Double Jeopardy:

Homophobic Attacks on the Press around the World Since 1990" (New York: Committee to Protect Journalists, 1995), p. 2.

56   "Rossiskoi ugolovnoi kodeks."

57   *Esche*, no. 4/16.

58   "The Dirty Peckers of Komsomol Members: Boris Moiseev about Himself and the Past" (in Russian), *Eshche*, no. 4/16.

59   Published under the heading "Bizarre Station" with the subheading "Sound Tracks" "Gay Thunder is Rumbling under the Pop Scene and Its Name is Boris Moiseev" (in Russian), *Moskovskii komsomolets*, 11 August 1993, p. 4.

60   Gessen, "Double Jeopardy," p. 37.

61   Interview with Mogutin, March 1994.

62   Actually, the interview contained in "Dirty Peckers" was originally published in the erotic weekly *Eshche*, no. 4/16.

63   The *Kuranty* article was entitled "Caught in the Act of Hooliganism," thereby apparently implying that the author felt the prosecutor was correct to charge Mogutin and his editor under Article 206.2, a fact which did not endear the author to Mogutin. Mogutin responded with an article in *Novyi vzgliad*, no. 38 (1993), p. 3, entitled "Dirty Peckers: The Second Duel" (in Russian). In this article, Mogutin derides not only *Kuranty*'s seeming alliance with the prosecutor by pointing out that the "foul language" was not his, but Moiseev's, and was marked in the article as quotations. He also points out that the article was originally published in *Esche* and then later published in *Moskovskii komsomolets*, but it was only *Novyi vzgliad* that was being charged. Furthermore, Mogutin sarcastically asks how the *Kuranty* author (to whom he refers as a "journalist-ka", a grammatically correct but certainly pejorative female diminutive ending for journalist) could possibly tell that the naked men in the pictures were in fact gay.

64   My translation. Author's copy of letter sent by the Russian PEN Center to the Prosecutor's Office of the Krasnopresnenski region of Moscow on 9 November 1993.

65   The article contained a highly taboo form of cursing in Russian known as *mat*. *Mat* is never, ever spoken in public, nor is it considered acceptable for women or the intelligentsia to speak in *mat*.

66   Interview with Y. Mogutin, March 1994.

67   A telephone interview with R. Fillipini, Mogutin's partner, in October 1994 revealed that the case had been dropped. Correspondence in February 1995 with Mogutin indicated that although the case had been dropped, it had been turned over to the federal prosecutor for the possibility of reopening it. In the meantime, Mogutin was allowed to obtain a foreign passport and could, ostensibly, escape Moscow in the event that his case was pursued further.

68   Field notes, April 1994. For a more detailed account of Mogutin's paralegal prosecution, see Masha Gessen's *Dead Again: The Russian Intelligentsia after Communism* (London: Verso, 1997), pp. 195–97. Gessen also discusses Mogutin's attempted marriage to his American boyfriend (see below).

69   A legal system actively prosecuted Mogutin for publicly revealing transgressive

desires. Surely in Moscow, where pornography is now sold on every corner and pornographic images crop up on everything from grocery bags to air fresheners, public sexual desires are no longer criminal, nor is exploiting those desires for profit. What continues to be criminal is desiring queerly.

70   The idea of marginal conflicts is indebted to Gayle Rubin's work on the emergence of S/M communities in the United States. In Rubin's view, "The sexual system is not a monolithic, omnipotent structure. . . . In addition to definitional and legal wars, there are less obvious forms of sexual political conflict which I call the territorial and border wars." "Thinking Sex: Notes for a Radical Theory of the Politics of Sexuality," in Carole S. Vance, ed., *Pleasure and Danger: Exploring Female Sexuality* (Boston: Routledge & Kegan Paul, 1984), p. 294.

71   De Certeau describes the power of the subject/ed: "Without leaving the place where he has no choice but to live and which lays down its law for him, he establishes within it a degree of *plurality* and creativity. By an art of being in between, he draws unexpected results from his situation." " 'Making Do': Uses and Tactics," in Michel de Certeau, *The Practice of Everyday Life*, trans. Steven Rendall (Berkeley: University of California Press, 1984), p. 30.

72   Indeed, the same journalist who was simultaneously "subjected" to the law against "criminal hooliganism."

73   Interview with Mogutin and Fillipini, March 1994. Filippini actually said "anything queer in the press is good no matter how it's perceived because it's a public forum." Mogutin added that the number of new stories written about the event will set a precedent in the law, since anything that is not disallowed is allowed.

74   Interview with Mogutin and Fillipini, March 1994.

75   Phone conversation with Filippini, April 1994.

76   Number 4 is the only palace that serves foreign citizens marrying Russians, although this was undoubtedly their most foreign affair.

77   Interestingly enough, both *Inostranets* and *Komsomol'skaia pravda* described the black leather of the groom. *Inostranets*, 13 April 1994; *Komsomol'skaia pravda*, 16 April 1994.

78   Field notes, 12 April 1994.

79   A *dezhurnaia* is a decidedly Soviet being, a woman, usually older, who watches over everything from museums to hotels for foreigners. To use *dezhurnaia* as an adjective is always pejorative since they are known for their rudeness, stupidity, spying, and not being very attractive—thus a *dezhurnaia*-like smile implies the government stooge aspects of the job/vocation. Stepan Builo, "The Setting Right of Russian-American Relations is Delayed" (in Russian), *Segodnia*, 13 April 1994.

80   *Komsomol'skaia pravda*, 15–18 April 1994.

81   Interview with Masel'skii, August 1994. Despite the fact that the group has been turned down twice for official registration, some members of the group were convinced the problem was the term "All-Russian" in the group's name. The group was going to try to register as a Moscow-based group, rather than claim a national status, which they were unable to substantiate. Unfortunately, the group folded before they actually attempted to register under the new name.

82   I am not claiming that oppression necessarily or even ever creates subjectivity.

This is in direct contrast to some historians of homosexuality in the United States who have assumed that it was the juridicomedical complex's harassment of lesbians and gays in the 1950s and 60s which politicized the movement. For instance, John D'Emilio claims that "the oppression of lesbians and gay men was the force that propelled the movement into existence." See John D'Emilio's "Capitalism and Gay Identity," in Ann Snitow, Christine Stansell, and Sharon Thompson, eds., *Powers of Desire: The Politics of Sexuality* (New York: Monthly Review Press, 1983), pp. 107–8. To the contrary, oppressive regimes make resistance necessary, but they do not necessarily bring resistance into being nor crystallize that resistance into a sense of self.

83   Such state intervention occurred in November of 1993 when several of Moscow's Special Forces (OMON) descended on the city's first gay bar, the Underground. The bar, which is relatively small, was occupied by twenty troops, dressed in combat uniforms and equipped with semiautomatic weapons, who searched the bar's customers and employees. The "reason" for the search was the murder of a U.S. citizen "known" to have been gay. It is a significant sign that the law "knows" (read: uses surveillance on) the sexual practices of some, and that a murder of a "known" homosexual would necessarily be connected to the victim's sexual practices, and that these practices could be translated into the more specific (and smaller) location of a queer community (i.e., the bar). *Kuranty,* 19 November 1993, p. 3.

84   I myself often encountered the law as "indifference to the point of hostility." For instance, a Moscow gay disco (MELS) was notorious for being dangerous for its clientele. Several times a night large bands of *remontniki* (literally "fixers") would descend on groups of people who were often too afraid to report the robberies and beatings to the police (i.e., because of fear of being outed to their family or employers). Even when larger numbers of police were posted at the nearby metro station, the police often chose to ignore the violence. According to one victim of such an attack, she went to the police inside the disco and insisted that they write up a report and arrest the attackers, but the police refused to do either and instead suggested that no one leave the disco until the next morning.

85   "Foucault points out that juridical systems of power *produce* the subjects they subsequently come to represent." Judith Butler, *Gender Trouble: Feminism and the Subversion of Identity* (New York: Routledge, 1990), p. 2. This is the productive sense of power which Foucault was exploring in *The History of Sexuality,* vol. 1, *An Introduction* (New York: Vintage Books, 1978), as well as in *Discipline and Punish: The Birth of the Prison* (New York: Vintage, 1977).

86   For example, see I. Shchadin, "About the Qualifications of Sexual Crimes" (in Russian), *Zakonnost',* 1994, no. 12, pp. 30–32. Shchadin says that *muzhelozhstvo* "is understood to be an unnatural sexual act . . . accomplished by means of the penis entering into the anus." Other forms of sexual relations between two men do not constitute *muzhelozhstvo.*

87   Gessen tells the story of how the law against male-male sexual contacts helped her to understand that she too was a homosexual. According to Gessen, as a young

child she discovered a copy of the legal code in her home. The code had been torn in half and the first page was now Article 121. As soon as she read the code against "men lying together," Gessen understood that she was the same as those men. Although an unusually literal case of the law shaping lesbian identities, Gessen may not be the only woman to identify herself in the illegal acts of others.

88 Several years ago, an interview with a doctor of juridical science was published in a Moscow daily. The doctor offered the opinion that prison is much more difficult for women, in part because women are more concerned with emotional connections than are men. The doctor continued: "In women's colonies, there are 'familial pairs.' This is complicated not only physiologically[!], but it's a morally complicated process for them as well. We shouldn't close our eyes to these sorts of relationships since up to 40% of sentenced women participate in them." Viktor Loshak, "Personality behind the Wire" (in Russian), *Moskovskie novosti*, no. 38 (8 September 1988), p. 11.

89 Consider L: "I was young and very naive, stupid. . . . She was older and had grown up in youth camps so she knew all about these things. She was an *aktivnaia*, so I thought I was *pasivnaia*, but then I realized I'm an *aktivnaia* lesbian." Or B: "In youth camp [Internat] I was very popular with my age mates. But at night we all slept together and the older girls would take turns coming to my bed at night."

90 Olga Zhuk, "The Lesbian Subculture: The Historical Roots of Lesbianism in the Former USSR" (in Russian), *Gay, Slaviane!*, no. 1 (1993), p. 18.

2 THE EXPERT GAZE 2: THE CURE

The epigraph is taken from Ippolit Tarnovskii, *Izvrashchenie polovogo chuvstva u zhenshchin* (St. Petersburg: Tipografiia S. N. Khudekova, 1895), as excerpted in Laura Engelstein, "Lesbian Vignettes: A Russian Triptych from the 1890s," *Signs* 15, no. 4 (1990), p. 824.

1 Mention of female homosexuality was extremely rare. Moreover, there was an "unwillingness of nineteenth-century Russian physicians to stigmatize sexual perversion as socially marginal and organically pathological." Ibid., p. 817.

2 Engelstein, *The Keys to Happiness: Sex and the Search for Modernity in Fin-de-Siècle Russia* (Ithaca, N.Y.: Cornell University Press, 1992), pp. 155–57, 162.

3 The Western writers most often cited in Russian writings about sexual deviance include Richard von Krafft-Ebing, Havelock Ellis, and Magnus Hirschfeld. For a fuller list, see Engelstein, "Lesbian Vignettes," p. 814.

4 I chose to look more closely at Weininger because he is the pre-Soviet theorist from the West that I have heard mentioned most often by queers in Russia today. Many queer intellectuals told me that Weininger's work was important to their own understanding and compared it favorably to Rozanov (see note 10 below). It is also worth noting that although the book was highly criticized in Russia for its misogyny, its anti-Semitism received scant notice. Engelstein, *The Keys to Happiness*.

5 Ibid., pp. 293, 301–2, 310–11.

6   According to Weininger, "[maleness and femaleness] are distributed in the living world in every possible proportion." Otto Weininger, *Sex and Character* (New York: AMS Press, 1975), p. 26.

7   Aleksander Etkind, *Eros of the Impossible: A History of Psychoanalysis in Russian* (in Russian) (Moscow: Gnozis, 1994), p. 44.

8   Published in 1899, *People of the Moonlight* [Liudi lunnogo sveta] maintains a certain poetic resonance in Russian as a synonym for queers. V. V. Rozanov, *People of the Moonlight: The Metaphysics of Christianity* (in Russian) (Moscow: Druzhba naradov, 1990).

9   Etkind, p. 45.

10   Rozanov believed that homosexuals (sodomites) are a different species than heterosexuals. "Sodomites" find heterosexual unions and their childbearing functions as unpalatable as "normal" people find sodomy. Not only are "sodomites" different in thought and deed, they are physiologically different from normal people: "The eye of a sodomite is different. . . . Their smile is completely different." Rozanov, pp. 73–74.

11   The medicopsychiatric complex's search for a cure is not unique to Russia. In the United States, although the American Psychiatric Association (APA) removed homosexuality from its list of psychiatric disorders in 1974 (John D'Emilio and Estelle B. Freedman, *Intimate Matters: A History of Sexuality in America* [New York: Harper & Row, 1988], p. 324), not all of its members followed suit. For instance, the National Association for Research and Therapy of Homosexuality and its leader, Dr. Charles W. Socarides, continue to search for the Cure (as cited in David W. Dunlap, "Shameless Homophobia and the 'Jenny Jones' Murder," *New York Times*, 18 March 1995, p. 16). The "healing" professions have either continued to pathologize or ignore entirely other forms of queerness. For instance, transsexualism was not even considered by the APA until 1980. Once it was considered, it was considered a "clinical condition" in need of heroic intervention (e.g., therapy, surgery). For instance, see Leslie Martin Lothstein, *Female-to-Male Transsexualism: Historical, Clinical and Theoretical Issues* (Boston: Routledge & Kegan Paul, 1984), pp. 4–5.

12   The statement of the AIDS specialist quoted in the epigraph to this section was made during the U.S./Soviet Women's Summit in May of 1990. Much to the dismay of her interpreter, the doctor insisted on making this statement even after she was asked if she had properly understood the question (author's conversation with interpreter, Susan Heuman, March 1995). The doctor stated privately the next day that she referred to a sex change operation since as she understood lesbians, they were actually men who happened to have the bodies of women (author's conversation with doctor, May 1990).

13   Of course, many men became the objects of medical and psychiatric interventions. But since men could be sent to prison for engaging in homosexual acts, that is, since they were accountable for those acts, they were not the most obvious candidates for "curing." The gender implications of the differing expert gazes will be taken up throughout the rest of this chapter.

14   Masha Gessen, *The Rights of Lesbians and Gay Men in the Russian Federation* (San Francisco: IGLHRC, 1993), p. 17.

15   In my research, most of the women-oriented women were or are married to men. Sometimes this is for uniquely Soviet reasons, like the impossibility of getting an apartment without being married. Sometimes it is part of a "closet," a closing off of one's sexuality from the public's prying eyes. These relationships tend not to be sexual. At other times, it stems from a desire to have children. I have met several women who married and had children while simultaneously maintaining a relationship with another woman (with and without their husbands' knowledge). Even the most "out" activists, such as E. Debrianskaia and M. Gessen, are or have been married to men. One of the interesting things about these marriages is that they are rarely, if ever, just marriages of convenience. Most of the women consider their relationships with their husbands to be important.

16   A told me that the KGB wanted her to report on all her contacts with foreigners. If she did not, she could have her only child taken away from her. "What choice did I have? Of course I reported to them." Field notes, Leningrad, 1989. N told me that some boys from the local police department in her town in Siberia had raped her and her girlfriend. They told her she could not make a complaint to their bosses because if they did, they'd be thrown in the "crazyhouse." Field notes, 1991.

17   Author's interviews with eight women from 1989 to 1994. Also see Gessen, p. 18.

18   Gessen, pp. 52–53. Also, Igor Kon, "Sexual Minorities," in Igor Kon and James Riordan, *Sex and Russian Society* (Bloomington: Indiana University Press, 1993), pp. 93–94.

19   In 1994 I met two young women who had recently been released from psychiatric hospitals. Both had been committed against their will for same-sex relationships.

20   If men are in fact no longer pursued for same-sex attraction by the law, they will undoubtedly come under increasing pressure for medicopsychiatric treatment.

21   A comprehensive review would be nearly impossible, since professional publications about sexuality are only available within the particular institutes in which they are written (interviews with D. Isaev and I. Kon). The decentralized location of materials, the lack of infrastructure supports such as computer-accessible listings of holdings and interlibrary loans, and the general user-unfriendly nature of doing research in Russian libraries made such a review too time-consuming for this project.

22   More exactly, these were various "experts" whose names were often mentioned during the course of my research as important influences in helping queers understand their sexuality better.

23   At least three of the handful of experts most popular among queers in Russia are rumored to be gay themselves, but they all insist that they are heterosexual.

24   Interview with G, 1994 (unless otherwise specified, all interviews are by the author). Of course, if homosexuals are not mentally ill, then presumably they do not warrant research by an expert on mental illnesses.

25   Interview with M, 1994. Although this particular expert is rumored to be gay and

openly admits that he is not a "masculine" man, he insists that he does not have relationships with men. Two of his male patients told me that they were in therapy with this psychiatrist who had admitted to them that he had homoerotic fantasies (April 1994), and another gay man insists he slept with this doctor. The doctor, however, maintains his objectifying stance, always speaking in the third person about "those people."

26 David Tuller's interview with D. Isaev, 1991. This interview was unpublished and given to author by Tuller in 1994.

27 Interview with Isaev, August 1994.

28 Interview with Kon, July 1994.

29 Again, I'm considering those experts known to groups of sexual minorities with whom I had contact in Moscow and St. Petersburg.

30 Of course, the source of these percentages is unclear. Isaev and his colleagues conducted a telephone survey of 435 randomly chosen persons in St. Petersburg. The respondents were asked if they had ever had homosexual encounters—about 3 percent of the men admitted to such encounters and 2 percent of the women. But these numbers do not reflect self-identified homosexuals (since no one described him/herself as homosexual) nor can it be assumed that most respondents answered truthfully. This is especially the case in Russia, where it is not "acceptable" (priniato) to discuss homosexuality and phones have often been tapped by an ever vigilant state. Author's interview, August 1994. Even less clear is why Isaev traces these percentages to "ancient" times. After all, classical Athens, which teemed with male-male relationships both in the form of prostitution and in the form of man-boy citizen bonds, surely had a higher percentage of "homosexuals," if there was such a person at all, than contemporary Russia or the United States. See David M. Halperin, "The Democratic Body: Prostitution and Citizenship in Classical Athens," *Differences* 2 (Spring 1990), pp. 1–28.

31 D. D. Isaev, "Psychosomatic Relationships in the Etiology of Homosexuality" (in Russian), 1989 (unpublished manuscript, copy given to author by Isaev, 1994).

32 It is interesting to note that Isaev allows many persons to engage in same-sex contact without being labeled homosexual. For instance, anonymous contact in a bathhouse would not threaten one's heterosexual status. Nor does same-sex contact in a same-sex environment, such as a prison or workers' dormitory. Isaev elaborates this point in another article when he and his coauthors say that homosexuality in prison "has nothing in common with homosexuality as a sexual orientation to persons of the same sex." A. D. Borokhov, D. D. Isaev, A. V. Stoliarov, "Sociopsychological Factors of Homosexual Behavior among Prisoners" (in Russian), *Sotsiologicheskie issledovaniia*, no. 6 (1990), p. 94. But if persons in prison are exempt from being labeled queer, perhaps persons in society should be exempted from being labeled straight? After all, in a society with "compulsory heterosexuality," being queer is not necessarily any more of an option than being straight is in prison.

33 This is from a slightly reworked English version of Isaev's unpublished manu-

script "Psychosomatic Relationships in the Etiology of Homosexuality." The article is entitled "Homosexuality and Its Etiologic Models," *Bekhterev Review of Psychiatry and Medical Psychology* 2 (1991), pp. 39–40.

34   Ibid., p. 40. Clearly Isaev is relying on a system of rigid gender differentiation to show the biological roots of homosexuality. He also assumes that gender transgressions are often, if not always, the same as transgressions of heterosexuality. Even more remarkably, he makes "maleness" visible in women by "high levels of intelligence."

35   Note that Isaev pathologizes "secondary" homosexuality in men, but allows women an "out"—which relies on that old but oft cited bit of folk wisdom that lesbians just haven't met the right man yet. Ibid., p. 41.

36   Isaev, "Psychosomatic Relations in the Etiology of Homosexuality."

37   Isaev, "Homosexuality and Its Etiologic Models," p. 41.

38   Special person, *liubimyi chelovek*, sometimes denotes a lover in Russian, but may also just signify a romantic but not necessarily sexual relationship.

39   Interview by David Tuller with Isaev, 1991.

40   D. Isaev, "Particularities of Sexual Identification and Psychological Orientation among Persons with Homosexual Orientations/Attractions," unpublished paper, V. M. Bekhterev Psychoneurological Institute, St. Petersburg, Russia.

41   Isaev's theory is mirrored in the research done by Aleksei Andreev in Rostov during the 1980s. According to Andreev, there are homosexuals who have a hormonal abnormality (i.e., primary homosexuality) and then there are those who are "unsure" of their sexuality (i.e., secondary homosexuality). The latter group might become heterosexual, or, if "recruited," might become homosexual. See Robert Cullen's *Citizen X* (New York: Ivy Books, 1993) for a journalistic description of Andreev's work, pp. 102–3.

42   In fact, "primary" homosexuals saw themselves as like women at a ratio of 3 to 1, while "secondary" homosexuals identified this way at a ratio of 3 to 7. Isaev, p. 4.

43   Ibid., pp. 4–9.

44   Unpublished interview conducted by David Tuller (May 1995) who attended the MiR meetings during a research trip to Moscow in 1991. According to Igor Kon, eighty people met weekly at MiR in 1991–92. Kon, p. 109.

45   As evidenced by the fact that when regularly occurring gay discos and meeting places appeared in Moscow, MiR and its meetings were no longer of interest to most people.

46   The actual phrase the sexologist uses here is *neustoichivost' polovoi roli*, which could also mean "instability of *sexual* role" since *pol* means "sex" (as in male or female), but this is also considered to imply "gender" (as in masculine or feminine). Unpublished interview conducted by David Tuller with a sexologist from MiR, 1991, pp. 4–5. Manuscript of interview was given to author in 1994.

47   Ibid., pp. 2–3, 5.

48   Ibid., pp. 7–8.

49   It is unclear whether it is completely a result of social prejudices since "[t]here are

those people who as a form of sport seduce naturals [heterosexuals], lead them to homosexual contacts." Ibid., p. 28.

50   Ibid., pp. 25–27.

51   Ibid., p. 9.

52   In the United States, transsexualism works somewhat differently than in Russia/the former Soviet Union. As in Russia, success is measured by heterosexuality. One of the top specialists in transsexualism, Dr. Stanley Biber, points out that his operations are quite successful since a large percentage of "these folks go on to get married and adopt children." But in the United States, the "change" is more literal—a literal resculpting of the human body, of sex, is required in order to officially change sex (despite the fact that the operation is misnamed "gender reassignment surgery" in English). In Russia, on the other hand, the successful enactment of the other gender is sufficient to change "sex" (regardless of contradictory embodiments). Of course, another major difference is that, in the United States, far more sex change operations are performed on male bodies than female ones. In part, this may be due to the cost differentials between male-to-female ($10,000) and female-to-male ($30,000) operations. See Elizabeth Cohen, "Biber-people," *OUT*, May 1995, pp. 87–90.

53   Interviews with Isaev and MiR sexologist. It is not clear who initiates the treatment, the expert or the patient. Isaev insists that he himself has never advised someone to have a sex change operation. In fact, in his view, lesbians who cannot accept their sexuality read articles about transsexualism and therefore begin to identify as men (unpublished interview with Isaev by David Tuller). This, however, does not explain how operations were performed since at least the early 1970s, well before any articles were published in the press about such things (interview by David Tuller with MiR sexologists). I have been told by three women who identify as "transsexuals" that they didn't know what they were until they ended up in a psychiatric hospital and were told by medicopsychiatric experts that they were transsexuals. In two of the three cases, the women expressed relief that they were not lesbians. On the other hand, I have met women who read about transsexualism in the press and then began to identify that way.

54   Unpublished interview with Isaev conducted by Tuller, p. 10. "*Delo v tom, shto chast' gomoseksualov sostavliaiut takie vot miagkie formy transseksyalov.*"

55   Ibid., p. 11.

56   Unpublished interview with Isaev conducted by Tuller, 1991.

57   Isaev actually feels that transsexualism is not about sexual behavior, but sexual identity (*pol'ovaia*). Although most women have the operation because of the urging of a partner, Isaev still believes they would never be able to live as lesbians nor would they ever find sexual satisfaction in their own bodies. Isaev also feels that because he only ever gives permission, never the advice to have a sex change operation, he is in fact doing the best he can for the women. He is however more careful about giving such permission to men, since men often change their mind in a few years and are able to live as gay men. Author's interview with Isaev, Au-

gust 1994. It is interesting that in published accounts, Isaev does not say that the women were lesbians, but instead insists they were transsexuals. In an interview reported in *A i F Peterburg*, Isaev says, "An operation is only necessary in the case where a conflict with one's own body is unresolved. When [the body] is so disgusting that a person does not allow himself to be touched, is embarrassed to undress even in front of his lover. . . . Thus I don't give permission for the operation to about half of my patients." In "When I Was a Woman . . ." (in Russian), *A i F Peterburg*, no. 25 (1994), p. 3.

58 Ibid., pp. 10–11.

59 Tuller interview with MiR sexologist, p. 13.

60 Ibid., pp. 13–14.

61 Low-level transsexuals are in fact "feminine homosexuals" according to this system. Ibid., pp. 13, 15.

62 Author's interview with Isaev, August 1994.

63 Tuller interview with MiR sexologist, pp. 16–17. Another theory offered by the doctor from MiR is that "in this society the male role is much more prestigious," p. 14.

64 *Diagnostic and Statistical Manual of Mental Disorders*, 4th ed. (Washington, D.C.: American Psychiatric Association, 1994), pp. 536–37. Of course, the more "advanced" American experts no longer list homosexuality as a disorder, although other sexual hierarchies are in place. For instance, sexual desires structured around cross-dressing or power exchanges (i.e., sadism/masochism) are still pathologized.

65 The sexologists from MiR even go so far as to suggest that there are "biological roots" to the "dogmatic" thinking of transsexuals; these "roots" are their low "intellect" and emotional development. Tuller interview with MiR, p. 14.

66 The tendency of those identified as gays and lesbians to distance themselves from other sexual "deviants" is highly pronounced in the United States. For instance, lesbian feminists often want to separate themselves not only from "perverts," such as transsexuals, fetishists, and pedophiles but also from homosexual men as well. Instead, they ally themselves with all women (except, presumably, those who were also "perverse"). For example, see Alice, Gordon, Debbie, and Mary, "Problems of Our Movement," in Sarah Lucia Hoagland, *For Lesbians Only: A Separatist Anthology* (London: Onlywomen Press, 1988), p. 392. Even scholars of gay/lesbian history mark their self-separation from sexual deviance by ignoring all other forms of queerness. Consider how a 428-page history of sexuality doesn't list transsexualism in its index (although it does include cross-dressing, which apparently does not cross the line between acceptable and unacceptable deviance): John D'Emilio and Estelle B. Freedman, *Intimate Matters: A History of Sexuality in America* (New York: Harper & Row, 1988). This tendency also appears among gay/lesbian activists in Russia. For instance, Kukharskii, the founder/president of Krylia, told me that his organization does not use the term "sexual minority" because it includes pederasts, zoophiles, and other perverts. Of course, since this is Russia, transsexualism is not on the list of unacceptable sociosexual practices. Thus some members of Krylia do identify as transsexuals.

67 "Sexual hierarchies" is an idea Gayle Rubin explores in her "Thinking Sex: Notes

for a Progressive Theory of the Politics of Sexuality," in Carole S. Vance, ed., *Plea-sure and Danger: Exploring Female Sexuality* (Boston: Routledge & Kegan Paul, 1984). The part transsexualism has historically played in sexual hierarchies as well as its role as a particular, but not unique, site of gender/sexuality is taken up by Sandy Stone in "The Empire Strikes Back: A Posttranssexual Manifesto," in Julia Epstein and Kristina Straub, eds., *Body Guards: The Cultural Politics of Gender Ambiguity* (New York: Routledge, 1991).

68   I have changed the names and some of the biographical details of all the transsexu-als in hopes of maintaining the anonymity of the speakers. In the case of Roma, a single story is actually a composite of several persons. One of the Romas was inter-viewed not by myself, but by David Tuller in 1991. In the past four years I have inter-viewed around ten women who identify as "transsexuals." I have met many more.

69   This story was cited several times by both "transsexuals" and "experts" as an im-portant catalyst for women becoming transsexuals.

70   What is known as "stone butch" in English.

71   The organization is discussed in chapter 3, "Identity Politics and the Politics of Identity."

72   The biographical details from this section are primarily from a series of unpub-lished interviews done by D. Tuller with a female-to-male transsexual in 1991.

73   Misha's first sexual experience with another woman came at the age of twelve. Around the same time a male friend had tried to have sex with Misha, but Misha found it "revolting." Misha had always desired the attention of girls—girls who thought of him as a boy. When Misha was six, he noticed two very pretty girls riding horses. "They were wearing mini-skirts and they had very beautiful legs and I was very attracted to them. I tried to trip them and they said to me 'Boy, why are you acting like a hooligan'—and I was so happy that they called me a boy."

74   Not only did Misha lose his wife, but he also lost his apartment, since the wife's mother was officially registered there with her daughter. In other words, the gov-ernment continues to allot insufficient housing even to those who are officially recognized as "family." Since Misha was not officially a man, he and his wife could not register in the apartment as "man and wife." This detail offers a glimpse into the myriad reasons why a woman who desires women would prefer being a man.

75   In some ways, Misha may have been referring to finding a woman who would treat him like a man. Misha's wife never let him perform household tasks such as vacu-uming and washing dishes. She would remind him that "a man shouldn't do such things."

76   It was not just the operation that offered Misha comfort after his wife's death. He also found comfort in his new identity as a transsexual (previously he had identi-fied as a man). Misha met a male-to-female transsexual who brought him into a group of other transsexuals associated with the organization Krylia. "I came here [to Krylia] and saw that there were people just like me. I thought: God, why do I torture myself so? Here are people with the exact same problems as myself. They can understand me. . . . I decided that I can save people from loneliness with the written word, by writing them answers."

77   The details of Roma's life are mostly based on personal acquaintances, although a few are added from unpublished interviews conducted by Tuller.

78   When asked whether she considered Roma a man or a woman, Ira answered: "To me he is a man—he couldn't be a woman. I am not a lesbian." Roma adds, "I'm not a lesbian either."

79   According to John, an American medical student interning at a psychiatric hospital in Moscow in 1994, it is still common practice for severely "schizophrenic" patients to be put into a diabetic coma as a means of curing them. The patients are kept in the coma for up to two weeks. Interview with student, spring 1994.

80   It is interesting to note that the doctor apparently referred to Roma as "he."

81   As opposed to the United States, where transsexual activists and communities, like the one on the Internet, are creating public space for permanent identities.

82   Interview with Kevin Gardner, September 1994.

83   Ezop o SPIDe, (Moscow: Wellcome Foundation, Tsentr EZOP, Gazeta 1/10), 1993. Another Moscow AIDS organization, AIDS Infoshare, is privately funded and thus less susceptible to state intervention. At the same time, the organization is mostly staffed by persons who identify as "straight." An informational bulletin put out by Infoshare, R.A.R. Info, also mentions, "This disease affects us all." R.A.R. Info, no. 1, 1994 (bulletin pages not numbered, on the eleventh page). The bulletin also does not seem to be aimed at a queer audience. It mentions no organizations of sexual minorities in a list of AIDS organizations and states that it is for "everyone interested in the problems connected to AIDS."

84   It is unclear whether homosexuals are a separate category all together or are assumed to be those who are promiscuous and have a venereal disease. "Instructions for the Procedure of Inspection of Donors and the Population for AIDS and the Conduct of Sanitarium Surveillance for Persons Infected with the Human Immune-Deficiency Virus" (in Russian) (Moskva: Ministerstvo zdravookhraneniia SSSR, 1987), pp. 1–2.

85   David Ljunggren, "Russian Parliament Approves Amended AIDS Law," Reuters World Service, 24 February 1995.

86   Field notes from press conference, June 10, 1994. Bella Denisenko, head of the Duma's health committee, also noted that contact with a foreigner is "100 times more dangerous than with a Russian," as cited in Anna Husarska, "Repression of Homosexuals Still Rules in Russia," Ottawa Citizen, 14 January 1995, p. B4.

87   Field notes from press conference. Also see Husarska.

88   Field notes from press conference.

89   Ibid.

90   In a newsletter of the Moscow Library of Lesbians and Gays, V. Oboin points out that the connection between homosexuality and criminality is all too evident in the press, which portrays homosexuals as "monsters who abduct children." Zerkalo, no. 1 (1995), p. 1.

91   Cullen, p. 106.

92   Ibid., pp. 106–7, 114.

93   Tat'iana Bystrova, "Chikatilo and Company" (in Russian), *Trud*, no. 201, 29 October 1994, p. 2.

94   Oleg Karmaza. "Sexual Maniacs for Some Reason Always Have Long Hands" (in Russian), *Komosomol'skaia pravda*, no. 179, 6 October 1994, p. 2.

95   Arkadii Sosnov, "Dissertation Helped to Catch a Maniac" (in Russian), *Moskovskie novosti*, 4–11 December 1994, p. 5.

96   Oleg Karmaza, "Bloodsucker" (in Russian), *Komsomol'skaia pravda*, 19 September 1994. It was not just homosexuality that signalled Azimov's perversity. The article concludes with the fact that Azimov carried a copy of Karl Marx's *Das Kapital* with him while fleeing the authorities on bicycle. In post-Communist Russia, such reading habits are read as symptomatic of serious illness.

97   Vadim Serebriakov, "Sexual Maniac? No, Just a Drinking Buddy," *Tsentr Plus*, 15 August 1994, p. 6. Note that the violent act of murdering someone by anally raping him is printable, but the word faggot is not.

3   IDENTITY POLITICS AND THE POLITICS OF IDENTITY

1   Kathy E. Ferguson devotes a chapter to "mobile subjectivities" in *The Man Question: Visions of Subjectivity in Feminist Theory* (Berkeley: University of California Press, 1993). Despite claims to a true self, we know that the identities we inhabit are never fully our own. There is always the danger of not "being" a "real" man, a "real" African American, a "real" lesbian. Identities are tightly scripted and sometimes we are unable or unwilling to perform. In this sense, identities "happen to us, positions through which we move and which move through us and each other." Ferguson, p. 169.

2   Of course, there were some officially sanctioned identities—such as being a party member.

3   I was personally associated with some of the members of the *Gruppa doveriia*, a Moscow-based peace group, as well as an underground feminist group that produced the samizdat feminist journal *Zhenskoe chtenie*. A good source on these and other groups is Helsinki Watch, *From Below: Independent Peace and Environmental Movements in Eastern Europe and the USSR* (New York: Helsinki Watch, 1987).

4   I am not suggesting that it is political failure per se that created the possibility for identity politics. Surely there are a variety of conditions—economic, social, discursive, and even individual—that are necessary to propel a taxonomy like sexuality into a source of self and social action. John D'Emilio has outlined many of the economic conditions upon which a gay/lesbian identity was built. See D'Emilio, "Capitalism and Gay Identity," in Ann Snitow, Christine Stansell, and Sharon Thompson, eds., *Powers of Desire: The Politics of Sexuality* (New York: Monthly Review Press, 1983). More recently, George Chauncey has given us a history of the rich cultural traditions that existed in the first half of the century, traditions upon which any later movements surely were built: *Gay New York: Gender, Urban Culture, and*

the Making of the Gay Male World, 1890–1940 (New York: Basic Books, 1994). I would argue, however, that the breakup of the Soviet Union created space—political, public, ethical—that allowed previously invisible subjectivities to take up a place in the public sphere. This is similar to Harrison White's formulation of identity creation as occurring when a preexisting identity breaks down. See White, *Action and Organization: Identity as Control in Social Networks* (Princeton: Princeton University Press, 1991).

5   For more on the historical moment when identity and identity politics seemed to be the future of Russia, see Judith B. Sedaitis and Jim Butterfield, eds., *Perestroika from Below: Social Movements in the Soviet Union* (Boulder, Colo.: Westview Press, 1991).

6   In June, 1969, a gay bar in Greenwich Village, the Stonewall Inn, became the site of a battle between queers and the police. The Stonewall Riots were, at least to many queer scholars and activists, a "watershed event in the lives of millions of American lesbians and gay men. Beginning with Stonewall, an isolated and stig-matized group of individuals transformed themselves into a vital and influential movement." Andrea Weiss and Greta Schiller, *Before Stonewall: The Making of Gay and Lesbian Community* (Tallahassee, Fl.: Naiad Press, 1988), p. 6.

7   A series of seminars and public demonstrations was even coined "Soviet Stone-wall." For more on this event, see below.

8   For instance, two Russian women told a Western reporter how they were lovers wrenched apart by family and society. As a modern day Juliet and Juliet, they were very touching. The only problem was, none of it was true. When asked why they lied, they pointed out that Westerners would want to hear that Russian queers were oppressed and needed to be saved. Of course, the women were probably cor-rect in their assessment of what was wanted from them.

9   As one American activist who has worked for years in Moscow told me: "There is a gay movement here. Of course, it may be a bowel movement, but it's a move-ment." One of many pithy insights into queer politics in Moscow made to the author by AIDS activist Kevin Gardner.

10 As was pointed out in chapter 2, marriage is not easily ignored when employment and housing are still contingent upon it.

11 See chapter 2.

12 Introduction by one of the journal's editors, Tat'yana Mamonova, to the English-language *Women and Russia: Feminist Writings from the Soviet Union*, ed. Tat'yana Mamonova (Boston: Beacon Press, 1984), p. xiii.

13 The sort of essentializing move that Mamonova makes in her claim that all women "give life" and are nonviolent does not allow for women who do not give life and advocate violence. These women fall into the liminal space of not "real" women (and not "real" men). A good critique of this sort of feminism can be found in Ferguson, p. 81.

14 The essay's author argues that the position of homosexuals is no different from the position of other dissidents, "those who think otherwise," since "the same methods of suppression used against dissidents are used against lesbians." An-

other essay in the same volume, "Mistress of the High Mountain" by Lyubov Razu-movskaya, tells the story of a young girl from the Urals who finds herself in love with a Leningrad actress. Eventually the young woman finds herself in Leningrad and even manages to meet the actress a few times. Although the relationship is never sexual, the sexual component of the attraction is clear, as is the immuta-bility of homosexual desires, evidenced by the fact that the author's "attraction" dates from her childhood. *Women and Russia*, p. 144.

15   Mamonova, *Women and Russia*, p. xv.

16   Ibid., p. ix. As well as private conversations with Mamonova in the spring of 1989.

17   Interview with Aleksandr Zaremba, August 1994.

18   This is according to Gay Laboratory member Sergei P. Shcherbakov's article "On the Relationship between the Leningrad Gay Community and the Legal Authori-ties in the 1970's and 1980's," in Udo Parikas and Teet Veispak, eds., *Sexual Minori-ties and Society: The Changing Attitudes toward Homosexuality in the 20th Century Europe* (Tallinn: Conference Papers, 1991), p. 101. Apparently the group's AIDS work con-sisted of warning Russians of the dangers of having sex with foreigners.

19   Shcherbakov, p. 102, and interview with Zaremba.

20   Interviews with Debrianskaia, December 1989.

21   In fact, the Libertarian Party was the direct descendent of the Russian Radical Party, a branch of the Italian Radical Party for Peace and Freedom. I myself wit-nessed representatives of the Italian Radical Party supplying its Russian counter-part with party literature as well as more mundane gifts, like large amounts of cash. Needless to say, the influence of the sexually libertarian Italian party was great.

22   Professional in the sense that it was Debrianskaia's vocation, not in the sense that she received reimbursement for it.

23   Conversations with Trust members Nikolai Khramov, Aleksandr Rubchenko, and E. Debrianskaia, 1989.

24   Interview with Debrianskaia, December 1989.

25   Of course, many of the political dissidents refused to acknowledge the importance of sexual dissidents. Instead, Debrianskaia was often insulted and even abused by many of her (male) "comrades" in the dissident movement. A particularly violent episode of harassment occurred within the Democratic Union. Debrianskaia even-tually left the DS and formed the Radical Party. Interview with Debrianskaia, 1989.

26   According to Debrianskaia, she was jailed numerous times, suffered KGB harass-ment and threats, was not allowed to work, and saw many friends and loved ones subject to KGB scrutiny because of her political and personal activities. She was not, however, sentenced to a prison term. Various interviews with Debrianskaia, 1989.

27   According to the association's original "manifesto," as published in the first issue of *Tema*, the first meeting was held on 15 October 1989. Debrianskaia's leadership position happened sometime after that.

28   *Tema* or "theme" refers to Russian slang for gay—as in "he's on the theme" or "he's a thematic person."

29   With the exception of Debrianskaia, most of the conference participants were under twenty-five, many of them university students. Masha Gessen, "Moscow Activists Push for Gay Glasnost," *Advocate*, 18 December 1990, p. 50.

30   Actually, some press reports claim that only Debrianskaia stated her full name. For instance, see Will Englund, "Gay Union to Seek Decriminalization of Homosexual Acts," *Baltimore Sun*, 18 February 1990, n.p. In subsequent interviews with both Debrianskaia and Kalinin, however, they both recalled Kalinin's stating his full name.

31   I am grateful to Masha Gessen for pointing out Debrianskaia's unique position as a well-known dissident *and* a queer leader. Interview with Gessen, February 1994.

32   Englund.

33   Gessen, p. 50.

34   In the summer of 1991, I was able to find *Tema* near the Bolshoi Theater (a gay cruising area), and I was told it could be found at a few metro stations in the city.

35   *Tema*, March 1990.

36   Roman Kalinin as quoted in *Treugol'nik*, no. 1 (1993), p. 7.

37   Dave Tuller, "Gay Liberation Russian-Style," *Advocate*, 3 December 1991, p. 44. *Tema*, March 1990. A more detailed analysis of *Tema* and some of the other queer periodicals appears below.

38   Telephone conversation with Debrianskaia, October 1990.

39   "Soviet Gay, Hookers Leader Leaves for U.S." (in Russian), TASS, 15 October 1990.

40   Officially at that time there were only forty cases of AIDS in the entire Soviet Union. Considering the lack of prophylactics as well as disposable syringes, this figure was highly suspect and made obtaining scarce resources for the fight against AIDS even more difficult. Treatment for AIDS patients, even in Moscow, often consisted of aspirin and sleeping pills. The demonstration took place on 7 November 1990, and I was one of about a dozen participants. Gessen mentions it in "Moscow Activists Push for Gay Glasnost," p. 50.

41   Articles were written in the *Advocate*, *Windy City Times*, and *Visibilities*. Contacts were made with a variety of groups including Parents and Friends of Lesbians and Gays (P-FLAG), Gay and Lesbian Alliance Against Defamation (GLAAD), International Gay and Lesbian Association (ILGA), San Francisco–based International Gay and Lesbian Human Rights Commission (IGLHRC) and New York's ACT-UP and Uncommon Women.

42   *Advocate*, 31 December 1991, pp. 34–35.

43   I provide a fuller account of the name change in chapter 6, "Patriots and Perverts."

44   Interview with Debrianskaia, July 1992.

45   Ibid.

46   1/10: *Gazeta dlia vsekh*, no. 4 (1993), pp. 1–2.

47   Conversations with Lipovskaia, November/December 1990.

48   Rich's essay has become a canon of lesbian-feminism. In it Rich argues that lesbianism is a far more "natural" choice than heterosexuality. The naturalness of lesbian attraction, however, is hidden within a system of stories about the necessity of heterosexuality. See Adrienne Rich, "Compulsory Heterosexuality and Lesbian

Existence," in Ann Snitow, Christine Stansell, and Sharon Thompson, eds., pp. 177–205.

49 *Zhenskoe chtenie*, no. 6, May 1990. There were two stories by Tat'yana Mamonova, one of the editors of the 1979/80 underground feminist journal *Women and Russia* (see above), as well as the by now famous article by Olga Zhuk, "Lesbian Subculture," describing the "Historical Roots of Lesbianism in the Former USSR," as the Stalinist camp system (in Russian). The articles were accompanied by homoerotic illustrations. The young graphic artist, herself a lesbian, did not want to depict lesbian sex acts so she drew men. Conversation with Lipovskaia, December 1990.

50 The Tchaikovsky Fund was named after the composer, Peter Tchaikovsky, who is known as homosexual among many Russian queers. The full name of the organization is the Tchaikovsky Fund for Cultural Initiatives for the Defense of Sexual Minorities.

51 Debrianskaia initially told me of the charge against Zhuk in the summer of 1991.

52 Interview with Iuri Ereev, July 1994.

53 The festivals were mainly funded by German organizations, although several local groups, including the Center for Gender Issues, the Human Rights Center, and two local lesbian groups (Sappho Peter and the Club of Independent Women) endorsed them. In 1994 the festival did not happen, in large part because German funding for it had dried up. Interviews with Ereev, July and August 1994, as well as fundraising literature for the 1992 festival.

54 Named after the heart of Greenwich Village and the location of the Stonewall Riots, the "beginning" of the U.S. gay/lesbian movement.

55 Festival fundraising literature, 1991. The 1993 festival was denied a permit for a rally and instead planned "organized walks." Ereev, by then the president of the fund, called the denial of a permit "a display of homophobia on the part of city hall and (Mayor) Anatoly Sobchak." "Homosexual Festival in St. Petersburg," A-Wlre, 12 June 1993.

56 See chapter 6.

57 Rex Wockner, "Soviet Stonewall: Russian Activists Clash over Tactics," *Outlines*, October 1991, p. 11.

58 The members answered letters from women sent to Ortanov's magazine, *RISK*.

59 Interviews with MOLLI founders, Liubov Zinoveva and Liudmila Ugolkova, conducted primarily in February/March 1994 but also in the summers of 1993 and 1994.

60 Interview with Kukharskii, August 1994.

61 Ibid. "Wings" refers to a novel by early twentieth-century writer Mikhail Kuzmin. Kuzmin wrote openly homoerotic prose and poetry.

62 Interview with Kukharskii, August 1994.

63 See Gessen's *The Rights of Lesbians and Gay Men in the Russian Federation* (San Francisco: IGLHRC), 1994.

64 In fact, to a certain degree this has already happened. Certain activists have gained reputations as substance abusers who cannot be relied upon to handle logistic or pecuniary affairs. Still, many Western groups continue to attempt to work with

Russian radical queers, in large part, it appears, because they are better known than the compromise-oriented ones. This is clear when one considers that Ereev and the Tchaikovsky Fund received a large grant recently from the International Lesbian and Gay Association (ILGA), despite previous reports that Ereev is an "alcoholic" who allows large numbers of "prostitutes" and "thieves" to spend time in the fund's headquarters.

65 Kalinin was twenty-three when he became involved in queer activism. Debrian-skaia, although already in her late thirties, had long been involved in "dissident" activities and had never had an officially sanctioned career. Zhuk also had contacts with the dissident community and has long been struggling with a drug addiction, which makes questions of further criminalization or marginalization moot.

66 Consider that most of the activists at the original Moscow Association press conference were under twenty-five years of age.

67 Ortanov had a very successful career in a scientific institute. Conversation with Ortanov, May 1994.

68 Tuller, "Gay Liberation Russian-Style," p. 43.

69 Interview with Kukharskii, August 1994.

70 For instance, at the 1992 March on Washington I witnessed conservatively dressed participants insulting women in S/M attire for "looking that way when you know that's the image that's going to be shown on television." At the twenty-fifth anniversary of Stonewall, several hundred thousand participants split from the officially sanctioned march from the United Nations to Central Park in order to march along Fifth Avenue (the "normal" route of all parades in New York City). The clothing (or lack thereof) of the "official" and "unofficial" marchers revealed more than a topographical division. As the official marchers divided by nation behind large solemn flags, the unofficial marchers tended to divide by sexual tastes, many of which were shocking by contemporary gay/lesbian standards (e.g., North American Man/Boy Love Association).

71 This "universal" model of sexual identity politics—which is really just the history of the United States and a few Western European countries—is constantly imposed on Russians. See chapter 6 for a more detailed description of how many Western activists came to view Russian queers as "like the U.S. in the 1960s."

72 And, of course, the tale of U.S. sexual otherness is far more complex than the Les-BiGay activists will admit. Plenty of women continued to relish the pre-Stonewall roles of butch/femme even after it was no longer "lesbian" to do so. Plenty of men crossed gender lines even when they were told they were merely living out "internalized homophobia." It is unclear whether the movement became more complex in the 1980s and began to accept a variety of sexual others, or a large divide appeared between activists fixated on the heterosexual/homosexual divide and those who wished to question this previously hegemonic binary opposition.

73 Interview with Ivanova, July 1992.

74 Treugol'nik, no. 1 (1993), p. 2.

75 1/10: Gazeta dlia vsekh, no. 4 (1993), p. 7.

76 Of course, it wasn't just sexual identity politics. There was great faith on the part

of many persons (Russian and Western) that groups that had formed around the environment, feminism, or even class would continue growing into mass proportions. This has certainly not happened for any groups other than those based on national/ethnic identity.

77 Hopes for political lobbying groups, national networks, crisis hotlines, and community centers are some of the dreams I heard about in the summers of 1991 and 1992.

78 Michael Specter, "Gay Russians are 'Free' Now But Still Stay in Fearful Closet," New York Times, 8 July 1995, p. 4.

79 For example, Ivanova, the brave young woman from Krasnoiarsk who began her own lesbian radio show was permanently cut off from her family for her activism. Personal correspondence, fall 1992. Olga Krauze, a St. Petersburg activist, feels that her long career as a folk singer was nearly ruined by her reputation as a lesbian activist. "It's not that my circle ever minded my being a lesbian—they're artists after all—but being associated with criminals [i.e., queer activists] . . ." Interview with Krause, February 1994.

80 Interviews with various Triangle members, including Debrianskaia, M. Gessen, and P. Masel'skii, spring 1994.

81 Debrianskaia, who had never been allowed to be employed under the Soviet regime, suddenly found herself a businesswoman. She owns a newsstand, and she and her partner work from very early in the morning to late in the evening. To find much time for anything besides attending a Saturday meeting of Triangle is extremely difficult for her. Several other Triangle members, like many people in post-Soviet Russia, are unemployed and are forced to rely on others for the little money they have.

82 When they occurred at P's home a Russian also had to get by the fact that P did not speak much Russian, which made finding out exact addresses or entry codes from the host even more intimidating for a non-English speaker.

83 At another time, an argument ensued over whether electronic mail would be a useful tool for the organization. Several members there had never even heard of electronic mail, and some had never even seen a modem. Field notes from a Triangle meeting, April 1994.

84 Of the five or six Americans who were regularly involved with Triangle, most had at least a master's degree (and in all cases except one from an Ivy League university).

85 Given that Triangle was envisioned as an umbrella organization and informational center, networking and informing seemed like obvious group goals to me, but discussion often ensued over whether or not the group was responsible for contacting other groups or whether other groups should contact them.

86 I was struck by how "faundraizng" (fundraising) was a concept without a context and an activity without a goal.

87 In fact, almost a third of the money ended up being spent on getting a passport for one of the organization's members—hardly a goal that would have been mentioned to potential donors, especially since the passport was never used for any organization-related traveling. Field notes, May 1994.

88   The session was held at Masha Gessen's, and in addition to myself and my host there were a couple of regular members plus a visitor from Novosibirsk as well as Olga Lipovskaia, head of the Gender Center in St. Petersburg. Only one person from Triangle's governing board, V. Kurskaia, had bothered to show up.

89   Field notes, August 1994.

90   I myself had invited a couple of women who were previously involved with MOLLI to one of these public Triangle meetings. This was not, of course, the first or last time I performed tasks for Triangle and other queer organizations in Russia. I informed English-language newspapers of events, I translated many documents and letters into English, I covertly paid costs for some activists who were too poor to attend various events (e.g., fundraisers, film festivals), typed newsletters and flyers into my computer, and in general tried to be as helpful as possible. I did try not to participate in any of the debates that came up—not in order to maintain some imaginary "professional distance," but because I do not live in Moscow permanently and sincerely believe such matters are better left to Muscovites.

91   Interview with Kurskaia after the meeting.

92   After nearly a half an hour I convinced the Triangle members to address the group. They discussed plans for Triangle's second national conference. An argument arose over Triangle's plan to charge an admission fee for the conference. "Why should I pay any money to Triangle when it won't be very interesting and the Americans came here and organized a conference for nothing and it was a hundred times more interesting?" asked one particularly skeptical woman. The only answer the Triangle members could come up with was that it was "the only organization out there and we have to support it." Another woman added, "We can't rely on the Americans to do everything for us. We have to help ourselves." "Sure," responded the first speaker, "but I'm still not going to pay money to go to some seminar I know will be boring." At this point, many of the women discussed how they are not interested in Triangle or their conference. The women seemed far more concerned with their own group, Klub Svecha (Club Candlelight), which was also having trouble raising enough funds to organize its various social events. Various strategies, including membership fees and an art auction, were discussed. Unlike at Triangle, no one mentioned the possibility of finding Western "sponsors," either through a fundraiser or some other means. Field notes, June 1994.

93   Tea dances are a gay male tradition in the United States. Held during teatime (or more accurately, happy hour), the events almost always occur in bars and/or discos.

94   Plane fare for Debrianskaia had been offered by the event's organizers, but when she could not attend they would not give the money to anyone else (presumably, because Debrianskaia is quite well known among many U.S. activists, they apparently wanted someone with enough name recognition to be worth the price of a ticket). Some members felt that plane fare should be found from the organization's coffers for someone else. Ultimately it was decided that the organization would not send anyone to New York, although a few members did travel on their own.

95   Triangle meetings, May–June 1994. I found myself located at the center of one of these interpersonal storms when I refused a last-minute request to put up one of Triangle's leaders in my New York apartment. I was already housing four extra persons, and this particular leader had stayed at my apartment before and shown himself to be less than an ideal house guest. When I returned from New York at the beginning of July, at least two Triangle members were angry with me. The potential house guest refused to return any of my phone calls after this point.

96   Field notes, August 1994.

97   Series of telephone and E-mail correspondences with M. Gessen and D. Tuller, spring/summer 1995.

      In fact, Triangle was brought back from the dead by foreign activists in the form of the International Lesbian and Gay Association (ILGA). ILGA, working through a European Union group known as Phare/Tacis Democracy, found funds for five cities, the three Baltic capitals plus Moscow and St. Petersburg. The result was the equivalent of several hundred thousand dollars to support organizations of sexual identity in Russia. The purpose of this money was "to build democracy, and what better way than to support a part of society that suffers society's greatest preju-dices and oppression" (E-mail correspondence with project coordinator, Andy Quan). Unfortunately, ILGA did not consider whether such organizations actually existed or whether giving them large amounts of money would be helpful in the long run. The upshot is that a group of activists, headed by American Kevin Gar-dener, formed an executive board, which was to oversee the handling of various projects, allot salaries, and expenses. They called the board Treugol'nik, although this was a bit like calling Dr. Frankenstein's monster by his pre-death name. A similar structure was set up by ILGA in St. Petersburg. Large amounts of money were then funneled through the Tchaikovsky Fund, another "organization" that was in fact not actually functioning before ILGA revived it. Although the results of ILGA's large-scale involvement are yet to be seen, the implications of such a paternalistic, if not imperialist, relationship can be considered immediately. See chapter 6, "Patriots and Perverts."

98   Interviews with Miller and Ugolkova, February, March, June, August, 1994. In fact, Ugolkova later began another journal, *Sappho*, dedicated to women's culture.

99   Including a small amount of money from the author.

100   The concerts also took place in a highly respected small Moscow theater (*Teatr u Nikitskikh Vorot*), a significant fact considering the near erasure of lesbianism in Russian society.

101   In fact, MOLLI is the only queer group to consistently cultivate contacts with feminist groups. They were represented at the first national feminist conference in Dubna. MOLLI also is closely allied with feminist activist Tatiana Lipovskaia's women's consciousness-raising group in Moscow. Interviews with Ugolkova, July 1992 and February 1994, and T. Lipovskaia, April 1994.

102   Many of her former colleagues from the fund blame an addiction to drugs for what they described as "erratic" and "paranoid" behavior. In August 1994 I interviewed Zhuk several times. She was, in fact, extremely depressed and kept discussing

suicide. Zhuk also exhibited a certain amount of paranoia when she showed me her recently completed manuscript on lesbianism in Russia and then feared that I would use all her ideas for myself—an unlikely prospect, I assured her.

103   Interview with Ereev, July 1994.

104   As I already noted, the festivals relied solely on outside money. Ereev told me in July 1994 that the Germans had refused to renew financing, and although they appealed to Dutch organizations as well as local businesses, no one seemed interested in putting up the approximately ten thousand dollars for such an event.

105   The apartment is located along one of Petersburg's major canals, a short walk from the main thoroughfare, Nevskii Prospekt. The main room in which everyone meets consists of a long table and chairs, walls filled with Tom of Finland posters, a couple of paintings that can only be described as pornographic-religious, as well as posters of various queer events and organizations (in several languages). In addition to Ereev, continuously smoking *papirosi* (cheap Russian cigarettes), is his ever present mother, who graciously serves tea to the fund's "guests."

106   My assessment of the Tchaikovsky Fund as a salon, not an organization, is based on my observations of the group throughout 1994, as well as a series of interviews with Ereev, Zhuk, and various persons who have worked on projects cosponsored (but not initiated) by the fund. In my interviews with Ereev he described the fund as "working on" various projects, such as the German-sponsored film festival or a large disco called Golden Cocks. In fact, none of these events seemed to be initiated by the fund, and literature distributed at festivals and discos lists the fund as one of several cosponsors.

107   See note 97 on the potential transformation of the fund by a large grant from ILGA.

108   It is interesting that both Kukharskii and Ereev met with Congressman Barney Frank (D-Mass.) when he visited in 1991. Apparently Frank told the activists that they should not rely on help from the West but should work for themselves. Ereev cited this as evidence that Frank understood "nothing about our situation. . . . [N]o businessmen here are going to invest in anything here because they don't want to be connected with gay groups." Kukharskii cited Frank's statement as an example of how well he understood the situation in Russia, where most leaders of the gay movement are supposedly only interested in getting money from the West. It is either ironic or just that Kukharskii's group receives no money, while Ereev's group receives large amounts from Western groups.

109   Kukharskii told me that thirty persons had attended the AIDS memorials, but pictures of the event (provided by Kukharskii himself) showed far fewer attendees (under ten). Interview with Kurkharskii, August 1994.

110   At the roundtable, Russia's foremost gay writer, Gennadi Trifonov, gave those queers trying to write poems and prose criticism. I say more about Trifonov in chapter 4.

111   Interview with Kurkharskii, August 1994.

112   See chapter 5, "Clothes Make the Man," for the gender/sexuality nexus caught up in this dismissal.

113 I summoned up my courage to go the next night only after I was reassured several times that there would definitely be a disco. After traveling the same remarkable distance, I was informed again by the club manager that the women's dance had been canceled (this time because Sappho Peter was unable to come up with the money to pay the club's rent).

114 See chapter 2, "The Cure," for more on the gender implications of "sexual" identity. As for the term "natural/ka" for heterosexual, suffice it to say that some words are burdened with an excess of significance. Needless to say, the term naturalizes heterosexuality while making homosexuality unnatural. At the same time, since the term does not preclude same-sex relationships, it allows some of those who participate in homosexual sex to be naturalized by virtue of adhering to the rules of gendered behavior.

115 This was actually how the club began in the early 1990s. When I first met them they were a very informal group of women who would meet at a local dairy bar (molochnyi kafe). Interviews with ten women in the dairy bar group, August 1992, as well as with N from Sappho Peter, August 1994.

116 The journal's distribution was about five thousand per issue. Interview with Krauze, April 1994.

117 Ibid. Krauze believed keeping the magazine fiscally accessible was an extremely important act, since those women who might feel the most isolated would be able to buy space. Yet Krause was herself extremely impoverished. She and her girlfriend would "smoke rather than eat because it's cheaper." Although her logic was unclear, her need was not.

118 Interview with Kurskaia, August 1994.

119 Interview with Kurskaia, June 1994.

120 In June, when a planned picnic had to be postponed because of rain, I was phoned with the cancellation and again with the new date and time.

121 For example, nearly half of the initial participants at the Golubki consciousness-raising sessions were women, almost all of them members of Candlelight. Or nearly all the persons who attended a Triangle meeting at the Underground were women, even though nearly everyone said they were uninterested in Triangle and far more interested in Candlelight's work. Field notes, June, August 1994.

122 Interview with Kurskaia, August 1994.

123 Again, Russians often do this importation, but that does not lessen the foreignness of it.

124 Donna Haraway, "A Manifesto for Cyborgs: Science, Technology, and Socialist Feminism in the 1980s," Socialist Review, no. 15 (March/April 1985), p. 73.

125 Other than Haraway, "postidentity" thinkers who offer similar visions of a coalitional politics that does not require a common identity include Judith Butler (see "From Parody to Politics," in Gender Trouble); Kathy E. Ferguson (see "Mobile Subjectivities," in The Man Question) and Nancy Fraser and Linda J. Nicholson (see "Social Criticism without Philosophy," in Nicholson, ed., Feminism/Postmodernism [New York: Routledge], 1990).

126 Of course, none of the postidentity thinkers was "thinking" of Russia, where no

strong "identity" politics existed in order to be resisted. Instead, Haraway et al. were describing the United States, a place so different that it is surprising that the concept of postidentity translates at all.

4 QUEER SUBJECTS AND SUBJECTIVITIES

1   Georg Lukacs first theorized a more true way of knowing, what he called "standpoint epistemology," among the working class. More recently, other identity activists have taken up the notion of "standpoint epistemology" (e.g., Nancy Hartsock posits a more true way of seeing among women, a "standpoint feminism," in her *Money, Sex, and Power: Toward a Feminist Historical Materialism* [New York: Longman, 1983]). The term "false consciousness" quickly became the complement of "standpoint epistemology." "False consciousness" is used to explain why oppressed groups do not possess a more true or a more critical knowledge of power. Activists of all sorts (e.g., communist, lesbian, feminist) have used "false consciousness" to describe those who do not think or behave in agreed-upon ways. Thus "standpoint epistemology" and "false consciousness" both valorize oppressed groups while threatening individual members of those groups with a complete disavowal of their thinking by labeling it "false."

2   There seems to be agreement among many sociologists that if people believe something to be real then it is real. But this ignores how "reality" is continuously contested, even within individuals. Believing and creating our reality requires continual negotiations with the phantasmagoria of the "unreal." Being straight requires constant negotiation with queerness (and vice versa).

3   Subculture, according to Dick Hebdige, is "the expressive forms and rituals of . . . subordinate groups." The "subordinate groups" must constantly contest the dominant culture's definition of them. The result of subculture's clash with culture is a style (e.g., of dress, of speech, of theater, of music) that can be recognized by both the dominant and the subcultures. Dick Hebdige, *Subculture: The Meaning of Style* (London: Routledge, 1979), pp. 3, 87. Hebdige later disavowed the explanatory power of "subculture" for separating off into bounded territories what is in fact a shifting and unbounded landscape. Instead Hebdige offers the idea of temporary alliances "organized around contradictory and conflicting social-sexual appetencies, aspirations, inclinations, dispositions, drives." Dick Hebdige, *Hiding in the Light: On Images and Things* (London: Routledge, 1988), p. 212.

   Hebdige may be right that subculture and culture make divisions too simple and too neat to describe the messiness of social life (let alone sexual lives), but I am not ready to give up the notion of abiding notions of self. To recognize that persons who lack a common identity can participate in common practices and events (e.g., attend a theater performance) should not exclude the possibility that the practices and events themselves depend upon a common, if complex, language of self. If culture and subculture are not useful descriptions of this common language, then subjectivity is.

4   Straight friends told me that the Sadko was a gay (*goluboi*) café.

5   Field notes, December 1989. The *Washington Post* wrote about the Sadko in the mid-80s. "The Grapevine Bills It as the Only Bar for Homosexuals," 12 December 1985, n.p.

6   The bar was called the Underground in both Russian and English. As I discuss below, "underground" is a highly meaningful term in Russian.

7   See chapter 3 for more on Kalinin.

8   In fact, the Underground's central location aroused suspicion among many of the former habitués of the Sadko. One man told me that he and all his friends were convinced that the Underground obtained its desirable location because it is actually a "KGB collection center." "How could Kalinin open a gay bar right at the walls of the Kremlin? A regular business couldn't open up there." Interview with I, July 1994.

9   For instance, in early 1994 the entrance fee was 4,000 rubles (about $2.50 at the time), while most of the discos were charging at least 12,000 rubles.

10   E.g., $2.50 for a beer, $5.00 for something stronger.

11   I never saw more than five women in the bar at any time, and generally there were only two or three women.

12   Based on thirteen visits to the Underground in 1994.

13   This information comes from a press account in *Segodnia*, no. 92 (19 May 1994), p. 6. Unfortunately I did not get into the restaurant. I went there once and found it closed (without explanation).

14   I was told by a contact that it was "one of our cafés," but I certainly would not have known about it otherwise.

15   The host's counterpart, the bartender, sported earrings, mascara, eye shadow, and a long ponytail. For more on gender transgression and signaling queerness, see chapter 5.

16   E.g., in July 1994 it was $4.00 for a beet salad, $1.50 for an espresso.

17   Based on four evenings in the Kafe Kat in July and August 1994.

18   Although I attended two of the St. Petersburg discos several times during 1994, I concentrate on describing the Moscow "scene" due to my far greater familiarity with the discos there. Not only did I attend the Moscow queer discos over thirty times, but I also went to other sorts of discos there. I also met and interviewed far more people in Moscow who go to discos than I did in St. Petersburg, where my contacts tended to be older and/or too poor to go to the discos.

19   These numbers are an average of my best "guesstimates" since counting dancing and mingling bodies is always an imprecise science. I always tried to count at 1 A.M. I would count one-fourth of the room and multiply by four.

20   Twenty-five thousand rubles or about $12.00 at the time.

21   Generally, 80 percent of the disco patrons were men. Given the inaccuracy of counting as well as the fact that gender, especially in a queer bar, is not always what it appears, I hesitate to make the claim that there were many more men than women (but it certainly seemed that way).

22   I only went to MELZ twice in 1994 because both times there was violence. Once a

knife fight broke out between two nearby dancers, and once some patrons arrived bloody from a "gay bashing" that had occurred right outside the door in full view of some local police.

23 Generally the stories were the same. Individuals or even groups of persons were attacked by a group of young men known as *remontniki*, or fixers. The victims were robbed and often beaten. Many of the victims did not report the incidents because they were afraid the police would blackmail them also (with threats of "outing" them to families or employers) or that the police were being paid by the *remontniki* to ignore the bashings, which were occurring regularly outside MELZ.

24 An article in *Nizavisimaia gazeta* told of a night at Premier that attracted so many queers that it felt like a "metro car at rush hour." Among the crowd were several notable celebrities, including pop star Boris Moiseev, who apparently passed out with his face in a plate of food. Aleksandr Kulish, "Goluboi vagon," *Nezavisimaia gazeta*, no. 169 (5 September 1994), p. 7. On another night, Moiseev was joined by Sergei Penkin (another singer who is far less out) and theater director, Roman Viktiuk ("in a yellow jacket surrounded by young men"). *Moskovskii komsomolets* (3 June 1994), p. 4.

25 These were not generally ways people felt comfortable dressing on the streets, and I always noticed disco patrons changing clothes in the morning before braving the Moscow metro. Again, see chapter 5 for more on the ways in which queerness was signaled through gender transgression in the discos.

26 No one who ran the disco discouraged such public displays of queer desires. Compare this "sexually liberated" space to the Kafe Kat or early bars in the United States, which catered to a queer clientele but also feared police and community harassment. For instance, see the description of queer bars in Buffalo, New York, mid-century in Elizabeth Lapovsky Kennedy and Madeline D. Davis, *Boots of Leather, Slippers of Gold: The History of a Lesbian Community* (New York: Routledge, 1993).

27 It seems public toilets are rarely, if ever, put to such uses by women. With the exception of sex workers, none of the Russian women I interviewed described public toilets as a potential place of anonymous lesbian encounters.

28 Even the most postmodern of theorists must admit to the difficulty of a person without a penis trying to embody herself as male in a public toilet. Perhaps with the right sort of dildo (e.g., one which not only looked "real" but could simulate urination as well) and the right amount of confidence, such a feat could be achieved. I shall leave it to braver and better-equipped researchers than I.

29 Field notes, July 1994.

30 Many of the samples that follow are from an unpublished paper, "Sources for Russian Gay History" (in Russian) by Viktor Oboin (pseudonym), 1994. According to Oboin, such homoerotic graffiti is visible in "a large number of public toilets" (i.e., not just those near cruising strips), p. 2.

31 Oboin, p. 3. Note that "Zhana" used the female form of "I'm ready" (*gotova*) as well as a woman's name to entice a partner "with a place."

32 Ibid.

33   Although some of the graffiti did indeed include possible meeting times for poten-
      tial readers/sex partners, most did not.

34   According to several interviews at the Bolshoi pleshka, sex usually occurs either in
      someone's home or in one of the nearby public rest rooms. Occasionally, espe-
      cially late at night, it might occur in a more public location, like behind some
      hedges, but the threat of police and criminal interference makes such encounters
      far more dangerous. Field notes, June–July 1994.

35   Pleshka may be the diminutive of the word for bald spot (plesh'), indicating the older
      man/younger boy (commercial) relationships that are often enacted there. It may
      also be derived from the French word for "place" since black marketeers, pros-
      titutes, and hippies in Russia also used it. See Vladimir Kozlovsky, Argo Russkoy
      gomoseksual'noy subkul'tury: Source Materials (in Russian) (Benson, Vt.: Chalidze Pub-
      lications, 1986), p. 60.

36   See Wayne Kostenbaum's The Queen's Throat: Opera, Homosexuality, and the Mystery of
      Desire (New York: Vintage Books, 1993) for more on the attraction of opera for
      queers.

37   The pleshka does not seem to exist for women. In the 1980s, women did sometimes
      congregate in the square next to the Bolshoi (ironically enough, at a statue of Karl
      Marx). Although I sometimes found groups of women in 1989, I had trouble find-
      ing them as early as 1991. By 1994, I never saw women congregate there, but a few
      women would come to the male pleshka across the street. One young woman I met
      there in 1994 identified herself as a "gay man," although she did not have sex with
      the men there. One of the Bolshoi pleshka regulars believed that with the creation
      of other places to meet (e.g., discos, political organizations), women did not need
      the pleshka since for them the primary purpose was "meeting one another, not
      sex." Without more information from the women who used to gather there, it is
      difficult to say why the women's pleshka came into being and just as mysteriously
      disappeared.

38   All of the older men whom I approached refused to talk to me, with the exception
      of one man who initially mistook me for a young man and then punched me when
      he found out that I wasn't (completely) a man.

39   In Moscow, the pleshkas I "cruised" were the Bolshoi, Kitaigorod, and Gogolov-
      skii Boulevard. In St. Petersburg I met men near the Central Department Store, in
      front of the Kazan Cathedral, and in front of the statue of Catherine the Great.

40   Dmitrii Lychev, as quoted in Sander Thoenes, "Gay Scene Shifts from Shadows
      into the Neon," Moscow Times, no. 537 (31 August 1994), pp. 1–2. Many people I
      interviewed used pleshka as a pejorative term for anonymous sex. For instance, one
      man said that "being with men was never about the pleshka. I can only be with a
      man I love. It's more than sex." Interview with L (and his partner), June 1994.

41   Although I was told a woman in Moscow sold all the queer press at a stand on
      Pushkin Square, I was unable to find her, even after phoning her several times to
      confirm that she would indeed be there (which means that potential consumers
      were not very likely to find her either).

42   See chapter 3, "Identity Politics and the Politics of Identity," for more on *Tema's* history. Again, *tema* means "theme," Russian slang for "queer."

43   The distinction between samizdat and unofficial publications is that the former were self-produced and often quite primitive while the latter appeared during the last years of the Soviet Union when it was possible to produce a highly commercial and slick magazine or newspaper, but official registration of the publication had not been obtained.

44   *Tema: Izdanie assotsiatsii seksual'nykh menshinstv*, no. 1 (February 1990). Two issues later, the *Tema* staff was still not revealing itself, although Roman Kalinin, the chief editor, was using his first initials. *Tema*, no. 3 (1990).

45   There were articles by Tat'yana Mamonova (the founder of the 1979 samizdat *Women and Russia*) and Olga Zhuk (the leader of Leningrad's Tchaikovsky Fund for Cultural Initiatives and the Defense of Sexual Minorities), as well as a reprint of an English-language cartoon depicting the birth of Jesus with the Wise Men announcing that the Christ child "is a lesbian."

46   *Tema*, no. 1 (1991).

47   A very popular artist of a particular type of homosexual and homoerotic aesthetic, Tom of Finland's images are always muscular, young, explicitly sexual, and male.

48   *Tema*, no. 1 (1992).

49   As I discussed in chapter 3, RISK was meant to be a less controversial alternative to *Tema* and the Moscow Association of Sexual Minorities.

50   Ortanov continued to edit the journal until September 1993, when he and his publishing company, ARGO, sold RISK to start a specifically erotic journal. The erotic journal was to be a "gay *Playboy*," with the "greatest concentration on sex, erotic, safe behavior." The sexual was to be interspersed with some interviews, articles, and humor. V. Ortanov, letter to readers, RISK, no. 3/4 (1993), p. 3.

51   Of course, there were a few exceptions. Liubov Zinovieva wrote occasionally for RISK, as did a few other women. For example, Inna Perova, "With Your Loved Ones Do Not Part" (in Russian), RISK, no. 1/2 (1993), p. 19. This article actually contained a photograph of two women in bed. Generally, the few images of women tended to be far less sexual than the images of men.

52   One exception was a young woman who was "theoretically" a lesbian, who wanted to find a gay man to marry. In exchange for financial support from her future husband, she would make a "cozy" home. Ibid.

53   The title 1/10 refers to the oft-cited statistic that one in ten persons is homosexual.

54   The woman apparently unsuccessfully masturbated with a nightstick, which separated inside of her, resulting in a trip to the local clinic. Vitalii Lazarenko, "Madam Mikriutishna and the Nightstick" (in Russian), 1/10, no. 6 (1993), p. 27.

55   Perhaps 1/10 did become slightly more "serious," with more articles about political events and an end to the gay horoscopes and crosswords that graced earlier journals.

56   *Ty*, no. 1 (1992) (this issue of the journal did not include a date or number, but it seems to have been the first and done in 1992).

57   *Impul's: deistvie-zhizn'!* (*Impulse: Action-Life!*).

58 Compiled by Dmitrii Lychev, *Other: An Anthology of Gay Fiction* (in Russian), (Moscow: ARGO-RISK, 1993).

59 This journal, put out by the Klub nezavisamykh zhenshchin (Club of Independent Women) was discussed in chapter 3 for its lesbian acquaintance service. The lesbian journal was originally published as *Arabesques*. *Arabesques* described itself as "the voice of women about women" without using the word "lesbian," displayed so prominently on the cover of its successor, *Awakening*. The content of *Arabesques* was also quite different from that of *Awakening*. While *Arabesques* contained translations of Sappho and poems by contemporary Russian women, *Awakening* focused on "movement" news. It contained a news digest of events, both nationally and internationally, of interest to queers (e.g., Romanian laws against male and female homosexuality and a Russian citizen's receipt of political refugee status in Finland because of the existence at the time of his departure of antisodomy laws) as well as lists of local queer organizations and meeting places. *Probuzhdenie (Awakening)*, March 1994, p. 3 (journal pages are not numbered). The more political journal did contain some poetry and prose by its creator, Krause, but this was limited to two pages (out of eighteen). The rest of the journal (about six pages) was given over to the acquaintance service.

60 Eight issues of Triangle's newsletter appeared during the course of 1993–94. The first several issues were published under the name *Treugol'nik (Triangle)* and the editorship of V. Lazarenko, while the last couple were published under *Treugol'nik soobschaet (Triangle Informs)*. According to its first issue, the purpose of the newsletter was "to inform Russian and Western mass media about what is happening in the gay movement in Russia today. The bulletin will also be distributed among gay publications, organizations, and private persons." See *Triangle*, no. 1 (November 1993), p. 1. The bulletin did indeed act as a sort of gay news service. It informed its readers of recent and upcoming events (e.g., classes in self-defense for lesbians). It also contained short interviews with various queer leaders on both national and local issues. The newsletter focused on the queer movement and its leaders, as well as social and organizational events (e.g., discos, meetings, bars). Unlike *Tema* and commercial magazines, the bulletin did not seem to be writing about or for a primarily or exclusively male readership. There were no photographs, or personals, or letters to the editor to create an exclusively male atmosphere, and the stories themselves did not focus only on men. The newsletter did occasionally publish comics, almost always of gay (male) content. The comics took up a relatively small part of the newsletter. The only letter to the editor was also by a gay man and was male-homosexual in character, since its writer fantasized about receiving nude photographs and a used condom from the subject of a story from an earlier issue. *Triangle*, no. 4 (January 1994), p. 3. Of course, the bulletin did more than report queer news, it created it as well. Several issues contained sensational revelations or easily reprinted soundbites. For instance, the first issue had Dmitrii Lychev, the editor of 1/10, saying that he and many other gay men supported the president because Yeltsin "is the true sex symbol of Russia." ITAR-TASS immediately (mis)quoted Lychev's pronouncement of politicosexual admiration and *Kom-*

somol'skaia pravda reprinted some of the information in an article entitled "Where Were the Gays in October?" (in Russian), *Komsomol'skaia pravda*, 11 November 1993. A later issue of the newsletter outed Vladimir Zhirinovskii, leader of the quasifascist Liberal Democrats. *Triangle*, no. 2 (December 1993), p. 1, and Mariia Korolov, "The Genius Populist at Home" (in Russian), *Triangle Informs*, no. 2 (1994).

61   *Gay, Slaviane!* never sparked the interest of Russia's queer readers, but it was a truly remarkable publication (the journal had a print run of five thousand, but it sold rather slowly, with copies from 1993 still being sold a year later). Although only a couple of issues appeared in the course of 1993–94, the journal was unique for consisting solely of essays and literature that were original and/or new to a readership in Russia. Its format, known in Russian as a "thick journal," was familiar to the Russian reader as the form "intellectual" publications (both samizdat and official) took in the Soviet years. The journal was edited not just by queer activists, but by literary heavyweight Gennadi Trifonov. During the Soviet regime, Trifonov was considered by many "the most subtle, most bitter, most loved poet of Leningrad," but until recently his work was never published in Russia. Instead, Trifonov gained a reputation in the United States after publishing a cycle of homoerotic poems. Unfortunately, the publication of Trifonov's material abroad moved the Soviet authorities to arrest him on charges of sodomy. In 1976 Trifonov was sentenced to five years in prison for representing queerness in his poetry. Officially, of course, Trifonov was guilty of other crimes, not all of which were sexual. An official version of Trifonov's arrest, printed in the weekly *Ogonek*, revealed the poet's "true" crime as treason (anti-Soviet behavior). Trifonov's years in jail did not diminish his growing reputation, abroad and at home, as a writer of some importance. Thus it was undoubtedly Trifonov's influence that made *Gay, Slaviane!* not just a queer journal, but a highly respected literary one as well. See K. Kuz'minskii as cited in Vladimir Kozlovsky, p. 180. Kozlovsky, pp. 180–82; A. Kostrov, "The Second Hypothesis of Theodore Foort" (in Russian), *Ogonek*, no. 27 (July 1977); *Gay, Slaviane!*, no. 1 (1993) and no. 2 (1994). Also see chapter 1 for more on Trifonov.

62   See chapter 3 for more on the history of these organizations.

63   In 1994, *Awakening's* creator, Olga Krause, began to publish a separate issue for men, which published much of the same material as the lesbian edition, but with a male-to-male acquaintance service. In this way, she assured the continued lesbian orientation of her publication.

64   Earning less money and having primary responsibility for children and the home are some of the obvious structural reasons for the lack of queer women's subjectivities. For instance, see my article (with T. Mamonova) "Perestroika for Women?" in Judith Sedaitis and Jim Butterfield, eds., *Perestroika from Below* (Boulder: Colo.: Westview Press, 1991). Not only do women tend to be too poor and too overburdened with their double burden of work and home to write or act or sing for free, but there are very few women who can act as sponsors for such things.

65   Queer is also popular in other forms, such as pop music and fashion. I explore some of these other "popular" genres of queer in chapter 5.

66   *Wings* tells the story of an adolescent aristocrat's growing awareness that he is

in love with an older "bachelor." The nature of the men's relationship is clear, if not explicit. In fact the only explicit mention of sex is by a male prostitute who is overheard by the nascent homosexual, Vania, to speak of "hanky panky" going on between the "boys" (sex workers) and the gentlemen who patronize them. See *Wings* in *Selected Poetry and Prose of Mikhail Kuzmin*, ed. and trans. Michael Green (Ann Arbor: Ardis, 1980), p. 39. Even a church canon admits that love between men is not necessarily a sin. "What's important in every action is one's attitude toward it. . . . [A]ctions in themselves are merely the mechanical movements of our bodies and cannot offend anyone, much less the Good Lord." Ibid., p. 107.

In *Wings*, Kuzmin argues for the primacy of love, regardless of societal judgments. One character, a teacher of Greek no less, explains that "what matters is that love, whatever its nature, can never be depraved except in the eyes of a cynic." The belief that love and acts of love are never sinful is repeated by other characters throughout the text.

67   This according to interviews with several queers, including Gennadi Trifonov, who told me that Kuzmin and other queer classics were always available to the highly motivated. Conversation with Trifonov, August 1994.

68   See chapter 3.

69   For instance, Trifonov listed Kuzmin's work as one of several homoerotic pieces he read in his youth. Interview, August 1994.

70   See Sonja Franeta's "After the Thaw," *Lambda Book Report*, no. 2 (Jan./Feb. 1994), p. 9.

71   To substantiate Tsvetaeva's status as lesbian icon, I offer the reader several facts. One, upon my departure from Moscow I received Tsvetaeva's poetry from nine different people (quite astonishing, considering I dislike her work). Two, quoting Tsvetaeva was a common way for women to introduce themselves to me at social gatherings. Three, at least one folk singer uses Tsvetaeva's work, in part as a way of covertly signaling her sexual practices to a subgroup of her listeners who "know" what invoking Tsvetaeva's work means. At a festival for Tsvetaeva, this singer attracted an enthusiastic group of listeners, including a contingent of lesbian friends (with whom I attended the concert).

72   Although not necessarily her lesboerotic ones, since, like Kuzmin's work, they were only widely available for the past few years.

73   Many editions of Tsvetaeva do not include the lesboerotic poems. A recent edition that does is *Marina Tsvetaeva: Sobranie sochinenii v semi tomakh* (vol. 1) (Moscow: Ellis Lak, 1994). The poem "Girlfriend" ("Podruga") includes a note, which says, "This cycle of poems was addressed to the poetess Sophia Parnok (1885–1933), with whom Tsvetaeva had a passionate friendship-love in 1914–1915," p. 599. The first cycle of "Girlfriend" says "I love you—Like a thunder cloud / Over you—sin . . . / For this shivering. For that there is no way / I am dreaming?— / For this ironic enchantment, / For that you are not he."

74   Of course, Wilde's works are elliptically queer, reveling in the aesthetic of dandyism, but not openly speaking the love that dare not speak its name. Still, it is difficult to read Wilde and not read queerness into him. Although one of Wilde's

most homoerotic works, *The Picture of Dorian Gray*, is often kept out of Russian anthologies (e.g., Oscar Wilde, *Skaski-Rasskazy* [Moscow: Khodozhestvennaia literatura, 1993]), it is a story that many queers seemed to know (many queers listed Wilde as an important writer when asked which writers were important to them). Also, see chapter 6, note 55. In *The Picture of Dorian Gray*, Dorian is clearly pursued by Lord Henry Wotton and Basil Hallward. Hallward, the portraitist, confesses that Gray is "absolutely necessary to [him]" and that he "couldn't be happy if [he] didn't see him every day." Lord Wotton is equally enthralled with Gray's beauty; "[H]is finely-curved scarlet lips, his frank blue eyes, his . . . passionate purity. . . . No wonder Basil Hallward worshiped him." Describing Hallward's relationship to Gray as something Plato had analyzed and Michelangelo Buonarotti, a great lover of men, had written about, Lord Wotton decides that he too would like to have that sort of relationship to Gray. Wotton decides to "dominate" Gray, to make "that wonderful spirit his own." The rest of Wilde's tale centers on the adoration and destruction of Gray by his two admirers in a way that is homoerotically charged without being homosexually identified. Isobel Murray, ed., *The Oxford Authors: Oscar Wilde* (Oxford: Oxford University Press, 1989), pp. 53, 59–60, 75.

75   Interview with Shatalov, July 1994.

76   All footnotes refer not to Shatalov's trailblazing edition, of which I never obtained a copy, but to Eduard Limonov, *Eto Ia, Edichka* (*It's Me, Eddie*) (Voronezh: Tsentral'no Chernozemnoe Knizhnoe Izdatel'stvo, 1993).

77   The KGB suppressed Kharitonov's work during his life. After he died, Kharitonov's mother, who did not want her son's openly homoerotic works to become known, refused to allow publication. Significantly, Shatalov convinced the writer's mother that her son was a "great writer" regardless of his subject matter. Franeta, p. 9.

78   Shatolov had plans to publish Judy Grahn's *Another Mother Tongue*, a book written in 1984 at the height of homosexual searches for mythical origins. Interview with Shatalov, July 1994. See Judy Grahn, *Another Mother Tongue* (Boston: Beacon Press), 1984.

79   James Baldwin, *Giovanni's Room* (New York: Laurel, 1956); William R. Burroughs, *Naked Lunch* (New York: Grover Press, 1959). All future references to these works are from these editions.

80   Shatalov has published one nonliterary book, an academic monograph by a Yale professor on the suicide and homosexuality of the composer Tchaikovsky. See Aleksandr Poznanskii, *Samoubiistvo Chaikovskogo* (Moscow: Glagol, 1993). Again, the composer's (homo)sexuality is separated from today's readers by a century.

81   Interview with Shatalov, July 1994.

82   Baldwin, p. 137.

83   Burroughs, p. 1.

84   Kharitonov was not only religious, but fervently nationalist as well. Kharitonov was also openly anti-Semitic and may have had ties with quasi-fascist leaders who were part of the underground Pamiat'. The anti-Semitism is certainly evident in his writing where he wrote phases like "the Hebrew danger" (*Evreiskaia opasnost*)

and "a generic kike-Masonic secretive mind" (*obshchii zhidomasonskii tainyi um*). For more on Kharitonov's anti-Semitism, see Yaroslav Mogutin, "The Other Kharitonov" (in Russian), *Nezavisimaia gazeta*, 7 April 1993, p. 5. Mogutin proposes an interesting hypothesis, based on the work of the nineteenth-century Austrian sexologist Otto Weininger (see chapter 2 for more on Weininger's significance among Russian queers) that "for a homosexual person Jewishness personifies the female part of humanity, which cannot elicit from him any positive emotions."

85   Mogutin speaks of this "double life" of Kharitonov, who was the nationally recognized expert on the artistry of mime, and founded the theater group Poslednnii Shans (Last Chance) which was still carrying on over a decade after his death in 1981. Yaroslav Mogutin, "Above Ground at Last," *Moscow Guardian*, 19 February 1993, p. 26.

86   *Uiti iz podpol'ia*. "Underground" is a term overburdened with significance in Russian. Underground is, of course, the metaphor many nineteenth-century writers used for the seamier side of life. To come out from underground, then, is to move from the dark and dirty vermin-filled spaces beneath the floorboards into the light and clean places of respectability.

87   For example, see the encounter between Eddie and a homeless man in Limonov, pp. 329–31.

88   For example, Giovanni and David discuss their female "mistresses" with each other, a subject that seems to arouse neither disgust nor jealousy. Baldwin, pp. 104, 215.

89   An article in a gay magazine about gay men married to women began, "From the point of view of society a normal person must be married. This is how it's supposed to be. This is acceptable. . . . Currently many gays are, in the eyes of the law, in heterosexual unions." Oleg Zobnin, "A Married Gay Man" (in Russian), RISK, no. 3/4 (1993), p. 20.

90   For example, Evgeniia Debrianskaia, the first and undoubtedly most famous public queer, has been married twice to men. Viktor Oboin (a pseudonym) has gathered the only gay/lesbian archive and library in Moscow, but he lives with his wife, who knows nothing about his queerness. In contrast, his boyfriend knows everything about the wife.

91   Interview with A, May 1994.

92   It is interesting to note that Roman Viktiuk and Evgenii Kharitonov (discussed above) were "friends—and in many ways—colleagues." Yaroslav Mogutin, "A Waltz in a Wheelchair" (in Russian), *Nezavisimaia gazeta*, 9 September 1993, p. 7.

93   In Viktiuk's production, the women are played by male actors. The Soviet censor read this as "perverted" and audience responses also acknowledged the play's queerness. For more on Viktiuk's gender subversion as a representation of queerness, see chapter 5.

94   "Viktiuk Only Plays with Youths" (in Russian), *Moskovskii komsomolets*, 27 October 1993.

95   Viktiuk acknowledged the historical importance of *Ragadka* by inviting a large

number of queer activists and personalities to the play's opening. Interviews with E. Debrianskaia, M. Gessen, V. Kurskaia, and others.

96   The neighbor is aptly named Larissa Dobropozhalovat' (Welcome).

97   Field notes, May 1994.

98   One person who hated Rogatka was Yaroslav Mogutin, who wrote a highly critical review of Viktiuk's more recent work entitled "Viktiuk Is Killing It Outright" (the "it" seems to be art) (in Russian). Yaroslav Mogutin, *Nezavisimaia gazeta*, 5 January 1994, p. 7.

99   Although it is impossible to provide a measurement of so immeasurable a concept as popular imagination/culture, it is obvious to even the casual reader of the Russian press that "queer selves" are widely represented. The mass media is not, of course, a "true" indicator of popular imagination. For one thing, Russian newspapers and journals are aimed at different, often very specific, audiences. Papers and journals are, however, accessible to a large portion of the population, since they're relatively inexpensive and sold on nearly every street corner. If even major publications give some space over to queer subjects then almost everyone has the opportunity to consume queer subjectivities, and queer subjectivities are potentially a part of almost everyone's imagination. In other words, as imperfect a measure as it is, the press does give some insight into the popular imagination. For a (partial) list of major publications that in the course of 1994 either listed queer self-representations (e.g., movies, books, plays written by queers) or allowed queers space to speak for themselves, see *Argumenty i fakty*, *Izvestiia*, *Kommersant*, *Kuranty*, *Moskovskii komsomolets*, *Moskovskaia pravda*, *Nezavisimaia gazeta*, *Penthouse Rossiia*, *Segodnia*, and *Stolitsa*. Of course, smaller publications like *Eshche* and *Novyi vzgliad* often allowed even more space for queer subjectivities. Since most of the popularizations of queer were either by queers or persons who admired a particular queer subjectivity (e.g., a Viktiuk play), they lacked the homophobic undertones of the perestroika press—which tended to objectify queer others. Yet even the few homophobic public descriptions of same-sex attraction that remained admitted that they were writing against the "propagandists of same-sex love." For instance, in a review of the *Men's Ballet of Russia*, the author bemoans the post-perestroika development of an "entire stratum of tasteless propaganda for same-sex love." The author makes clear that the *Men's Ballet* is not part of this stratum, although he does single out Roman Viktiuk and singer Boris Moiseev for his vitriol. Aleksei Belyi, "Pointshoes Size Forty Three" (in Russian), *Moskovskaia pravda*, 11 June 1994, p. 4.

5   CLOTHES MAKE THE MAN: GENDER TRANSGRESSION AND PUBLIC QUEERNESS

1   *New York Times* editorial, "Invisible People Made Visible," 28 June 1994, p. A16.

2   I cannot emphasize enough that the reading of sexuality is furtive. Whenever I have presented this work at conferences, including queer studies conferences, I

have been told that "you can't tell by looking." But what is it I cannot tell? What a person does in bed or fantasizes about doing? Of course I cannot tell that. Nor can I tell whether someone has a vagina or a penis or whether they were born with one or the other or both. But I always read that person through a prism of gender (and race and class and sexuality and nation). I do this not at a conscious level, but at the level of habit. Reading social divisions through sartorial significations is something we all learn to do in a society structured around and on those divisions.

3   Judith Butler, *Gender Trouble: Feminism and the Subversion of Identity* (New York: Routledge, 1990), p. 140.

4   Habitus is "an objective basis for regular modes of behavior and thus for the regularity of modes of practice." Pierre Bourdieu and Loic J. D. Wacquant, *An Invitation to Reflexive Sociology* (Chicago: University of Chicago Press, 1992), pp. 13, 77.

5   See Judith Butler, "Critically Queer," *GLQ: A Journal of Lesbian and Gay Studies* 1, no. 1 (1993), p. 21. Bourdieu's conceptualization of habitus is also a nonvoluntaristic account. For Bourdieu, habitus is similar to a game. A good player understands all the possible moves, and yet the rules of the game are so inscribed as to be invisible. "The habitus as the feel for the game is the social game embodied and turned into a second nature." What Bourdieu is proposing here is a model which counters structuralism by allowing the subject to "play," but denying the existence of an unconstrained subject able to act freely and rationally. Pierre Bourdieu, *In Other Words: Essays Towards a Reflexive Sociology* (Stanford: Stanford University Press, 1990), pp. 13, 47, 63.

6   "*Molodoi chelovek, brat, synok, devushka, dorogaia, shto vy takoi, mushchina ili zhenshchina, pederast, lesbukha.*"

7   Butler, p. 151, n. 6.

8   Vladimir Kozlovsky, *Argo Russkoy gomoseksual'noy Subkul'tury: Source Materials* (in Russian) (Benson, Vt.: Chalidze Publications, 1986), pp. 39–74.

9   Kozlovsky actually compiled most of the gay "argot" in 1973–74. Ibid., p. 38.

10 For more on the popularity and popularization of "transsexualism" among women-oriented women in Russia see chapter 2, "The Cure."

11 Still, an extremely "obvious" or sexually active lesbian, a dyke, is a *lesbukha*, which is feminine.

12 John M. Clum, *Acting Gay: Male Homosexuality in Modern Drama* (New York: Columbia University Press, 1994), p. 205.

13 Interview with S. Zarubin, who has played the role of Monsieur since the play first opened in 1989. February 1994.

14 Actually it is not clear that *The Maids* was about homosexuality at all. When the play was first put on in 1946 by Louis Jouvet, all the female roles were played by women. According to Jean-Paul Sartre and Roger Stephane, Genet had wanted men to play the maids. According to Jacques Derrida, Genet later denied making such a comment. See Edmund White, *Genet: A Biography* (New York: Knopf, 1993), pp. 298–303, 572. Regardless of Genet's intent, the maids are often played by men. Viktiuk's production is homoerotic precisely because of the play on gender.

15 Again, whether or not Genet made these remarks is unclear, but in the intro-

duction to *The Maids* by Jean-Paul Sartre, Sartre argues that Genet means to have men play the roles of women in order to show the "impossibility of living as a woman . . . to present to us femininity without woman." Sartre's argument here is not unlike Butler's conception of gender. According to Sartre, the men playing the roles of women will make the "spiritualized female appear as an invention of man . . . which cannot sustain itself unaided." Jean Genet, *The Maids and Death-watch*, trans. Bernard Frechtman (New York: Grove Weidenfeld, 1954), pp. 9–11.

16   It is interesting to note the similarities between Viktiuk's use of "art" and the arguments made to support the display of Robert Mapplethorpe's homo and S/M erotic photographs.

17   Interview with Zarubin, March 1994.

18   Dorinne K. Kondo, "*M. Butterfly*: Orientalism, Gender, and a Critique of Essential-ist Identity," *Cultural Critique* (Fall 1990), p. 15.

19   Note that Song is not only an inappropriate gender for Réné, but also an inap-propriate nationality (i.e., Chinese, not Japanese). Thus Réné is seduced by the appearance of an appropriately dominated nation as well as gender. This is one of the many ways that David Henry Hwang, the playwright, is positing identity as existing in multiple power relations, including those between nations. Ibid.

20   Wayne Kostenbaum, *The Queen's Throat: Opera, Homosexuality, and the Mystery of Desire* (New York: Vintage Books, 1993), pp. 59 and 95.

21   Author's interview, July 15.

22   Between January and September of 1994, I visited Chance twelve times, each time for an average of four hours. I went to Premera five times, and MELZ twice. In St. Petersburg, I went to both the Café Caprice and Na Mokhovoy two times each. I also attended several one-time only discos, such as the Treugol'nik tea dance at Moscow's Sports Bar and the first women-only night disco in Petersburg, orga-nized in conjunction with a gay and lesbian film festival held in May 1994.

23   This quote is a response to author's survey.

24   As was discussed in chapter 2, "The Cure," making desire for a woman, whether experienced by a man or a woman, male is further reinforced among Russian les-bians by certain experts who have suggested that a woman who cannot be "cured" (read "rid") of her desire for other women must "really" be a man. Thus many women who desire women consider themselves to be men. Some of these women identify as transsexual, which does not always translate into a desire for a penis as much as it does a desire for a male gender.

25   This is an interesting example of how the mere act of looking upon the female objects of desire was not disturbing but the refusal to maintain an objectifying (male) gaze was. Indeed, V lost his subject status by desiring to become the ob-jects of male desire (both in his wardrobe and his bed).

26   Pugachova's reputation might best be compared to those of Madonna, Bette Midler, and Liza Minnelli rolled into one.

27   Interview with Boris Moiseev, 9 May 1994.

28   *Chasnaia zhizn'* no. 6, (November 1994), p. 3.

29   *Eshche*, no. 4/16 (1993), p. 2.

30   Mercury, a singer for the rock group Queen, died of AIDS and is considered by some Moscow and St. Petersburg queers to be a gay icon.

31   I would like to thank Moiseev who showed me many of his video clips during an interview with him (March 1994).

32   *Komsomol'skaia pravda*, 24 May 1994, p. 6.

33   Actually, Penkin's enigmatic sexuality has become part of his public image as well. Like Ellen Degeneres's admission of being a "Lebanese" (before her debut as a lesbian), Penkin tells his audience that he is "green" (a play on Russian slang for a gay man—"light blue"/*goluboi*).

34   Sergei Penkin, "Holiday," "Lad," on the CD A/O, Moscow, Russia.

35   " 'The Morality Police': We Really Love Grannies and Pops" (in Russian), *My*, no. 7 (1994), pp. 173–76.

36   I saw the Morality Police once in 1994 in St. Petersburg.

37   One of the singers said in an interview, "We happily work in the gay clubs. They [gays] want us like crazy. . . . And already the lesbians do too." Ibid., p. 175.

38   Perhaps the Morality Police's lesboerotica is better described as a gimmick than an act. The women were previously known as Lady Style and were far more conventional-looking and acting as well as far less popular.

39   Ibid., pp. 174–75.

40   None of the four women in the staged lesbian duos seems to have a last name (at least not in interviews).

41   "The Main Impulse in Sex Is Inventiveness" (in Russian), *Penthouse Rossiia*, no. 6 (1993), p. 66.

42   The very fact that I split these respondents into male and female, as though that division were both obvious and natural, shows the extent to which we all participate in replicating the heterosexual matrix. On the questionnaire, I tried to assess gender and sex with the following questions: "What sex do you consider yourself?," "What sex is written on your passport?," but still this misses so many subtleties, such as a person born a female who has a sex change operation and makes the corresponding change on her/his passport, which would be lost in the shallowness of survey methodology.

43   Thirteen said there are no such signs and twenty-two respondents said they didn't know (usually "*ne znaiu*"). Five didn't answer the question.

44   Interview with R: "If I've just had my head shaved or my boyfriend and I are walking together, the *militsia* can see it, see we're gay, and they always ask for our papers." "Once my boyfriend and I were having a fight on the metro and when he left there were tears in my eyes and these *remontniki* almost beat me up because they could see we were together." Although the law against sodomy was repealed in April 1993, harassment of some gay men and lesbians by the police and other local authorities continued to come up in author's interviews.

45   Eve Kosofsky Sedgwick, "Privilege of Unknowing: Diderot's The Nun," in *Tendencies* (Durham, N.C.: Duke University Press, 1993), pp. 23, 25.

46   Gender is not the only knowledge that requires ignorance. As Evelyn Brooks Higginbotham points out, the discourse of race in nineteenth-century United

States often rested upon the erasure of gender among African Americans. For example, railroad cars had both a gender and a race, but the "ladies" car was not accessible to black women. Instead, they were forced to sit either in the "colored" cars or even the "smoking" (i.e., male) ones. Evelyn Brooks Higginbotham, "African American Women's History and the Metalanguage of Race," *Signs* 17, no. 2 (Winter 1992), p. 262.

6   PATRIOTS AND PERVERTS: THE INTERSECTION OF NATIONAL AND SEXUAL IDENTITIES

1   Eve Sedgwick speaks about the invisibility, the "naturalness," of U.S. nationalism, a nationalism that forms the "overarching ideology of our age." In a telling example, Sedgwick considers weather maps in U.S. newspapers, maps which drop off precipitously at the (imaginary) border with Canada—as though the weather in Toronto would be of no interest in Detroit while the weather in Atlanta would be. Or worse, as though Canada is not connected to the United States, which floats alone in the world, secure from the influence of "foreign" storms. Eve Sedgwick, "Nationalism and Sexualities in the Age of Wilde," in Andrew Parker, Mary Russo, Doris Sommer, and Patricia Yaeger, eds., *Nationalisms and Sexualities* (New York: Routledge, 1992), pp. 238, 240–41.

2   Ibid., p. 239.

3   Benedict Anderson, *Imagined Communities: Reflections on the Origin and Spread of Nationalism* (London: Verso, 1983), p. 4. Interestingly enough, Anderson dates the nationality/ism to the nineteenth century, to the same moment in time when the homosexual, an identity almost as modular as nationality, attached itself to the person and thereby stabilized and essentialized itself. (See introduction for a fuller discussion.)

4   Greta N. Slobin explores how Russia has always been Other to Western Europe/North America, but it has relied on its own "others" to be European. In particular, Slobin considers ideas of Russian nation as defined by its difference from the Crimea. "Revolution Must Come First: Reading V. Aksenov's *Island of the Crimea*," in Parker et al. Interestingly enough, Slobin acts as though heterosexuality were the only sexuality in Aksenov's work, when homosexuality is more obviously connected with nationalism. In the course of the book, a Crimean Russian nationalist, a Russian Russian nationalist, and communist nationalists are not only homosexuals, but the only homosexuals, thus reinforcing a notion of nationalism as a queer affair. See V. Aksenov, *The Island of the Crimea*, trans. Michael Henry Heim (London: Hutchinson, 1985).

5   Benedict Anderson points out the connection between gender and nationality when he says "in the modern world everyone can, should, will 'have' a nationality, as he or she 'has' a gender." Anderson, p. 5.

6   As Parker et al. point out in the introduction to *Nationalisms and Sexualities* (p. 6), "This trope of the nation-as-woman of course depends for its representational

efficacy on a particular image of woman as chaste, dutiful, daughterly or maternal. . . . [T]his iconography operates despite or rather *because* of the actual experiences of their female populations. . . . Their claims to nationhood frequently dependent upon marriage to a male citizen, women have been 'subsumed only symbolically into the national body politic.' "

7   Ibid. A compelling example of homosexual "containment" among men comes in the same volume in a chapter by Lee Edelman. Edelman explores the 1964 scandal surrounding Lyndon Johnson's chief of staff, Walter Jenkins. Jenkins was found with another man in a public restroom not far from the White House. What is interesting about this case, and more recent cases like it, is that it was written about as an issue of *national* security—a case of a representative of the nation who is subject to penetration by other nations through the form of blackmail. See Edelman, "Tearooms and Sympathy, or, The Epistemology of the Water Closet."

8   Pierre Bourdieu works out a theory of complex social space in which persons can be both dominant and dominating (e.g., upper-class women). See Bourdieu, *Distinction: A Social Critique of the Judgement of Taste*, trans. Richard Nice (Cambridge, Mass.: Harvard University Press, 1984).

9   See chapter 3 for more on Debrianskaia's role as a dissident and activist for sexual minorities.

10   Interview with Debrianskaia, December 1989.

11   Interview with Debrianskaia, fall 1990.

12   Unlike many postcolonial theorists, I would not describe the adoption of Western notions of sexuality and identity politics as mimicry. "Mimicry" seems to denote a set of practices whereby the mimic tries to be more authentic than the original. For example, a colonized Indian being more British than the British colonizer. In Russia, the use of Western notions of politics and sexuality is always framed as being Russified. Without this necessary Russification, an appropriation loses legitimacy. For instance, at a press conference on AIDS, every participant insisted on establishing his Russianness before presenting information critical of the government response to the disease. Yet most of these participants were affiliated with Western organizations (such as the NAMES Project).

13   In my survey of twenty-one persons who described themselves as "bisexual," only two were women. Most women who used labels used "homosexual" or "lesbians."

14   Conversation with anonymous receptionist in the Golubka offices, 4 August 1994.

15   Flyer put out by the Tsentr sotsial'no-prakticheskogo prosveshcheniia 'golubka,' Moscow, 1994.

16   Field notes.

17   Interviews with Ereev, August 1994.

18   Interview with Debrianskaia, August 1994.

19   Both myself and David Tuller conducted the interview on 9 August 1994. The third organizer was George Lakey, a sociologist who claims to have led more than a thousand seminars on four continents.

20   Goals listed at the seminar and also by Beck during interview, August 1994.

21   Interview with M. Gessen, February 1994.

22   Interview with Kevin Gardner, August 1994.

23   As I discussed in chapter 3, Kurskaia was an active member of Triangle and a leader of Klub Svecha.

24   Interview with Kurskaia, August 1994.

25   Gessen told me that Roman Kalinin (Moscow Association of Gays and Lesbians) provided logistical help. Other Moscow-based activists were either unable or unwilling to help. In fact, several activists confided that they thought the festival a "dangerous" and "unnecessary" event. I am surely obligated to tell the reader that I myself was in Moscow at the time, but did not feel that participating in the events was something I could do in good conscience, since I was in principle opposed to staging any event in Russia without the initiative and energy coming from Russians. I must also confess that since that time I have come to see the events as extremely complex and might not in fact make the same decision now that I did in 1991.

26   Interviews with various persons involved in the Soviet Stonewall events, including M. Gessen, S. Helfrich, O. Lipovskaia.

27   Interview with Gessen, February 1994.

28   Rex Wockner, "Moscow/Leningrad Pride Events Called Soviet 'Stonewall,'" *Outlines* 5, no. 4 (September 1991), pp. 10, 12.

29   Ibid.

30   The canonical book on colonial literature is Edward W. Said's *Orientalism* (New York: Vintage Books, 1979). More recently, Anne McClintock has examined the plots of other colonial texts, such as soap ads. See McClintock, *Imperial Leather: Race, Gender, and Sexuality in the Colonial Context* (New York: Routledge, 1995).

31   Debrianskaia and L. Ugolkova (Moscow Organization of Lesbians in Literature and Art) both felt that they should have been consulted during the planning stages of Stonewall rather than have the agenda set from San Francisco. Interviews with Debrianskaia and Ugolkova, summer 1991. I conducted over twelve interviews with Moscow activists that summer—persons already involved in some sort of organization—and with the exception of Kalinin very few of them felt as though the Soviet Stonewall had anything to do with Russia or Russians.

32   Interview with N. Ivanova, July 1991 and 1992.

33   Interview with Gessen, February 1994.

34   The question asks "What sort of social events have influenced your understanding of sexual identity (e.g., some sort of film festival)?" Only twenty-one persons listed such events—and of those twenty-one, eight listed Soviet Stonewall.

35   McDonald's is in fact considered by many Muscovites a good restaurant, and many of my teenage friends in Moscow—regardless of their educational/class backgrounds—consider working at McDonald's "prestigious." In America McDonald's is usually read differently.

36   Almost all of the quotes from German-speakers in this section were either translated into Russian by an interpreter (and then into English by the author) or spoken in English by nonnative speakers. There is little doubt that some miscom-

munication took place. All references, unless otherwise noted, refer to author's field notes of 15–23 May 1994.

37 Interview with Mahita Lein, April 1994. The single Russian participant was Olga Zhuk. As I discussed in chapter 3, Zhuk founded the Tchaikovsky Fund. Shortly thereafter she moved to Berlin. She ended her association with the festival because she did not believe the films chosen by the Germans were going to make sense in St. Petersburg. She was particularly disturbed by depictions of lesbian S/M sex. Interview with Olga Zhuk, August 1994.

38 The festival was held 15–23 May 1994 in the movie theater Spartak in St. Petersburg.

39 From the introduction of *Grani liubvi — drugoi vzgliad* (*The Boundaries of Love — A Different View*), Mahita Lein and Andreas Shtrofeldt, eds. (Berlin–St. Petersburg, 1994).

40 Another lesbian film was also quite controversial. The film, Angela Scheirl's *Red Ears*, is a futuristic film with a contemporary twist. Women rule the world, but not all women are welcome in the inner circle. In particular, practitioners of "kinky" sex are being systematically persecuted. Audience discussion after the film included a question about why swastikas were used. Scheirl: "I believe that every symbol has a variety of ways it can be read." No doubt Scheirl's film was read differently in St. Petersburg than it was in Berlin. From questions posed to audience members the politics of "sex wars" seemed lost on most, but not the ironic use of imagery typical of 1960s Japanese-made sci-fi films (e.g., *Godzilla*). Four audience members told me they appreciated the slick style of the film, although they were not sure if they understood what it was about. (Like many Japanese sci-fi thrillers from the mid-century, the simultaneous translation was not perfect and may have accounted for some confusion.) Zhuk told me that she decided to end her association with the festival organizers after they insisted that *Red Ears*—which she saw as "too cold" for a Russian audience—be included despite her vehement opposition. Interview with Zhuk, August 1994.

41 In all there were eight Germans, four Russians, and myself.

42 Both translators and one filmmaker paid the cover charge.

43 Interview with V, May 1994. I later heard that V had moved to Berlin and was soon to be married to a German citizen.

44 The woman seemed anxious to introduce me to someone until the end of the interview, when I told her I was Jewish.

45 I am using the term "nationalist" to describe persons who not only identify by nation state (e.g., Russian, American), but believe that this identity is central to their core sense of self (e.g., "I am Russian") and that their national self is both different from other nation systems and superior to it. It is difficult to discuss how many of the country's queer leaders are themselves nationalist—especially when what may appear nationalist to me may not be perceived as such by them (the objective/subjective labeling do not necessarily coincide). For that reason, I chose Mogutin and Debrianskaia since their own sense of self was not that different from my sense of them.

46   Interview with Debrianskaia, July 1992.

47   Interviews with Debrianskaia, August 1994; Gessen, February 1994.

48   For the reader who is not familiar with the Soviet/post-Soviet political landscape, Pamiat', which means memory, began in the late 1980s and has evolved into a powerful political force. It is paramilitaristic and quasi-fascist—supporting bands of black-shirted, black-booted youths roaming the streets of Moscow. My first encounter with Pamiat' was in 1989, when they arrived at the Central House of Artists in order to protest the exhibit of a Russian Jewish artist as too "Western." When they arrived, my companion looked at me and burst out laughing. "You look like a Pamiat'nik," he said. I looked down and realized that I too was wearing black boots, black pants, and a black shirt. Worse, I had just cut my hair into a crewcut, all signs which in New York spelled "fashion," in Moscow "fascist." I went down to the museum's café to wait out the Pamiat' protest and was called a fascist by several other museum-goers who were doing the same.

49   Interview with Debrianskaia, August 1994.

50   At this point in the interview I was struck by the Foucauldian criticism of Western/liberal notions of freedom that Debrianskaia was making. Debrianskaia seemed to be saying the liberal notion of freedom—which involves freedom to do/say/write, and so on—was not nearly as compelling to her as the freedom to *not* do/say/write. The freedom to "exit" from the public sphere completely—to live a duplicitous but anarchic existence. When I suggested this to Debrianskaia and explained some of Foucault's critique of liberalism, particularly his critique of sexual identity, Debrianskaia nodded her head and said "exactly." Interview, August 1994.

51   Debrianskaia was probably referring to Wilde's *The Picture of Dorian Gray*, in which Lord Henry Wotton says, "There is no such thing as a good influence, Mr. Gray. All influence is immoral—immoral from the scientific point of view. . . . Because to influence a person is to give him one's own soul. He does not think his natural thoughts, or burn with his natural passions. . . . He becomes an echo of someone else's music, an actor of a part that has not been written for him." See Isobel Murray, ed., *The Oxford Authors: Oscar Wilde* (Oxford: Oxford University Press, 1989), p. 61.

52   Conversation with Debrianskaia, May 1994.

53   See chapter 1.

54   According to Mogutin he met Zhirinovskii on 10 October 1993. Shortly thereafter Zhirinovskii asked Mogutin to work for him.

55   Interview with Mogutin, August 1994.

56   Yaroslav Mogutin, "The Chechen Knot: 13 Theses" (in Russian), *Novyi vzgliad*, no. 3 (1995), p. 3.

57   From official decisions of the commission made available to Ya. Mogutin.

58   Phone interview with Mogutin, March 1995.

59   For instance, see articles by Anna Polikovskaia in *Obshchaia gazeta*, no. 9 (2–8 March 1995), p. 12, and Il'ia Samanchuk in *Vek*, no. 8 (1995).

60   Interview with Mogutin, May 1995.

61   "The Chechen Knot," p. 3.

62 Interviews with Mogutin, March and May 1995.

63 I myself pressed the U.S. Embassy in Moscow to give Mogutin a visa due to the imminent danger of arrest. I also wrote a memorandum outlining the details of the case for several human rights groups and newspapers. I was appalled by Mogutin's article, but I firmly believe that his prosecution was not connected to his nationalism but his homosexuality. Mogutin was given political refugee status in June 1996. See the introduction to Mogutin's homoerotic poetry collection *Exercises for the Tongue* (in Russian), (New York, 1997), p. 5.

64 See Polikovskaia and Samanchuk.

65 Interview with Mogutin, March 1995.

66 Eduard Limonov, *It's Me, Eddie*, trans. S. I. Campbell (New York: Random House, 1983).

67 Interview with Aleksandr Shatalov, July 1994.

68 For instance, an edition was put out by Tsentral'no-Chernozemnoe Knizhnoe Izdatel'stvo in Voronezh in 1993 and was easily found by the author in both Moscow and St. Petersburg in 1994.

69 Eddie is seeking erotic "otherness"—which is found in homosexuality, sex with the impoverished, and, of course, sex with racial "others." The unabashed racism of the hero is part of this search for sexual exotica. Eduard Limonov, *Eto Ia, Edichka* (Voronezh: Tsentral'no-Chernozemnoe Knizhnoe Izdatel'stvo, 1993), pp. 246–48.

70 Ibid., pp. 329–31.

71 Numerous examples of redemption through suffering in Russian literature come to mind, particularly the works of Dostoevsky. Consider many of the "camp" memoirs from the Soviet period, particularly N. Ratushinskaia's and Aleksandr Solzhenitsyn's. Eddie describes his "all-forgiving love," which was far too "powerful" to allow him to leave his lover begging for change. Ibid., p. 330.

72 Although Shatalov alone has published several homosexual/erotic works, including William Burroughs's *Naked Lunch* and James Baldwin's *Giovanni's Room*, literary production was much more controlled in 1990 when Limonov's work was first published. For a fuller discussion, see chapter 4.

73 Interview with Aleksandr Shatalov, July 1994. In fact, Shatalov does not seem to be upset by Limonov's politics per se, but by the influence of politics on "art." Shatalov's press, however, did publish Limonov's collection of articles defending the Russian-Soviet empire in 1992.

74 Limonov, *It's Me, Eddie*, p. 395.

75 Vanora Bennett, "Russia's Leather-Clad Bad Lad Says Zhirinovsky Not Nasty Enough," *Moscow Tribune*, 6 September 1994, pp. 1–2.

76 Davrell Tien, "Love, Sex, and Mother Russia," *Index on Censorship* 22, no. 10 (1993), p. 34.

77 Of course, the two may be related in Limonov's logic—since a Jew is not a Russian and a non-Russian is clearly not loyal to Russia and Russianness. In Stalinist terms, Jews are "Rootless Cosmopolites"—always a threat to a nationalistic-fascistic order.

78   Eduard Limonov, *Limonov against Zhirinovskii* (in Russian) (Moscow: Konets Veka, 1994), pp. 17, 41, 72.

79   Thus Limonov and his colleagues called for a boycott of all "foreign" goods in the fall of 1994—an idea that was more "symbolic" than actual, since Russian production has dropped drastically and even the organizers did not seem willing to forgo their American cigarettes. Bennett.

80   From party literature ending with "Praise Russia! The National Bolshevik Party" (National-Bol'shevistskaia Partiia).

81   This is a symbol used on Limonov's *Ischeznovenie varvarov* (Moscow: Glagol, 1992).

82   Tien.

83   Michael Specter, "The Great Russia Will Live Again," *New York Times Magazine*, 19 June 1994, pp. 28–29. Also, see Zhirinovskii's *The Last Strike to the South* (in Russian), (Moscow: Pisatel', 1993).

84   Although I did not see the appearance myself, many persons in Moscow—both within and without the community of queers with whom I worked—confirmed that Zhirinovskii did indeed say that the rights of sexual minorities would be protected if he were elected president. Unfortunately, numerous attempts by myself to speak to Zhirinovskii were unsuccessful.

85   Presentation of information on the state of affairs of queers vis-à-vis the Russian government by V. Ortanov at the ILGA Conference, Palanga, Lithuania, April 1994.

86   One Russian journalist told me of going to dinner at the same restaurant as Zhirinovskii. Zhirinovskii called the young man over to his table and put his hand on his knee. Eventually, Zhirinovskii spotted two pubescent boys and called them over to the table as well. At that point, Zhirinovskii supposedly began speaking about the need to discipline the boys, teach them "how to be a man." The journalist and his friend left in disgust since the boys were only twelve or thirteen years old. The story itself may or may not be true. What is interesting about it is it is one of literally a hundred stories I have heard about Zhirinovskii's queer sexual practices.

87   A St. Petersburg friend told of a young gay man who was being paid five hundred dollars a week to be one of Zhirinovskii's "guards." The requirements consisted mostly of "lying around on a couch all day" (i.e., in the decorative and sexualized sense).

88   Andrew Solomon, "Vlady's Conquests," *New Republic*, 20 June 1994, p. 14.

89   *Treugol'nik Soobshchaet*, no. 2 (1994), p. 1.

90   As cited in *Harper's*, 19 March 1994, p. 19, under the title "Bimbo Eruptions, Russian-Style."

91   Maria Korolov, "At Home," *Soobshchaet*, pp. 1–2.

92   For instance, see Limonov's own account in *Limonov against Zhirinovskii*, pp. 50–51.

93   Of course, this is not the only history of queerness in the United States. The ghost of Roy Cohn and other rabidly conservative and nationalist queers haunts the myth of solidarity among marginalized groups.

94   Frank Rector, *The Nazi Extermination of Homosexuals* (New York: Stein & Day, 1981), p. 161.

95   Ibid., p. 23.

96   Ibid., p. 34.

97   Rector, p. 54.

98   Hitler and Roehm had been friends since 1919. After the failed Beer Hall Putsch in 1923, Roehm left Germany only to be called back by Hitler to command the SA. Ibid., pp. 83–89.

99   Gay leader Kurt Hiller was arrested in March 1933, just months after Roehm's SA had celebrated Hitler's ascent to chancellor. In May 1933 the Nazis attacked the Hirschfeld Institute. Magnus Hirschfeld, a scholar of sexuality and himself a homosexual and transvestite, started the institute, one of the first of its kind. In fact, Hirschfeld coined the term "transvestite" to describe himself. James D. Steakley, *The Homosexual Emancipation Movement in Germany* (New York: Arno Press, 1975), pp. 87, 103. The attack was carried out by SA troops, many of whom were gay themselves. The SA destroyed over 12,000 manuscripts and 35,000 pictures. Rector, pp. 104–5. Many gays managed to ignore the antigay sentiment of the attack by reinscribing it as anti-Jewish. One Nazi official described Hirschfeld as the cause of anti-Semitic (not homophobic) rage. Steakley, p. 105; Plant, p. 52. Of course, there was also a gender variable in the violence against Hirschfeld. Hirschfeld, a cross-dresser, was "feminine," not the supermasculine gay many in the SA favored. Steakley, pp. 48–49. The gender equation is also evident in the fact that "feminine" gays were treated much more harshly in the camps than "masculine" ones. Rector, p. 157.

100   Steakley, p. 82.

101   Despite Nazi propaganda that condemned homosexuality, there was little persecution. For instance, in May 1928 the Nazis released an official statement that called the homosexual "our enemy," since the Nazis "reject anything that emasculates our people." Also, in 1933 the Nazi Party began a very active propaganda campaign against homosexuality. Rector, pp. 105–6.

102   Ibid., p. 83.

103   Ibid., p. 95.

104   Plant, p. 57.

105   Rector, p. 91.

106   Ibid., pp. 56, 67.

107   Plant, p. 67.

108   Ibid., p. 69. Anti-Jewish laws followed close on the heels of antigay legislation.

109   Steakley, p. 110.

110   Plant, p. 7.

111   Rector, p. 34.

112   Irene Elizabeth Stroud. Although the article was entitled "Queer Exile," the front page asked "Rebel or Racist?," NYQ 2 (24 April 1995), pp. 6–7.

113   See chapter 1, "The Law."

114   The raid occurred at the disco Chance. A similar raid occurred in July 1996. The government said it was looking for narcotics, but the owners say it is part of a plan to shut them down. E-mail correspondence with V. Also see *Sydney Morning Herald*, 14 February 1998.

CONCLUSION

The epigraph by Kate Bornstein is taken from Shannon Bell, "Kate Bornstein: A Transgender Transsexual Postmodern Tiresias," in Arthur and Marilouise Kroker, eds., *Feminism and Outlaw Bodies* (New York: St. Martin's Press, 1993), p. 104.

1   Actually, not just generic "fiction," but pieces of an actual fiction entitled *Losing Myself* that I've been working on at the same time I've been writing this more academic work.

2   For example, see Trinh T. Minh-Ha, *When the Moon Waxes Red: Representation, Gender, and Cultural Politics* (New York: Routledge, 1991).

3   Eve Kosofsky Sedgwick, "A Poem Is Being Written," *Tendencies* (Durham, N.C.: Duke University Press, 1993), pp. 110–43.

4   That the lips are "full" is important since racial otherness has always been imaged in the West as certain physical characteristics/stigmata. We only need to think of the fetishization of the "Hottentot Venus," Sarah Bartman's buttocks, or the "simian" features of the colonized, including the Irish, in Victorian England. See Anne McClintock, *Imperial Leather* (New York: Routledge, 1995).

5   Clearly blurring boundaries are not just confined to queers. One man I know in Moscow is considered by all, including himself, to be straight. He only ever has sex with women, but to have that sex he must pretend he is a lesbian. A lesbian, trapped in the trappings of a straight man.

bibliography

PRIMARY SOURCES

Books

Baldwin, James. *Giovanni's Room*. New York: Laurel, 1956.

Bol'shaia Sovetskaia entsiklopediia. Ed. B. A. Vvedinskii. Moscow: Gosudarstvennoe nauchnoe izdatel'stvo, 1952.

———. Moscow: Izdatel'stvo "Sovetskaia entsiklopediia," 1974.

Burroughs, William R. *Naked Lunch*. New York: Grove Press, 1959.

Gorky, Maksim. "Proletarskii gumanizm" ("Proletarian humanism"), *Sobranie sochinenii*
27, 1933–36. Moscow: State Publishers of Literary Texts, 1953.

Kommentarii k ugolovemu kodeksu Rossiiskoi Federatsii. Moscow: Verdikti, 1994.

Kon, Igor. "Sexual Minorities." In Igor Kon and James Riordan, eds., *Sex and Russian
Society*. Bloomington: Indiana University Press, 1993.

Kozlovsky, Vladimir. *Argo Russkoy gomoseksual'noy subkul'tury: Source Materials* (Argot of the
Russian gay subculture). Benson, Vt.: Chalidze Publications, 1986.

Kuzmin, Mikhail. "Wings." Michael Green, ed. and trans., *Selected Poetry and Prose of
Mikhail Kuzmin*. Ann Arbor: Ardis, 1980.

Limonov, Eduard. *Eto ia, Edichka* (It's Me, Eddie). Voronezh: Tsentral'no chernozemnoe
knizhnoe izdatel'stvo, 1993.

———. *Ischeznovenie varvarov* (The disappearance of the barbarians). Moscow: Glagol,
1992.

———. *Limonov protiv Zhirinovskogo* (Limonov against Zhirinovskii). Moscow: Konets Veka,
1994.

Lychev, Dmitrii, ed. *Drugoi: Sbornik gei-rasskazov* (Other: An anthology of gay fiction).
Moscow: ARGO-RISK, 1993.

Mamonova, Tat'yana, ed. *Women and Russia: Feminist Writings from the Soviet Union*. Boston:
Beacon Press, 1984.

Poznanskii, Aleksandr. *Samoubiistvo chaikovskogo* (Tchaikovsky's suicide). Moscow: Glagol,
1993.

Razumovskaya, Lyubov. "Mistress of the High Mountain." In Tat'yana Mamonova, ed.,
Women and Russia. Boston: Beacon, 1984.

Rozanov, V. V. *Liudi lunnogo sveta: Metafizika Khristianstva* (People of the moonlight: The
metaphysics of Christianity). Moscow: Druzhba narodov, 1990.

Shcherbakov, Sergei P., "On the Relationship between the Leningrad Gay Community and the Legal Authorities in the 1970's and 1980's." In Udo Parikas and Teet Veispak, eds., *Sexual Minorities and Society: The Changing Attitudes toward Homosexuality in the 20th Century Europe.* Tallinn: Conference Papers, 1991.

Trifonov, Gennadi. "Otkrytoe pis'mo." Reprinted in Vladimir Kozlovsky, *Argo Russkoy gomoseksual'noy subkul'tury: Source Materials* (Argot of the Russian gay subculture). Benson, Vt.: Chalidze Publications, 1986.

Tsvetaeva, Marina. *Marina Tsvetaeva: Sobranie sochinenii v semi tomakh. Vol. 1.* Moscow: Ellis Lak, 1994.

Ugolovnii kodeks RSFSR. Moscow: Iuridicheskaia literatura, 1987.

Ugolovnoe pravo Rossii osobennaia chast'. Moscow: Iurist, 1993.

Verkhovnyi Sud SSSR (Sekretnaia Chast'). Fond no. 9492, Opis no. 6c, Delo no. 69.

Weininger, Otto. *Sex and Character.* New York: AMS Press, 1975.

Wilde, Oscar. *Skazki-rasskazy.* Moscow: Khudozhestvennaia literatura, 1993.

Zhirinovskii, V. V. *Poslednii brosok na Iug* (The last strike to the south). Moscow: Pisatel', 1993.

Memos, Liner Notes, Periodicals, Pamphlets, and Unpublished Manuscripts and Interviews

Belyi, Aleksei. "Pointshoes Size Forty Three" (in Russian). *Moskovskaia pravda,* 11 June 1994.

Borokhov, A. D., D. D. Isaev, and A. V. Toliarov. "Sotsial'no-psichologicheskie faktory gomoseksual'nogo povedeniia u zakliuchenikh" (Sociopsychological factors of homosexual behavior among prisoners"). *Sotsiologicheskie issledovaniia,* no. 6 (1990).

Builo, Stepan. "The Setting Right of Russian-American Relations is Delayed" (in Russian). *Segodnia,* 13 April 1994.

Bystrova, Tat'iana. "Chikatilo and Company" (in Russian). *Trud,* no. 201, 29 October 1994.

Eshche. Weekly erotic newspaper. Moscow.

Ezop o SPIDe. Pamphlet. Moscow: Wellcome Foundation, Tsentr EZOP, Gazeta "1/10," 1993.

Gay, Slaviane! Occasional literary journal. G. Trifanov, ed. St. Petersburg.

Impul's: Deistvie-zhizn! Weekly newspaper. Moscow.

"Instruktsiia o poriadke obsledovaniia donorov i nacelaniia na SPID i provedeniia dispansernogo nabliudenia za litsami, infitsirovannymi virusom immunodefitsita cheloveka" ("Instructions for the procedure of inspection of donors and the populations for AIDS and the conduct of sanitarium surveillance for persons infected with the immune deficiency virus"). Moscow: Ministertvo zdravookhraneniia SSSR, 1987.

Isaev, D. D. "Gomoseksual'nye kontakty v mestakh zakliucheniia i problema SPIDa" ("Homosexual contact in places of imprisonment and the problem of AIDS"). Unpublished manuscript. 1989.

———. "Homosexuality and Its Etiological Models," *The Bekhterev Review of Psychiatry and Medical Psychology*, 1991, vol. 2.

———. Interview. In "Kogda ia byl zhenshchinoi" ("When I was a woman"). *A i F Peterburg*, no. 25 (1994).

———. "Particularities of Sexual Identification and Psychological Orientation among Persons with Homosexual Orientations/Attractions." Unpublished manuscript. V. M. Bekhterev Psychoneurological Institute, St. Petersburg, Russia.

———. "Psikhosomaticheskie otnosheniia v etiologii gomoseksualizma" ("Psychosomatic relations in the etiology of homosexuality"). Unpublished manuscript. 1989.

Karmaza, Oleg. "Bloodsucker" (in Russian). *Komsomol'skaia pravda*, 19 September 1994.

———. "Sexual Maniacs for Some Reason Always Have Long Hands" (in Russian). *Komsomol'skaia pravda*, 6 October 1994.

Khokli, Kris. "A Tabloid Makes the World a Happier Place" (in Russian). *Nezavisimaia gazeta*, 18 June 1991.

"Kommitet po okhrane zdorov'ia: Proekt" ("Committee for public health: Draft"), 24 May 1994.

Komov, Evgenii. "The Publisher of 'Esche' is Arrested" (in Russian). *Segodnia*, 8 February 1994.

Korolov, Maria. "At Home" (in Russian). *Soobshchaet*, no. 2 (1994).

Kostrov, A. "The Second Hypothesis of Theodore Foort" (in Russian). *Ogonek*, no. 27 (July 1977).

Kulish, Aleksandr. "Goluboi vagon" ("Blue wagon"). *Nezavisimaia gazeta*, no. 169 (5 September 1994).

Lein, Mahita, and Andreas Shrtofeldt, eds. *Grani liubvi-drugoi vzgliad* (The boundaries of love—a different view). Catalog of German film festival held in St. Petersburg, 1994.

Loshak, Viktor. "Lichnost' za provolokoi" ("Personality behind the wire"). *Moskovkie Novosti*, no. 38 (18 September 1988).

Mogutin, Yaroslav. "Above Ground at Last." *Moscow Guardian*, 19 February 1993.

———. "The Chechen Knot: 13 Theses" (in Russian). *Novyi vzgliad*, no. 3 (1995).

———. "Dirty Peckers: The Second Duel" (in Russian). *Novyi vzgliad*, no. 38 (1993).

———. " 'Drugoi' Kharitonov" ("The other Kharitonov"). *Nezavisimaia gazeta*, 7 April 1993.

———. "Val's v Invalidnoi Koliaske" ("Waltz in a wheelchair"). *Nezavisimaia gazeta*, 9 September 1993.

———. "Viktiuk Ubivaet Napoval" ("Viktiuk is killing outright"). *Nezavisimaia gazeta*, 5 January 1994.

———. *Uprazhneniia dlia iazika* (Exercises for the tongue). New York: n.p., 1997.

Moiseev, Boris. "The Dirty Peckers of Komsomol Members: Boris Moiseev about Himself and the Past" (in Russian). *Eshche*, no. 4/16.

Moscow PEN Center. Letter to the Krasnopresnenski Prosecutor's Office re. Y. Mogutin's Prosecution. Moscow, 9 November 1993.

Natsional-Bol'shevistskaia Partiia. Party literature.

Novyi vzgliad. Weekly newspaper. Moscow.

Oboin, Viktor. "Istochniki po russkoi gei-istorii" ("Sources for Russian gay history"). Unpublished manuscript. Moscow, 1994.

———. "Letter to the Editor" (in Russian). *Zerkalo*, no. 1 (1995).

1/10: *Gazeta dlia vsekh*. Weekly newspaper. Moscow.

Ortanov, V. "Letter to Readers" (in Russian). *RISK*, no. 3/4 (1993).

Penkin, Sergei. *Holiday*. Compact disc recording. Moscow: "Lad."

Perova, Inna. "With Your Loved Ones Do Not Part" (in Russian), *RISK*, no. 1/2 (1993).

Podrabin, Aleksander. "Commentary" (in Russian). *Ekspress-khronika*, 11 February 1994.

Probuzhdenie. Occasional self-published magazine. Ol'ga Krauze, ed., St. Petersburg.

R.A.R. Info. Occasional bulletin of the organization AIDSInfoshare, Moscow.

RISK. Monthly magazine. V. Ortanov, ed., Moscow.

Shchadin, Iu. "O kvalifikatsii polovykh prestuplenii" ("About the qualifications of sexual crimes"). *Zakonnost'*, no. 12 (1994).

Sosnov, Arkadii. "Dissertation Helped to Catch a Maniac" (in Russian). *Moskovskie novosti*, 4–11 December 1994.

"Soviet Gay, Hookers Leader Leaves for U.S." (in Russian). *TASS*, 15 October 1990.

Tema. Monthly self-published newspaper of the Moscow Association of Gays and Lesbians. Roman Kalinin, ed., Moscow.

Thoenes, Sander. "Gay Scene Shifts from Shadows into the Neon." *Moscow Times*, no. 537 (31 August 1994).

Treugol'nik (later series, *Treugol'nik soobschaet*). Monthly bulletin of the organization Treugol'nik, Moscow.

"Tsentr sotsial'no-prakticheskogo prosveshcheniia 'golubka.' " Flyer. Moscow, 1994.

Tuller, David. Interview with Dmitri Isaev, 1991.

———. Interviews with a female-to-male transsexuals, 1991.

———. Interview with unnamed sexologist from the Moscow Institute of Medicine and Reproduction (MiR), 1991.

Ty. Monthly magazine. Moscow.

Vil'mis, Maria. "Pornography" (in Russian). *Ekspress-khronika*, 1 April 1994.

Wockner, Rex. "Moscow/Leningrad pride events called Soviet 'Stonewall.' " *Outlines* 5, no. 4 (September 1991).

Zerkalo, no. 1 (1995). Occasional bulletin of the Moscow Library for Gays and Lesbians. Viktor Oboin, ed., Moscow.

Zhenskoe Chtenie. Occasional, self-published feminist literary journal. Ol'ga Lipovskaia, ed., St. Petersburg.

Zhuk, Olga. "Lesbiiskaia subkul'tura: Istoricheskie korni lesbiianstva v byvshem SSSR" ("Lesbian subculture: The historical roots of lesbianism in the former USSR"). *Gay, Slaviane!*, no. 1 (1993).

———. "Reportazh 1: Iablonevka" ("The first report: Iablonevka"). *Gay, Slaviane!*, no. 1 (1993).

Zobnin, Oleg. "A Married Gay Man" (in Russian). *RISK*, no. 3/4 (1993).

SECONDARY SOURCES

Aksenov, V. *The Island of the Crimea.* Trans. Michael Henry Heim. London: Hutchinson, 1985.

Anderson, Benedict. *Imagined Communities: Reflections on the Origin and Spread of Nationalism.* London: Verso, 1983.

Arguelles, Lourdes, and B. Ruby Rich. ". . . Understanding . . . the Cuban Lesbian and Gay Male Experience." In Estelle B. Freedman et al., eds., *The Lesbian Issue: Essays from "Signs."* Chicago: University of Chicago Press, 1985.

Bakhtin, Mikhail. *The Dialogic Imagination.* Austin: University of Texas Press, 1981.

Barthes, Roland. *Mythologies.* New York: Noonday Press, 1957.

Bell, Shannon. "Kate Bornstein: A Transgender Transsexual Postmodern Tiresias." In Arthur and Marilouise Kroker, eds. *Feminism and Outlaw Bodies.* New York: St. Martin's Press, 1993.

Bennett, Vanora. "Russia's Leather-Clad Bad Lad Says Zhirinovsky Not Nasty Enough." *Moscow Tribune,* 6 September 1994.

"Bizarre Station: Sound Tracks: Gay Thunder is Rumbling under the Pop Scene and Its Name is Boris Moiseev." *Moskovskii komsomolets,* 11 August 1993, p. 4.

Blackwood, Evelyn. "Sexuality and Gender in Certain Native American Tribes." In Estelle B. Freedman et al., eds., *The Lesbian Issue: Essays from "Signs."* Chicago: University of Chicago Press, 1985.

Bourdieu, Pierre. *Distinction: A Social Critique of the Judgement of Taste.* Trans. Richard Nice. Cambridge, Mass.: Harvard University Press, 1984.

———. *In Other Words: Essays Towards a Reflexive Sociology.* Trans. Matthew Adamson. Stanford: Stanford University Press, 1990.

Bourdieu, Pierre, and Loic J. D. Wacquant. *An Invitation to Reflexive Sociology.* Chicago: University of Chicago Press, 1992.

Butler, Judith. "Critically Queer." *GLQ: A Journal of Lesbian and Gay Studies* 1, no. 1 (1993), pp. 17–32.

———. *Gender Trouble: Feminism and the Subversion of Identity.* New York: Routledge, 1990.

Calhoun, Craig, ed. *Habermas and the Public Sphere.* Cambridge, Mass.: MIT Press, 1992.

Chauncey, George. *Gay New York: Gender, Urban Culture, and the Making of the Gay Male World, 1890–1940.* New York: Basic Books, 1994.

Clifford, James. *The Predicament of Culture: Twentieth-Century Ethnography, Literature, and Art.* Cambridge, Mass.: Harvard University Press, 1988.

Clum, John M. *Acting Gay: Male Homosexuality in Modern Drama.* New York: Columbia University Press, 1994.

Cohen, Ed. *Talk on the Wilde Side.* New York: Routledge, 1993.

Cohen, Elizabeth. "Biberpeople." *OUT,* May 1995, pp. 87–90.

Cullen, Robert. *Citizen X.* New York: Ivy Books, 1993.

De Certeau, Michel. *The Practice of Everyday Life.* Trans. Steven Rendall. Berkeley: University of California Press, 1984.

D'Emilio, John. "Capitalism and Gay Identity." In Ann Snitow, Christine Stansell, and

Sharon Thompson, eds., *Powers of Desire: The Politics of Sexuality*. New York: Monthly Review Press, 1983.

D'Emilio, John, and Estelle B. Freedman. *Intimate Matters: A History of Sexuality in America*. New York: Harper & Row, 1988.

Diagnostic and Statistical Manual of Mental Disorders. 4th ed., Washington, D.C.: American Psychiatric Association, 1994.

Dunlap, David W. "Shameless Homophobia and the 'Jenny Jones' Murder." *New York Times*, 18 March 1995.

Edelman, Lee. "Tearooms and Sympathy, or, The Epistemology of the Water Closet." In Andrew Parker, Mary Russo, Doris Sommer, and Patricia Yaeger, eds., *Nationalisms and Sexualities*. New York: Routledge, 1992.

Eley, Geoff. "Nations, Publics, and Political Cultures: Placing Habermas in the Nineteenth Century." In Craig Calhoun, ed., *Habermas and the Public Sphere*. Cambridge, Mass.: MIT Press, 1992.

Engelstein, Laura. *The Keys to Happiness: Sex and the Search for Modernity in Fin-de-Siècle Russia*. Ithaca, N.Y.: Cornell University Press, 1992.

———. "Lesbian Vignettes: A Russian Triptych from the 1890s." *Signs* 15, no. 4 (1990).

Englund, Will. "Gay Union to Seek Decriminalization of Homosexual Acts." *Baltimore Sun*, 18 February 1990.

Etkind, Aleksandr. *Eros Nivozmozhnogo: Istoriia Psikhoanaliza v Rossii* (Eros of the Impossible: A History of Psychoanalysis in Russia). Moscow: Gnozis, 1994.

Fajchman, John. *Michel Foucault: The Freedom of Philosophy*. New York: Columbia University Press, 1985.

Ferguson, Kathy E. *The Man Question: Visions of Subjectivity in Feminist Theory*. Berkeley: University of California Press, 1993.

Fitzpatrick, Sheila. *The Russian Revolution: 1917–1932*. Oxford: Oxford University Press, 1982.

Foucault, Michel. *The Archeology of Knowledge*. New York: Pantheon, 1972.

———. *Discipline and Punish: The Birth of the Prison*. Trans. Alan Sheridan. New York: Random House, 1979.

———. *The History of Sexuality, vol. I: An Introduction*. Trans. Robert Hurley. New York: Vintage, 1980.

———. "Lecture One: 7 January 1976." Reprinted in Michael Kelly, ed., *Critique and Power: Recasting the Foucault/Habermas Debate*. Cambridge, Mass.: MIT Press, 1994.

Franeta, Sonja. "After the Thaw." *Lambda Book Report*, no. 2 (Jan./Feb. 1994), pp. 8–9.

Geertz, Clifford. *The Interpretation of Cultures*. New York: Basic Books, 1973.

———. *Local Knowledge*. New York: Basic Books, 1983.

Genet, Jean. *The Maids and Deathwatch*. Trans. Bernard Frechtman. New York: Grove Weidenfeld, 1954.

Gessen, Masha. "Comrade in Arms," *Out/Look*, no. 12 (Spring 1991).

———. *Dead Again: The Russian Intelligentsia after Communism*. London: Verso, 1997.

———. "Double Jeopardy: Homophobic Attacks on the Press around the World Since 1990." Draft report. New York: Committee to Protect Journalists, 1995.

————. "Moscow Activists Push for Gay Glasnost." *Advocate*, no. 566, 18 December 1990.

————. *The Rights of Lesbians and Gay Men in the Russian Federation*. San Francisco: IGLHRC, 1994.

Grahn, Judy. *Another Mother Tongue*. Boston: Beacon Press, 1984.

Habermas, Jürgen. "The Critique of Reason as an Unmasking of the Human Sciences: Michel Foucault." In Michael Kelly, ed., *Critique and Power: Recasting the Foucault/Habermas Debate*. Cambridge, Mass.: MIT Press, 1994.

————. "Some Questions Concerning the Theory of Power: Foucault Again." In Michael Kelly, ed., *Critique and Power: Recasting the Foucault/Habermas Debate*. Cambridge, Mass.: MIT Press, 1994.

————. *The Structural Transformation of the Public Sphere*. Trans. T. Burger and F. Lawrence. Cambridge, Mass.: MIT Press, 1989.

Halperin, David M. "The Democratic Body: Prostitution and Citizenship in Classical Athens." *Differences* 2 (Spring 1990).

————. *One Hundred Years of Homosexuality*. New York: Routledge, 1990.

Haraway, Donna. "A Manifesto for Cyborgs: Science, Technology, and Socialist Feminism in the 1980s." *Socialist Review*, no. 15 (March/April 1985).

Hartsock, Nancy. "Foucault on Power: A Theory for Women?" In Linda J. Nicholson, ed., *Feminism/Postmodernism*. New York: Routledge, 1990.

————. *Money, Sex, and Power: Toward a Feminist Historical Materialism*. New York: Longman, 1983.

Hebdige, Dick. *Hiding in the Light: On Images and Things*. London: Routledge, 1988.

————. *Subculture: The Meaning of Style*. Routledge: London, 1979.

Helsinki Watch. *From Below: Independent Peace and Environmental Movements in Eastern Europe and the USSR*. New York: Helsinki Watch, 1987.

Higginbotham, Evelyn Brooks. "African American Women's History and the Metalanguage of Race." *Signs* 17, no. 2 (Winter 1992).

Hoagland, Sarah Lucia. *For Lesbians Only: A Separatist Anthology*. London: Onlywomen Press, 1988.

Husarska, Anna. "Repression of Homosexuals Still Rules in Russia." *Ottawa Citizen*, 14 January 1995.

Irigaray, Luce. *This Sex Which Is Not One*. Ithaca, N.Y.: Cornell University Press, 1985.

Karlinsky, Simon. "Russia's Gay Literature and Culture: The Impact of the October Revolution." In Martin Bauml Duberman et al., eds., *Hidden from History: Reclaiming the Gay and Lesbian Past*. New York: NAL Books, 1989.

Kennedy, Elizabeth Lapovsky, and Madeline D. Davis. *Boots of Leather, Slippers of Gold: The History of a Lesbian Community*. New York: Routledge, 1993.

Kondo, Dorinne K. "M. Butterfly: Orientalism, Gender, and a Critique of Essentialist Identity." *Cultural Critique* (Fall 1990).

Kostenbaum, Wayne. *The Queen's Throat: Opera, Homosexuality, and the Mystery of Desire*. New York: Vintage Books, 1993.

Limonov, Edward. *It's Me, Eddie*. Trans. S. I. Campbell. New York: Random House, 1983.

Ljunggren, David. "Russian Parliament Approves Amended AIDS Law." *Reuters World Service*, 24 February 1995.

Lothstein, Leslie Martin. *Female-to-Male Transsexualism: Historical, Clinical and Theoretical Issues.* Boston: Routledge & Kegan Paul, 1984.

McClintock, Anne. *Imperial Leather: Race, Gender, and Sexuality in the Colonial Contest.* New York: Routledge, 1995.

Mandelstam, Nadezhda. *Hope against Hope.* New York: Atheneum, 1970.

Maus, Marcel. "Techniques of the Body." 1934. Reprinted in *Economy and Society* 2, no. 1 (February 1973), pp. 70–88.

Minh-Ha, Trinh T. *When the Moon Waxes Red: Representation, Gender, and Cultural Politics.* New York: Routledge, 1991.

Murray, Isobel, ed. *The Oxford Authors: Oscar Wilde.* Oxford: Oxford University Press, 1989.

Nicholson, Linda J. "Social Criticism without Philosophy." In Linda J. Nicholson, ed., *Feminism/Postmodernism.* New York: Routledge, 1990.

Nietzsche, Friedrich. *The Genealogy of Morals.* Trans. Walter Kaufmann. New York: Vintage, 1969.

Parker, Andrew, Mary Russo, Doris Sommer, and Patricia Yaeger, eds. *Nationalisms and Sexualities.* New York: Routledge, 1992.

Plant, Richard. *The Pink Triangle: The Nazi War against Homosexuals.* New York: Henry Holt, 1986.

Radway, Janice. *Reading the Romance: Women, Patriarchy, and Popular Literature.* Chapel Hill: University of North Carolina Press, 1991.

Rector, Frank. *The Nazi Extermination of Homosexuals.* New York: Stein & Day, 1981.

Rich, Adrienne. "Compulsory Heterosexuality and Lesbian Existence." In Ann Snitow, Christine Stansell, and Sharon Thompson, eds., *Powers of Desire: The Politics of Sexuality.* New York: Monthly Review Press, 1983.

Rubin, Gayle. "Thinking Sex: Notes for a Radical Theory of the Politics of Sexuality." In Carole S. Vance, ed., *Pleasure and Danger: Exploring Female Sexuality.* Boston: Routledge & Kegan Paul, 1984.

Said, Edward W. *Orientalism.* New York: Vintage Books, 1979.

Sawicki, Jana. *Disciplining Foucault: Feminism, Power, and the Body.* New York: Routledge, 1991.

Schudson, Michael. "Was There Ever a Public Sphere? If So, When? Reflections on the American Case." In Craig Calhoun, ed., *Habermas and the Public Sphere.* Cambridge, Mass.: MIT Press, 1992.

Sedaitis, Judith B., and Jim Butterfield, eds. *Perestroika from Below: Social Movements in the Soviet Union.* Boulder, Colo.: Westview Press, 1991.

Sedgwick, Eve Kosofsky. "Nationalism and Sexualities in the Age of Wilde." In Andrew Parker, Mary Russo, Doris Sommer, and Patricia Yaeger, eds., *Nationalisms and Sexualities.* New York: Routledge, 1992.

———. *Tendencies.* Durham, N.C.: Duke University Press, 1993.

Slobin, Greta N. "Revolution Must Come First: Reading V. Aksenov's *Island of the Crimea.*" In Andrew Parker, Mary Russo, Doris Sommer, and Patricia Yaeger, eds., *Nationalisms and Sexualities.* New York: Routledge, 1992.

Solomon, Andrew. "Vlady's Conquests." *New Republic*, 20 June 1994.

Specter, Michael. "The Great Russia Will Live Again." *New York Times Magazine*, 19 June 1994.

Steakley, James D. *The Homosexual Emancipation Movement in Germany*. New York: Arno Press, 1975.

Stone, Sandy. "The Empire Strikes Back: A Posttranssexual Manifesto." In Julia Epstein and Kristina Straub, eds., *Body Guards: The Cultural Politics of Gender Ambiguity*. New York: Routledge, 1991.

Tien, Davrell. "Love, Sex, and Mother Russia." *Index on Censorship* 22, no. 10 (1993).

Treadgold, Donald W. *Twentieth-Century Russia*. Boulder, Colo.: Westview Press, 1981.

Tuller, Dave. *Cracks in the Iron Closet: Travels in Gay and Lesbian Russia*. Boston: Faber & Faber, 1996.

————. "Gay Liberation Russian-Style." *Advocate*, no. 591 (3 December 1991).

Vance, Carole, et al., eds. *Homosexuality, Which Homosexuality?* London: GMP Publishers, 1989.

Van Maanen, John. *Tales of the Field: On Writing Ethnography*. Chicago: University of Chicago Press, 1988.

Warner, Michael. "The Mass Public and the Mass Subject." In Craig Calhoun, ed., *Habermas and the Public Sphere*. Cambridge, Mass.: The MIT Press, 1992.

Weber, Max. *Economy and Society*. Trans. Guenther Roth and Claus Wittich. Berkeley: University of California Press, 1978.

Weiss, Andrea, and Greta Schiller. *Before Stonewall: The Making of Gay and Lesbian Community*. Tallahassee, Fl.: Naiad Press, 1988.

White, Edmund. *Genet: A Biography*. New York: Knopf, 1993.

White, Harrison. *Action and Organization: Identity as Control in Social Networks*. Princeton: Princeton University Press, 1991.

Wockner, Rex. "Soviet Stonewall: Russian Activists Clash over Tactics." *Outlines*, October 1991.

Wolfe, Susan J., and Julia Penelope. *Sexual Practice, Textual Theory: Lesbian Cultural Criticism*. Cambridge, Mass.: Blackwell, 1993.

Russian-Language Periodicals Reviewed for Mention of Homosexuality

Chasnaya zhizn'

Ekspress-khronika

Inostranets

Kommersant

Komsomol'skaia pravda

Kyranti

Megapolis ekspress

Moskovkaia pravda

Moskovskie novosti

Moskovskii komsomolets

The Moscow Times

The Moscow Tribune
My
Nezavisimaia gazeta
Novoe vremia
Novyi vzgliad
Obshchaia gazeta
Ogonek
Penthouse Rossiia
Rossiiskie vesti
Segodnia
Trud
Tsentr Plus
Vek

index

Laurie Essig is an independent scholar and writer.

Library of Congress Cataloging-in-Publication Data
Essig, Laurie.
Queer in Russia : a story of sex, self, and the other /
Laurie Essig.
p. cm.
Includes bibliographical references and index.
ISBN 0-8223-2312-5 (cloth : alk. paper).
—ISBN 0-8223-2346-X (paper : alk. paper)
1. Homosexuality—Russia (Federation)
2. Gays—Russia (Federation)   I. Title.
HQ76.3.R8E85   1999
306.76'6'0947—dc21   98-42134   CIP